Focus on Form in Classroom
Second Language Acquisition

THE CAMBRIDGE APPLIED LINGUISTICS SERIES

Series editors: Michael H. Long and Jack C. Richards

This series presents the findings of recent work in applied linguistics which are of direct relevance to language teaching and learning and of particular interest to applied linguists, researchers, language teachers, and teacher trainers.

In this series:

Interactive Approaches to Second Language Reading *edited by Patricia L. Carrell, Joanne Devine, and David E. Eskey*

Second Language Classrooms – Research on teaching and learning *by Craig Chaudron*

Language Learning and Deafness *edited by Michael Strong*

The Learner-Centered Curriculum *by David Nunan*

Language Transfer – Cross-linguistic influence in language learning *by Terence Odlin*

Linguistic Perspectives on Second Language Acquisition *edited by Susan M. Gass and Jaquelyn Schachter*

Learning Strategies in Second Language Acquisition *by J. Michael O'Malley and Anna Uhl Chamot*

The Development of Second Language Proficiency *edited by Birgit Harley, Patrick Allen, Jim Cummins and Merrill Swain*

Second Language Writing – Research insights for the classroom *edited by Barbara Kroll*

Genre Analysis – English in academic and research settings *by John M. Swales*

Evaluating Second Language Education *edited by J. Charles Alderson and Alan Beretta*

Perspectives on Pedagogical Grammar *edited by Terence Odlin*

Academic Listening *edited by John Flowerdew*

Power and Inequality in Language Education *edited by James W. Tollefson*

Language Program Evaluation –Theory and practice *by Brian K. Lynch*

Sociolinguistics and Language Teaching *edited by Sandra Lee McKay and Nancy H. Hornberger*

Contrastive Rhetoric – Cross-cultural aspects of second language writing *by Ulla Connor*

Teacher Cognition in Language Teaching *by Devon Woods*

Second Language Vocabulary Acquisition *edited by James Coady and Thomas Huckin*

Text, Role, and Context – Developing Academic Literacies *by Ann M. Johns*

Immersion Education: International Perspectives *edited by Robert Keith Johnson and Merrill Swain*

Focus on Form in Classroom Second Language Acquisition *edited by Catherine Doughty and Jessica Williams*

Interfaces Between Second Language Acquisition and Language Testing Research *edited by Lyle F. Bachman and Andrew D. Cohen*

Culture in Second Language Teaching and Learning *edited by Eli Hinkel*

Network-Based Language Teaching –Concepts and Practice *edited by Mark Warschauer and Richard Kern*

Focus on Form in Classroom Second Language Acquisition

Catherine Doughty

Georgetown University

and

Jessica Williams

University of Illinois at Chicago

CAMBRIDGE
UNIVERSITY PRESS

CAMBRIDGE UNIVERSITY PRESS
Cambridge, New York, Melbourne, Madrid, Cape Town, Singapore, São Paulo, Delhi

Cambridge University Press
32 Avenue of the Americas, New York, NY 10013–2473, USA

www.cambridge.org
Information on this title: www.cambridge.org/9780521625517

First published 1998
8th printing 2008

Printed in the United States of America

A catalog record for this publication is available from the British Library

Library of Congress Cataloging in Publication Data

Doughty, Catherine
Focus on form in classroom second language acquisition /
Catherine Doughty, Jessica Williams
p. cm. – (The Cambridge applied linguistics series)
Includes bibliographical references.
ISBN 978-0-521-62390-2 (hbk.) – ISBN 978-0-521-62551-7 (pbk.)
1. Language and languages – Study and teaching. 2. Second
language acquisition.
P51.F549 1998
407.1 – dc21

97-46568

ISBN 978-0-521-62390-2 hardback
ISBN 978-0-521-62551-7 paperback

To our mentor,

Tere Pica

Contents

Contributors

Robert M. DeKeyser, University of Pittsburgh
Catherine Doughty, Georgetown University, Washington, D.C.
Jacqueline Evans, University of Illinois at Chicago
Birgit Harley, Ontario Institute for Studies in Education, Toronto, Canada
Patsy M. Lightbown, Concordia University, Montreal, Canada
Michael H. Long, University of Hawaii at Manoa
Peter Robinson, Aoyama Gakuin University, Shibuya, Japan
Merrill Swain, Ontario Institute for Studies in Education, Toronto, Canada
Elizabeth Varela, Georgetown University, Washington, D.C.
Joanna White, Concordia University, Montreal, Canada
Jessica Williams, University of Illinois at Chicago

Series editors' preface

Although the terms have varied over the years, whether language is usefully treated as object in language learning, in or out of classrooms, or is better left to be acquired incidentally, while doing something else, has long been a central question for learners, teachers, and researchers alike. Views and (in theory, at least) language teaching practice have ranged from one extreme to another. Some practitioners have advocated systematic attention to a series of isolated target linguistic features, usually sequenced intuitively, utilizing various combinations of grammatical rule statements, implicit or explicit L1/L2 contrasts, structural pattern drills, "error correction," memorization, and translation. Others have eschewed such practices in favor of target language experiences much like those encountered by young children acquiring their first language – in other words, experiences that focus on "natural" exposure, on meaning and communication, not on language per se, and on implicit and incidental, rather than explicit, learning. Proponents of intermediate positions have argued for "eclectic" combinations of the first two, or for the use of each approach, but separately with different kinds of learners (e.g., adults or children), for different kinds of target language items (e.g., "complex" or "simple" rules), or at different proficiency levels (e.g., "elementary" or "advanced").

Rather than argue endlessly back and forth in a theoretical and empirical vacuum, as has been the case with some (although not all) debates on the issue in the pedagogtical literature, an increasing number of teachers and researchers (often people wearing both hats) have turned away from unsupported assertions and denials to confront the daunting, but ultimately essential, task of finding out what works the hard way – they have studied it. One such group and line of work, represented in this volume, coalesces around varying interpretations and classroom instantiations of *focus on form*. Occasionally reflecting somewhat differing theoretical allegiances, the chapters review a range of recent work relevant to the construct itself, report findings from new qualitative and quantitative laboratory and classroom studies, and make rationally argued, suitably modulated, suggestions for classroom practice. In addition to their common focus of inquiry, the contributors share a belief in the need for (S)LA theory and data-based SLA and L2 classroom research as crucial sources of information in the debate (not the only sources, of course). They also recognize that, although considerable progress has been made in this area, many issues remain unresolved.

Its treatment of a central issue in language learning and teaching via theoretically coherent empirical study makes *Focus on Form in Classroom Second Language Acquisition* a welcome and appropriate addition to the Cambridge Applied Linguistics Series. Catherine Doughty and Jessica Williams have made a valuable contribution to the field through their own substantive contributions to the research program, which are included here, and also in the meticulous way in which they have worked with the other contributing authors in refining their chapters. We think that the finished product will make a valuable addition to the libraries of many language teachers, SLA researchers, and applied linguists.

Michael H. Long
Jack C. Richards

Preface

This volume of ten original chapters presents the research and discussion from three recent, refereed conference symposia/colloquia on *focus on form* in second language instruction. One focus-on-form session took place at the 1994 Second Language Research Forum at Concordia and McGill Universities, Montreal, Canada (Doughty, 1994b); two were held at the 1995 meetings of the Amercian Association for Applied Linguistics and Teachers of English to Speakers of Other Languages, both of which took place in Long Beach, California (Doughty & Williams, 1995; Williams & Doughty, 1995). At the time of the conferences, the participants were invited to contribute their previously unpublished work to the current volume, which brings together expanded and revised versions of the focus-on-form conference presentations.

The conference audiences to which these papers concerning the theoretical perspectives, empirical studies, and classroom interpretations of the construct of *focus on form* were presented were composed of researchers and teachers alike. Researcher interest in this issue is keen, as can be gauged by attendance at the sessions and by the number of journal publications of numerous studies that address questions of formal instruction and second language learning. Initial reactions from practicing teachers have varied considerably and have led to debates among those holding three positions: (1) rejection of the notion of focus on form by purely communicatively oriented teachers, (2) eager, but inappropriate use of the notion to justify a return to discrete-point grammar instruction by more traditional language teachers, and (3) increasing enthusiasm for understanding more about the implementation of valid focus on form into communicative classrooms. Such a diversity of teacher reactions appears to stem from various misconstruals of the terms *focus* and *form* in the overall construct of *focus on form*. It is thus timely for classroom SLA researchers to discuss and clarify focus-on-form terminology and issues and to interpret the focus-on-form research within a classroom context in order to prevent a rejection of focus on form or a misguided swing of the pedagogical pendulum back toward the teaching of linguistic forms in isolation.

Indeed, it is the exploration of the nature and feasibility of *focus on form* that is the central aim of the chapters in this volume. Thus, particularly since the majority of studies have supported the efficacy of attention to form and have investigated and discussed the specific ways in which to achieve effective pedagogical intervention, this collection is intended for SLA researchers and language teaching practitioners as well as for graduate students in the field of applied linguistics.

Acknowledgments

Our collaboration on this book began years ago, grew during countless late-night discussions as roommates at SLRF and AAAL conferences, and finally coalesced after the SLRF Montreal symposium on focus on form, which inspired us to organize two subsequent colloquia and, ultimately, to invite contributions for this volume. Working together has been a rewarding and, we believe, fruitful experience. If it can be said that writing clarifies thinking, then it is true all the more so that collaborative writing enlightens scholarship. With the completion of the research, writing, and editing that we have done jointly throughout the preparation of this book, we feel truly gratified intellectually and are confidently hopeful that readers will find something of value in the discussion we present here.

We are deeply grateful to all of the authors for their participation in the conference sessions, for their thought-provoking ideas on *focus on form,* and, most of all, for their efforts given to the individual chapters in this book. We have also appreciated the expert guidance of Cambridge University Press during the preparation of the volume: The series editors have been very supportive, and the anonymous reviewers thorough. Finally, we wish especially to thank Olive Collen for her precision and expertise in copy editing.

Catherine Doughty
Jessica Williams

1   *Issues and terminology*

Catherine Doughty
Jessica Williams

Background

When we entered the field of second language acquisition (SLA) in 1980, SLA research and L2 teaching were seemingly intractably split. Some influential SLA researchers were claiming that instruction made no difference because natural language acquisition processes are all-powerful. Apart from those individuals for whom such pronouncements validated the widely popular "communicative approach" to language teaching, many teachers developed a mistrust of SLA, furthering the divide between researchers and practitioners (Clarke, 1994). For those researchers who were particularly interested in classroom language acquisition, whatever its nature might be, this disjunction between research and practice was frustrating at best, and unproductive for both theory and practice at worst.

Times have since changed for the better: There has been an increasing emphasis on classroom-oriented research that examines processes by instructed language learners. In addition, there has been a greater focus on the role that teachers can play in the research cycle (e.g., Bailey & Nunan, 1996; Crookes, 1993, 1997; Nunan, 1996; Pica, 1997; Schachter & Gass, 1996; Williams & Doughty, 1995). The cooperation between teacher-researchers and university researchers is also evident in this volume, as seen in the collaborative efforts reported in many of the chapters. These classroom SLA studies are not collaborative simply in the sense that teachers joined a research project; they also address issues that are of pedagogical importance.

Among the major issues raised by classroom SLA researchers is the controversial question of whether and how to include "grammar" in L2 instruction. The debate on the degree to which teacher or learner attention should be directed to linguistic features has a long history. It is perhaps unique among issues in SLA, given the extent to which such discussion brings together the concerns of researchers and practitioners and often goes to the heart of deeply held beliefs and strong views. Thus, we believe that the time has come to reexamine the question, this time in terms of the role of what has come to be known more recently as *focus on form* in second language learning and teaching.

The motivation for focus on form

Current interest in focus on form is motivated, in part, by the findings of immersion and naturalistic acquisition studies that suggest that when classroom second language learning is entirely experiential and meaning-focused, some linguistic features do not ultimately develop to targetlike levels (see, e.g., Harley, 1992; Harley & Swain, 1984; Vignola & Wesche, 1991). This is so despite years of meaningful input and opportunities for interaction. Thus, in contrast to natural first language acquisition, classroom (typically adult) SLA is variably successful. Findings of classroom research have begun to indicate, however, that pedagogical interventions embedded in primarily communicative activities can be effective in overcoming classroom limitations on SLA. For example, controlled effects-of-instruction studies and research on the negotiation of meaning suggest a positive influence for attention to form in interlanguage (IL) development (see Doughty, 1991, in press; Pica, 1994, for reviews). On the basis of this work, a strong claim has been made that focus on form may be necessary to push learners beyond communicatively effective language toward targetlike second language ability. A somewhat weaker claim is that, even if such a focus may not be absolutely necessary, it may be part of a more efficient language learning experience in that it can speed up natural acquisition processes.

Responses to the suggestion that second language teaching that is primarily meaning-focused could be improved with some degree of attention to form have often been heated, especially among classroom teachers. These responses have ranged from outright rejection by teachers whose orientation is wholly communicative, to an eager, if misguided, embrace by others, as justification for a return to explicit, discrete-point grammar instruction and as proof of what they have "known all along" was the correct path (Doughty, 1994a, 1997). Such diversity of responses stems, in part, from varied construals of how focus on form should be operationalized in the classroom. Indeed, diversity is apparent in this volume as well, although all contributors have as their point of departure that some, rather than no, attention to form in the second language classroom is beneficial. In light of these varied responses to focus on form, we believe that it is essential to define the term operationally if subsequent interpretations are to be assessable.

Defining focus on form

Most researchers currently investigating the role of attention to form attribute the reawakening of interest in this issue to Michael Long (1988a, 1991).[1] In that seminal work, Long distinguished between a *focus on formS,* which characterizes earlier, synthetic approaches to language teaching that have as their primary organizing principle for course design the accumulation of individual language elements (e.g., forms such as verb endings or agreement features, or even functions such as greetings or apologies) from what he (and now we) call *focus on form.* The crucial distinction – which can be seen in the two versions of Long's definitions of focus on form that follow – is that focus on form entails a prerequisite engagement in meaning before attention to linguistic features can be expected to be effective. The first definition is the more theoretical one, offering little specific applicability for classroom use. The second, more operational, definition, developed for this volume, offers researchers and practitioners greater direction for practical implementation.

> focus on *form* . . . overtly draws students' attention to linguistic elements as they arise incidentally in lessons whose overriding focus is on meaning or communication. (Long, 1991, pp. 45–46)

> focus on form often consists of an occasional shift of attention to linguistic code features – by the teacher and/or one or more students – triggered by perceived problems with comprehension or production. (Long & Robinson, this volume, p. 23).

The proposed advantage of focus on form over the traditional forms-in-isolation type of grammar teaching is the cognitive processing support provided by the "overriding focus . . . on meaning or communication." To state this advantage rather simply, the learner's attention is drawn precisely to a linguistic feature as necessitated by a communicative demand.

Since the notion of focus on form was introduced, there has been some confusion in the literature, which can be traced to imprecise use of terminology. It is important to sort out this confusion, for the lack of conformity in terminology has probably had its own part to play in generating the opposing "grammar must remain taboo" versus "grammar first" teacher reactions mentioned earlier. To be clear, it should be borne in mind that the traditional notion of *formS* always entails isolation or extraction of linguistic features from context or from communicative activity. Unfortunately, teachers and researchers have used a variety of

1 Long's paper, which was first presented in 1988 at the European-North-American Symposium on Needed Research in Foreign Language Education, Rockefeller Center, Bellagio, Italy, was widely circulated in that version prior to its 1991 publication.

terms to refer to instruction involving focus on formS, including *grammar instruction, formal instruction, form-focused instruction,* and *code-focused instruction.* This has led to confusion, because these terms inevitably have been juxtaposed to terms like *focus on meaning* or *communication.* We would like to stress that focus on formS and focus on form are *not* polar opposites in the way that *form* and *meaning* have often been considered to be. Rather, focus on form *entails* a focus on formal elements of language, whereas focus on formS is *limited* to such a focus, and focus on meaning *excludes* it. Most important, it should be kept in mind that the fundamental assumption of focus-on-form instruction is that meaning and use must already be evident to the learner at the time that attention is drawn to the linguistic apparatus needed to get the meaning across.

The greatest terminological difficulty is caused by the frequent use of the term *form-focused,* as in *form-focused instruction,* which most often describes instruction that is, in fact, formS-focused but sometimes can refer to instruction involving what we are calling *focus on form.* Thus, the phrase *form-focused instruction* is variously used to denote the teaching of linguistic formS in isolation, as well as to describe teaching that integrates attention to forms, meaning, and use.[2] For this reason, we believe that it will be best to avoid the term *form-focused* altogether in this volume as well as in future discussions of focus on form. This leaves us with something of a problem, however, for there is, as yet, no serviceable adjectival modifier when the intended meaning is *focus-on-form instruction.* Perhaps the acronym *FonF,* which has already come into colloquial use, will serve this purpose. In any case, in this volume, we opt to use the contrasting (but not opposite) terms *formS-focused instruction* and *FonF instruction.*

The chapters in this volume

Long is adamant that focus on form does not imply a focus on individual linguistic forms as a way of organizing language instruction, and that the primary focus in FonF instruction is never to be on anything other than meaningful activity (Long, 1991; Long & Robinson, this volume). This interpretation of focus on form is also seen in the studies in this volume by Doughty and Varela, White, and Williams and Evans. Yet, even in these studies, form may have a higher profile than Long anticipates. In some cases, the focus on form in activities was occasionally more than a brief diversion, and, in others, the tasks or techniques were designed a priori with a formal linguistic focus in mind, although, in each case, the

2 See Spada (1997) for a related discussion of the terms *form-focussed* and *focus on form.*

aim was to keep the primary focus on meaning. Nonetheless, these tasks and techniques are compatible with the operational definition of *focus on form,* since their use is always triggered by an analysis of learner need rather than being imposed externally by a linguistic syllabus. Other contributors seem to draw their definition of *focus on form* even less narrowly. Harley's learners, for instance, sometimes manipulated purely code-based aspects of the language, including metalinguistic terms, as part of their focus. Of course, not all the activities were this overt; nevertheless, Harley views this explicit focus as an important component of the overall unit on grammatical gender. Similarly, Swain proposes the use of metalinguistic reflection as one of the major roles for output practice in facilitating IL development. Students in the immersion classes she studied appeared to benefit from discussing their explicit knowledge of language rules. Thus, Long is at the most implicit end of the FonF continuum, with the narrowest interpretation of the term, whereas both DeKeyser and Lightbown, for instance, see at least some role for what Long would probably call *focus on formS.* It is important to note, however, that such explicit attention to form must occur within a particular cognitive window of opportunity if the learner is to be able to accomplish the kind of integration of forms and meaning advocated by Long. That is to say, DeKeyser and Lightbown propose that, even in advance of needing forms for communicative purposes, learners can hold them in mental representation (i.e., memory) for further processing. However, this cognitive ability is limited in the sense that, if no timely opportunity for use arises, the forms will no longer remain in memory.

Thus far, we have seen that there is considerable variation in how the term *focus on form* is understood and used. Now that we have defined and operationalized the term from theoretical and operational perspectives (see also Long & Robinson, this volume), the debate moves to questions of when and how classroom learners derive the most benefit from focus on form and, finally, to how focus on form is to be implemented from a pedagogical perspective. We have centered our discussion on four key issues and the questions they entail in the debate on the role of focus on form in second language learning and teaching:

1. *Timing of focus on form:* When should focus on form occur in the overall curriculum? Should it occur initially, continuously, or only after the communicative ability of L2 learners is well developed? When should focus on form occur in individual classrooms? Should it be planned a priori by the teacher or only when it seems necessary? Must all FonF activities be integrated into communicative ones? How long need the focus continue in order to be effective? (see chapters in this volume by DeKeyser; Doughty & Varela; Doughty & Williams; Lightbown; Long & Robinson).

2. *Forms to focus on:* Which forms are amenable to focus on form? Are some forms resistant to focus on form? Are forms that are persistent learning problems the ones best targeted for FonF treatment? Or is the acquisition of "easy" rules likely to be facilitated most by such instruction? Does the effectiveness of focus on form in instruction differ depending on the forms in focus? Are differences related to the forms themselves, that is, their complexity, prototypicality, and so on, or to the status of those forms in the learners' ILs? (see chapters in this volume by DeKeyser; Doughty & Williams; Harley; Williams & Evans).

3. *Classroom context for focus on form:* What factors are important to consider in deciding on the nature and degree of focus on form that would be most beneficial? Is it likely to be equally beneficial in all settings? How does effectiveness compare in immersion, intensive, and less intensive programs? Is age an important consideration in deciding on the degree and kind of focus on form? (see chapters in this volume by Harley and by Swain).

4. *Curricular decisions:* Can tasks and techniques be designed during which problematic forms are likely to arise so that an opportunity to focus on form can be provided? Should an entire segment of a curriculum be designed to highlight a particular form or set of related forms? Should focus on form be unobtrusive or overt? How might pedagogical intervention strategies be affected by the findings on timing, choice of form, and context? What is the role of feedback in the communicative classroom? Can it provide sufficient focus on form? (see chapters in this volume by DeKeyser; Doughty & Varela; Doughty & Williams; Harley; Swain; White; Williams & Evans).

Each of the chapters in this volume addresses at least one of these aspects of focus on form in SLA. In Chapter 2, Long and Robinson provide some historical context for focus on form, in both second language theory and pedagogy. They outline the problems of any language teaching syllabus that presents a predetermined sequence of items, whether they are grammatical forms, functions, or lexical items. Such syllabi cannot succeed, Long and Robinson claim, because to use them is to ignore basic acquisition processes. On the other hand, Long and Robinson maintain that a course design that focuses exclusively on meaning also has drawbacks, particularly for older learners. They point to the potential *need* for negative evidence to make it possible to learn some forms and to the *inefficiency* of leaving learners to their own devices when instruction might provide some useful shortcuts. Long and Robinson's shortcut of choice is focus on form. They draw an important distinction between focus on form as observable external behavior, especially on the part of teachers as they try to draw learners' attention to some formal linguistic feature, and the more important, internal mental state of the learner, or how focal attention is allocated (see also Sharwood Smith, 1991, 1993). They favor unobtrusive techniques, such as recasting, which are toward the most implicit end of the FonF continuum, and eschew any treatment of form that is extensive or separate. In support of their position, they review the findings of experimental studies on implicit and explicit learning and on focus on form versus focus on meaning, as well as quasi-experimental studies on focus on form.

DeKeyser and Swain see rule-based knowledge as a crucial aspect of SLA and, unlike Long and Robinson, suggest more explicit, metalinguistic components of FonF activities.

In Chapter 3, DeKeyser reviews ongoing research in cognitive psychology for evidence relevant to the debate on focus on form. He suggests that it is important to distinguish both between kinds of learning (explicit and implicit) and among kinds of linguistic rules (i.e., abstract rules and co-occurrence patterns). He argues that explicit learning is probably helpful, but only for abstract rules. DeKeyser then also considers the issue of timing, in this case by examining findings in cognitive psychology. He draws on the skill acquisition theory of John Anderson, suggesting ways in which different types of instructional intervention could facilitate acquisition of declarative knowledge, as well as the later proceduralization and automatization of that knowledge. He claims that many current methods, as well as those that have been used in the past, ignore these basics of skill acquisition and are, therefore, doomed to only partial success. Within the definition set forth by Long (1991) and Long and Robinson (this volume), DeKeyser's approach does not qualify as focus on form, since this skill-based treatment of explicit knowledge represents more than the brief diversion from meaningful content espoused by Long. DeKeyser defends his view by arguing that it is both possible and necessary to include "communicative drills" in second language instruction in which learners engage in meaningful communication while drawing on their declarative knowledge. To do this successfully, however, DeKeyser reasons that learners must have first developed this knowledge as part of activities that often are not integrated with meaningful communication. Furthermore, learners must have ample time to assimilate the knowledge before they are called upon to deploy it in the production or comprehension processes of communication.

Merrill Swain has documented the successes and shortcomings of immersion education in Ontario for the past 20 years (1984, 1991a; Swain & Lapkin, 1982). Although these learners are, in many ways, extremely proficient and exceptionally fluent, their accuracy lags far behind that of native speakers, and there also appears to be some restriction in the range of language functions they use. Swain has long advocated an important role for output in the development of IL toward target language levels of ability. In Chapter 4, she focuses expressly on the role of output, particularly that which is the result of dialogue, in prompting metalinguistic reflection. In producing the target language, the learners Swain studied often sensed that something was wrong and, during collaborative work, were able to work out what they thought was right. She reports on two exploratory studies that attempt to characterize what happens in such collaborative episodes and to determine whether there is any relationship between the conscious reflection in these episodes and learners' acquisition of reflected-upon linguistic features.

The next group of chapters in this volume (Part II) are primarily empirical in nature, attempting to answer some of the questions that we have posed here. White reports, in Chapter 5, on her work with children, using a relatively implicit technique that integrates focus on form and meaning to determine its effect on L1 French learners' use of possessive determiners in L2 English. Specifically, she tested the effect of typographical enhancement plus input flood, in combination with what she calls a *book flood*. The aim was to see whether the enhancement might increase learners' awareness of the English determiner system, which differs considerably from the French. This awareness might, in turn, be beneficial as the learners did the readings in the book flood, which presumably contained a plethora of natural examples of the form in focus. White found that the gains for the enhanced groups were initially significant but that, by the delayed posttest, the unenhanced, flood-only group had caught up (see Mellow, Reeder, & Forster, 1996, for a useful discussion of such findings). Post hoc comparisons with a group that had not received any flood material suggest that the learners in all the experimental groups benefited from the increased focus on form: Although the accuracy scores were not the most illuminating part of White's study, a developmental stage analysis reveals a complex picture of IL restructuring based on L1 influence, initial stage, FonF treatment, and testing procedures.

The aim of Doughty and Varela's study, reported in Chapter 6, was to determine whether it is possible to draw learners' attention to form successfully without distracting them from the educational aims of their content class. In this study, focus on form consisted of unobtrusive, but targeted, repetitions and recasts by the teacher of IL utterances intended to express past and conditional past during the reporting of experiments conducted in science class. Results of the study indicate that this focus, which was concentrated and yet not overt, was far superior to meaning-focused instruction alone in facilitating accuracy in the use of these forms, suggesting that it is indeed possible to have a dual focus on form and meaning. Doughty and Varela caution, however, that the treatment must be focused and concentrated. There would be little profit, they suggest, in trying to focus on multiple forms simultaneously.

In Chapter 7, Williams and Evans focus on the question of which forms to choose for FonF activities. They looked at two criteria in choosing forms: formal and functional complexity of the form and its status in the learners' ILs. One form had a straightforward form-function relationship (participial adjectives, e.g., *bored/boring*); and the other form, the passive, was chosen because it is complex in both form and use. Participial adjectives appeared regularly, though often incorrectly, in the learners' ILs. The passive, on the other hand, had yet to emerge in any significant way in their ILs. Williams and Evans used two instructional strategies: first, an implicit input flood containing the form, and second, the input flood plus brief, contextualized, but explicit instruction on rules for formation and use. For the participial adjectives, the explicitly instructed group showed the greatest gains. The flood group made more modest gains, but both groups performed significantly better than the control group. For the passive, although the two experimental groups did better than the control group, the difference between the learners in the two experimental groups was less clear. Williams and Evans claim that their findings are related to both the nature of the forms and developmental readiness. They reason that more explicit treatment may be better suited to relatively simple rules and forms. In addition, it may be that, in order for the more explicit treatment to be effective, the learners have to be ready for it.

Harley's learners are the youngest in the volume (Chapter 8). Harley deliberately chose this age group to determine whether early intervention could ameliorate the persistent problems with grammatical gender that such learners often experience throughout the immersion experience, in particular, by tapping into phonological learning processes documented in young L1 learners. She maintains that gender is especially problematic because it is an exclusively formal feature, and, for English speakers, it has no analog in the L1 that might predispose them to look for this feature in the L2. Instructional activities in her study varied in terms of the balance of focus on meaning or form. All instructional activities were more overt than those found in the other studies in this volume; some could even be viewed as focus on formS. The activities were aimed at getting learners to recognize the phonological, orthographic, and morphological cues that can help predict gender assignment. Harley's findings are twofold. First, she found a prevalence for item learning; that is, the students in the experimental classes were better at gender assignment in the words they had been exposed to and practiced in class. However, there was little evidence of system learning, that is, that they had extended their knowledge of these cues to novel words. Second, Harley's work has important pedagogical implications for using FonF activities with such young learners. Of particular importance, she found, were transparency of the L2 input and the compatibility of the tasks within the overall curriculum. If the FonF tasks did not fit in with what the class was doing, the teachers implicitly or explicitly rejected them.

The final part of this book (Part III) presents some pedagogical implications of focus-on-form research. In Chapter 9, Lightbown explores the important issue of timing. The term *timing* applies to two issues: developmental time and on-line "lesson" time. In the first case, Lightbown examines the relationship between developmental stages and focus on form, specifically, whether more benefits are derived from targeting forms in an immediately subsequent stage or from focusing on more advanced structures only and assuming that the easy ones will be acquired with little or no instructional intervention. The second notion of timing addresses the question of whether focus on form should be planned in advance or provided on an as-needed basis, as problems arise, as well as whether attention to form should be concurrent or separate. For the first question, Lightbown suggests that although this line of research is indeed promising, there is, for the moment, little evidence that instruction at levels far beyond the current stage is deleterious (contra Pienemann, 1984). She also counsels teachers to be cautious in shaping their instruction too narrowly around the "next" developmental stage, for the evidence "is far from overwhelming that learners benefit only from developmentally appropriate instruction" (this volume, p. 188). Rather, she suggests that teachers use their knowledge of acquisitional sequences to inform their teaching more generally and realistically to guide their expectations and feedback.

As for the question of the place of focus on form in relation to more meaning-focused activities, Lightbown rejects any blanket prescriptions. She cites affective, psycholinguistic, and pedagogical reasons for why it is possible, and sometimes preferable, to integrate focus on form and meaning in the same activity. On the other hand, she also sees a role for separate self-study of formal linguistic features. She points out that if teachers are to attract attention only briefly, as Long advises, learners must have knowledge, and a vocabulary of that knowledge, on which to draw. This view echoes the suggestions of DeKeyser's cognitive approach.

Finally, we return to the concerns of classroom teachers as they face daily decisions in implementing focus on form. In Chapter 10, we examine many of the issues that were explored in the empirical studies of this volume, as well as in other recent studies reported in journals, with a view to making six major decisions in implementing focus on form:

Decision 1   Whether or not to focus on form
Decision 2   Reactive versus proactive focus on form
Decision 3   The choice of linguistic form
Decision 4   Explicitness of focus on form
Decision 5   Sequential versus integrated focus on form
Decision 6   The role of focus on form in the curriculum

When implementing focus on form in the classroom, the teacher encounters broader considerations than those which can be addressed in any one empirical study: Should focus on form be planned in advance, or should it be primarily reactive? Should such activities focus overtly on forms, or should they be unobtrusive? How can FonF activities be categorized, and on what basis should choices among them be made? How should tasks be sequenced? In considering these questions, we have drawn together findings from a wide range of studies and have discussed their implications relative to the pedagogical issues we have raised. Finally, we present a taxonomy of tasks to help teachers relate various learner and learning considerations to the selection of FonF tasks.

Conclusion

The discussion throughout this volume leads to the conclusion that neither formS-based instruction nor meaning-based instruction alone can lead to complete second language acquisition. There is ample evidence here and elsewhere that this is the case. Furthermore, our own view is that some degree of carefully timed and delivered focus on form is likely to be appropriate in most cases of L2 learning difficulty. Taking the perspective that adult second language learning is, in many respects, fundamentally different from first language learning, we believe that leaving learners to discover form-function relationships and the intricacies of a new linguistic system wholly on their own makes little sense. This does not mean, however, that we advocate a constant focus on all forms for all learners all the time. Instead, our intention is to find a pedagogically sound and empirically grounded position between these two stances. In this regard, the contributions in this volume often present differing views of *how* focus on form is to be accomplished. In fact, readers will inevitably come to see that there is not, as yet, and probably never will be, any *single* solution to the intriguing problem of how to implement focus on form in communicative classrooms. Nonetheless, there are certain emerging pedagogical principles that can inform decisions about FonF implementation. At this point, it is our belief that the *ideal* delivery of focus on form is yet to be determined. Thus, it is for the reader to decide – on the basis of FonF pedagogical principles – exactly what the appropriate degree of explicitness of attention to form is to be in his or her classroom. The contributors have presented their diverse and occasionally conflicting perspectives on this question, but it is certain that the debate will not end with this collection.

PART I:
THEORETICAL FOUNDATIONS OF
FOCUS ON FORM

2 Focus on form
Theory, research, and practice

Michael H. Long
Peter Robinson

Introduction

This chapter consists of two main sections. In the first section, some of the historical context for focus on form in language teaching and in second language acquisition (SLA) theory is presented, suggesting a convergence of interest in the idea, and some support for it, in both fields. The second section offers a brief review of three bodies of research findings relevant to determining the strengths and limitations for language learning of a focus on form, a focus on formS, and a focus on meaning.

Options in language teaching

Focus on forms

Although by no means the only important issue underlying debate over approaches to language teaching down the years, implicit or explicit choice of the *learner* or the *language* to be taught as the starting point in course design remains one of the most critical. The popular position has long been that the teacher's or syllabus designer's first task is to analyze the target language (or more commonly to adopt an existing analysis, usually in the form of a pedagogical grammar or a textbook), that is, what Wilkins (1976) termed the *synthetic* approach (Figure 1, Option 1).

Depending on the analyst's linguistic preferences, the L2 is broken down into words and collocations, grammar rules, phonemes, intonation and stress patterns, structures, notions, or functions. The items in the resulting list(s) are then sequenced for presentation as *models* to learners in linear, additive fashion according to such criteria as (usually intuitively assessed) frequency, valence, or difficulty. Synthetic syllabi, still used in the vast majority of classrooms the world over, with the structural syllabus being the most common, are those in which:

parts of the language are taught separately and step by step so that acquisition is a process of gradual accumulation of parts until the whole structure of language has been built up. . . . At any one time the learner is being exposed to a deliberately limited sample of language. (Wilkins, 1976, p. 2)

Option 2	Option 3	Option 1
analytic	*analytic*	*synthetic*
focus on **meaning**	focus on **form**	focus on **formS**

←——→

Natural Approach	TBLT	GT, ALM, Silent Way, TPR
Immersion	Content-Based LT(?)	
Procedural Syllabus	Process Syllabus(?)	Structural/N-F Syllabuses
etc.	etc.	etc.

Figure 1   Options in language teaching (adapted from Long, in press).

The learner's role is to synthesize the pieces for use in communication. Synthetic syllabi, together with the corresponding materials, methodology, and classroom pedagogy, lead to lessons with a *focus on formS*. The syllabus consists of inductively or deductively presented information about the L2. Pedagogical materials and accompanying classroom procedures are designed to present and practice a series of linguistic items, or forms. They have no independent reason for existence.

Synthetic syllabi – lexical, structural, notional-functional, and in practice to date, topical and situational – and the synthetic "methods" (Grammar Translation, Audiolingual Method, Audiovisual Method, Silent Way, Noisy Method, Total Physical Response, etc.) and classroom practices (repetition of models, transformation exercises, display questions, explicit negative feedback, i.e., error "correction," etc.) commonly associated with them are generally produced and used, although they need not be, before a *needs analysis* is conducted for a particular group of learners. Moreover, synthetic syllabi, "methods," and classroom practices either largely ignore language learning processes or tacitly assume a discredited behaviorist model. Of the scores of detailed studies of naturalistic and classroom language learning reported over the past 30 years, none suggest, for example, that presentation of discrete points of grammar one at a time (albeit in "spiral" fashion), as dictated by a synthetic syllabus of some kind, bears any resemblance except an accidental one to either the order or the manner in which naturalistic or classroom acquirers learn those items. As Rutherford (1988) noted, SLA is not a process of accumulating entities.

Instead of learning discrete lexical, grammatical, or notional-functional items one at a time, research shows that both naturalistic and classroom learners rarely, if ever, exhibit sudden categorical acquisition of new forms or rules (for review, see, e.g., R. Ellis, 1994a; Gass & Selinker, 1994; Hatch, 1983; Larsen-Freeman & Long, 1991). Rather, they traverse what appear to be fixed developmental sequences in word order, relative clauses, negation, interrogatives, pronouns, and other grammatical domains (Brindley, 1991; R. Ellis, 1989; Felix & Hahn, 1985; Hyltenstam, 1977, 1984; Johnston, 1985; Meisel, Clahsen & Pienemann, 1981; Pavesi, 1986; Schumann, 1979), with L1-L2 relationships affecting rate of progress through a sequence and sometimes leading to additional substages within a sequence, but not altering the sequences themselves (Zobl, 1982). Far from moving from zero knowledge of a rule to mastery in one step, moreover – the result that language teaching methodologies associated with synthetic approaches try, and fail, to achieve – learners typically pass through stages of nontargetlike use of target forms, as well as targetlike and nontargetlike use of nontargetlike forms (see, e.g., Andersen, 1984; Huebner, 1983; Kumpf, 1984; Meisel, 1987; Sato, 1986, 1990). In other words, morphosyntactic development involves prolonged periods of form-function mapping. Progress is not necessarily unidirectional. There are often lengthy periods of highly variable, sometimes lexically conditioned, suppliance of even supposedly easily taught items like English plural -*s* (Pica, 1983; Young, 1988), zigzag developmental curves (Sato, 1990), temporary deterioration in learner performance (Meisel, Clahsen, & Pienemann, 1981), backsliding (Selinker & Lakshamanan, 1992), and so-called U-shaped behavior (Kellerman, 1985). Even a good deal of lexical acquisition is not sudden and categorical but exhibits developmental patterns (Blum & Levenston, 1978; Laufer, 1990; Meara, 1984; Shirai, 1990). None of this sits well with simplistic notions of "what you teach, when you teach it, is what they learn."

One attempt at ameliorating these problems is known as *consciousness-raising* (R. Ellis, 1991; Rutherford & Sharwood Smith, 1985; Sharwood Smith, 1981). The syllabus is still synthetic, and pedagogical materials are still designed with a specific linguistic focus (see, e.g., the innovative exercise types in Rutherford, 1988). Recognizing that sequential categorical mastery of items in the (overt or covert) grammatical syllabus is an unrealistic goal, however, teachers and materials writers seek instead to make students *aware* of new target language items, rules, or regularities by highlighting them in the input – more or less concisely or elaborately, and with greater or lesser explicitness and intensity (R. Ellis, 1991) – but not necessarily to encourage students to produce them, and certainly not correctly, right away. Consciousness-raising shows some respect for the learner's internal syllabus, but the content of the external syllabus is still the L2, and the sequencing and timing problems with synthetic syllabi remain. In more recent work, Sharwood Smith (1991, 1993) has abandoned consciousness-raising for *input enhancement*. The accent is now on the more readily verifiable creation of input salience, for example, by "flagging" target items (highlighting, underlining, coloring, rule giving, etc.), to direct the learner's attention to them, not on changes in the learner's internal mental state. The input enhancement notion avoids the problematic "consciousness" issue and the related fact that, just as teachers' attempts to correct errors may not result in error correction, teachers' attempts to raise consciousness may not result in consciousness-raising. Once again, however, syllabus content remains linguistic, and pedagogical materials continue to be linguistically motivated.

Focus on meaning

A growing sense that something was wrong, recognition that traditional synthetic syllabi and teaching procedures were not working as they were supposed to, and familiarity with the findings of studies of instructed interlanguage development have, over the years, led a small minority of experienced teachers and syllabus designers, and several SLA theorists, to advocate abandonment of a focus on formS in the L2 classroom in favor of an equally single-minded *focus on meaning* (Table 1, Option 2). Although the terminology has varied, some have gone so far as to claim that learning an L2 *incidentally* (i.e., without intention, while doing something else) or *implicitly* (i.e., without awareness) from exposure to comprehensible target language samples is *sufficient* for successful second or foreign language acquisition (L2A) by adolescents and adults, just as is it appears to be for first language acquisition (L1A) by young children (see, e.g., Corder, 1967; Dulay & Burt, 1973; Felix, 1981; Krashen, 1985; Wode, 1981). Others have suggested that harnessing L1A learning processes is adequate or even optimal as the basis for teaching a second or foreign language (see, e.g., Allwright, 1976; Krashen & Terrell, 1983; Newmark, 1966, 1971; Newmark & Reibel, 1968; Prahbu, 1987; Reibel, 1969). In fact, although the rationales have differed considerably, variants of the "noninterventionist" position go back hundreds of years, if not longer (see Howatt, 1984, pp. 192–208; Kelly, 1969, pp. 19–43). The essential claim is that people of all ages learn languages best, inside or outside a classroom, not by treating the languages as an object of study, but by experiencing them as a medium of communication. Language teaching syllabi of this second kind are what Wilkins (1976) termed *analytic:*

[P]rior analysis of the total language system into a set of discrete pieces of language that is a necessary precondition for the adoption of a synthetic approach is largely superfluous. Analytic approaches . . . are organized in terms of the purposes for which people are learning language and the kinds of language performance that are necessary to meet those purposes. (Wilkins, 1976, p. 13)

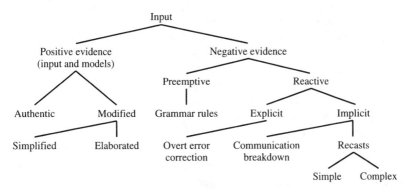

Figure 2   Data for SLA (adapted from Long, in press).

Although Wilkins's distinction focused on treatment of the language to be taught and said little about related learning processes, analytic syllabi assume, in current terminology, that adolescent and adult L2 learners are still capable, like young children, of (1) subconsciously analyzing linguistic input and inducing rules and/or forming new neural networks underlying what looks like rule-governed behavior, and/or (2) accessing, partially or completely, innate knowledge of linguistic universals and the way languages can vary. The emphasis, therefore, is on the provision of sufficient quantities of *positive evidence* about what is possible in the L2 (see Figure 2).

Some advocates of Option 2 claim that L2 samples may need to be modified in various ways in order to make them comprehensible to the learner, but that such modifications should be "natural." For example, modifications should be the result of negotiation for meaning in teachers' spontaneous attempts to communicate with less proficient speakers, and not the product of artificial linguistic "simplification," for example, through a priori manipulation of the lexical frequency, sentence length, and syntactic complexity of texts. A focus on meaning characterizes a variety of L2 classrooms, including those implementing Prabhu's procedural syllabus, Krashen and Terrell's Natural Approach, and some (but not all) content-based ESL instruction and immersion education.

Re-creating for older learners something akin to the conditions for child language acquisition would at first sight seem to be a reasonable proposal. Most child L1 or L2 learning is successful, after all, whereas most adolescent and adult L1 or L2 learning ends in at least partial failure even when motivation, intelligence, and opportunity are not at issue (for review, see Curtiss, 1988; Long, 1990; Newport, 1990) and despite the availability of (presumably advantageous) classroom instruction. Second, and of particular importance for some recent advocates of nonintervention (e.g., Krashen, 1985), there are the repeated findings of positive correlations between morpheme accuracy orders in naturalistic and instructed learners (for review, see Krashen, 1977; Larsen-Freeman & Long, 1991; Pica, 1984), methodological limitations of the morpheme studies notwithstanding (for review, see Long & Sato, 1984), as well as developmental sequences that do not appear to be modifiable by instruction (see, e.g., Lightbown, 1983; Pica, 1983; Pienemann, 1984, 1989). These results are to be expected if the primary constraints governing L2 development are universal cognitive ones and if new constructions must be comprehensible and processible before they are learnable and, therefore, teachable (Clahsen, 1987; Pienemann, 1989). The results provide support for the idea that the language teacher's primary function should be to facilitate the unfolding of what Corder recognized as the learner's powerful internal syllabus, not to try to impose an external one.

Another factor lending credence to the noninterventionist case, in this instance by default, is the diminishing credibility of many traditional instructional alternatives. Grammatical syllabi, linguistically "simplified" teaching materials, explicit grammar explanations, immediate forced student production, pattern practice, translation, error "correction," and other widely used teaching devices are often asserted by their advocates to account for classroom language learning success. As attested by the ratios of beginners and false beginners to finishers, however, the same phenomena are more frequently associated with failure, suggesting that the successful students may learn through them or in spite of them, not necessarily because of them.

Although more theoretically coherent than Option 1, Option 2 suffers from at least four problems. First, although the jury is still out, an increasing amount of evidence suggests that older learners no longer have the same capacity as young children to attain native norms in a new language simply from exposure to its use; that is, there appear to be maturational constraints on language learning (Hyltenstam, 1988; Long, 1990, 1993; Newport, 1990). Whether or not the explanation is biological, it is certainly the case that very few, if any, older learners achieve even near-native abilities, so at least when advanced proficiency is important, something will be needed to compensate for the loss. Second, studies show that adult acquirers with prolonged natural exposure may become fluent, but not nativelike, speakers (Long, 1997a; Pavesi, 1986; Schmidt, 1983); thus they reveal evidence of premature stabilization and of nonincorporation of input despite plenty of learning opportunity. Evaluations of French immersion programs in Canada, moreover, have found that although many child starters are successful in other subjects, eventually comprehend the L2 statistically indistinguishably from native speakers, and speak fluently, "their productive skills remain far from nativelike, particularly with respect to grammatical competence" (Swain, 1991a), even after more than 12 years of immersion at school and university in some cases. Some errors, such as failure to use the *vous* form appropriately, can be traced to infrequent exposure in classroom input (Harley & Swain, 1984), but others, such as failure to mark gender on articles correctly, cannot. Given that almost every utterance and sentence to which the students have been exposed throughout their schooling will have contained examples of gender-marked articles, it is unlikely that more exposure is all the students need. Rather, additional salience for the problematic features seems to be required, achieved either through enhancement of positive evidence or through provision of negative evidence of some kind (see Figure 1).

A third problem for purely analytic approaches, identified by L. White (1989, 1991) and others, is the unlearnability of some L1-L2 grammatical contrasts from positive evidence alone, for example, the English constraint barring adverb placement between verb and direct object, which is not observed by French speakers:

Je bois du café tous les jours.   I drink coffee every day.
Je bois tous les jours du café.   *I drink every day coffee.

An English speaker learning French should have no difficulty in learning the new verb-adverb-direct object option from its frequent occurrence in the input (positive evidence). The French speaker learning English, on the other hand, is faced with noticing the absence of the French option in the L2 English input, an unlikely outcome, as attested to by the persistence of this error in the speech even of many advanced French speakers of English. This is especially so, as L. White notes, since the deviant English structure (*He opened *carefully* the door) causes no breakdown in communication and is likely to be accepted by native speakers, leaving learners unaware of the existence of error.

Fourth, and finally, studies show that although learning much of an L2 through experiencing its use is possible, it is *inefficient*. There are rate advantages for learners who receive formal instruction of various kinds (for review, see R. Ellis, 1994a; Long, 1983a, 1988b), an issue of little theoretical significance but considerable practical importance for students.

Focus on form

There is a temptation for advocates of Options 1 and 2, traditional language teaching and nonintervention, to view problems with the rival position as support for their own. This is rarely justified, however, and can constitute yet another source of unproductive methodological pendulum swings. Evidence (see, e.g., R. Ellis, 1989; Lightbown, 1983) that developmental sequences do not reflect instructional sequences, for example, does not mean that attention to language as object is a waste of time. Some of the very studies (e.g., Pienemann, 1984, 1989) that have documented the robustness of developmental sequences, even in foreign and second language classroom settings, have simultaneously provided evidence of instruction's beneficial effects, for example, on the scope of application of a new rule or on the rate of acquisition. Further, theoretically motivated studies of classroom language learning (for review, see Mellow, 1992) have shown that instruction involving attention to code features can work, at least to induce short-term gains, as long as it is timed appropriately for particular groups of learners, apparently because it respects processing constraints on learnability (Pienemann, 1984). Similarly, evidence that some kind of instruction works does not mean that teachers should return to a focus on formS. Even if it were possible, for example, to sequence an entire structural syllabus to conform to learnability constraints, all the previously noted problems with Option 1 would remain. Probably the most intractable problem is the remote possibility that the timing of attention to a particular item would be right for all students in a class, given that placement testing is routinely based on the results of proficiency tests rather than on more appropriate interlanguage-sensitive measures.

Fortunately, the choice is not limited to either a focus on formS or a focus on meaning. Nor is it necessary to attempt to graft a synthetic syllabus, either lexical, as proposed by Willis (1993), or structural, as suggested by R. Ellis (1993), onto an analytic task-based one, the result of either of which process would be difficult to deliver in practice and theoretically unsatisfactory (for critiques of these proposals, see Long & Crookes, 1993a; and Robinson, 1994, respectively). A third option, which attempts to capture the strengths of an analytic approach while dealing with its limitations, is *focus on form* (FonF) (Long, 1988a, 1991; Long & Crookes, 1992). This approach is motivated (although by no means exclusively so) by the so-called Interaction Hypothesis (Long, 1981, 1983b, 1996), which holds that SLA is a process explicable by neither a purely linguistic nativist nor a purely environmentalist theory.

According to the Interaction Hypothesis, a crucial site for language development is interaction between learners and other speakers, especially, but not only, between learners and more proficient speakers and between learners and certain types of written texts, especially elaborated ones (Long, 1997b). Particularly important is the negotiation for meaning that can occur more or less predictably in certain interactions, for example, according to the kinds of tasks in which speakers are engaged and the prevailing task conditions. Among other benefits, modifications to the interactional structure of conversation that result from negotiation work (or from the elaboration of written texts; see Yano, Long, & Ross, 1994) increase input comprehensibility without denying learners access to unknown L2 vocabulary and grammatical forms, as tends to occur through linguistic "simplification" (Long & Ross, 1997), and provide important information about L2 form-function relationships. Negotiation work also elicits negative feedback, including recasts, that is, corrective reformulations of a child's or adult learner's (L1 or L2) utterances that preserve the learner's intended meaning. Such feedback draws learners' attention to mismatches between input and output, that is, causes them to focus on form, and can induce noticing of the kinds of forms for which a pure diet of comprehensible input will not suffice (e.g., items that are unlearnable from positive evidence or are rare, and/or semantically lightweight, and/or perceptually nonsalient, and/or cause little or no communicative distress – see Long, 1996; Pica, 1994; Pica, Lincoln-Porter, Paninos, & Linnell, 1996). In short,

[I]t is proposed that environmental contributions to acquisition are mediated by selective attention and the learner's developing L2 processing capacity, and these resources are brought together most usefully, although not exclusively, during *negotiation for meaning*. Negative feedback obtained in negotiation work or elsewhere may be facilitative of SL development, at least for vocabulary, morphology and language-specific syntax, and essential for learning certain specifiable L1-L2 contrasts. (Long, 1996, p. 414)

As indicated in Table 1, the syllabus for Option 3 is analytic, employing a nonlinguistic unit of analysis, such as task. Syllabus content is a series of *pedagogical tasks* (or, in some content-based approaches, curricular subject matter), the justification for which is that the content or tasks are related to the current or future needs of the particular group of learners to be served. As described elsewhere (Long, 1985, in press; Long & Crookes, 1992), pedagogical tasks are designed, with no specific linguistic focus, as successively more complex approximations to the *target tasks* that a task-based needs analysis has identified as facing the learner, such as attending a job interview, making an airline reservation, reading a restaurant menu or a journal abstract, writing a lab report, or taking a driving test. Attempts by the materials designer and teacher to make students notice the sorts of linguistic problems identified by L. White and others, described earlier, are not scheduled in advance by means of an external synthetic syllabus of some kind but, instead, exploit opportunities that arise naturally from the interaction of learners and tasks.

Focus on form refers to how focal attentional resources are allocated. Although there are degrees of attention, and although attention to forms and attention to meaning are not always mutually exclusive, during an otherwise meaning-focused classroom lesson, focus on form often consists of an occasional shift of attention to linguistic code features – by the teacher and/or one or more students – triggered by perceived problems with comprehension or production. This is similar to what happens when native speakers who are good writers pause to consider the appropriate form of address to use when composing a letter to a stranger, or when efficient readers suddenly "disconfirm a hypothesis" while reading and are momentarily obliged to retrace their steps in a text until they locate the item – perhaps a little *not* they had missed earlier in the sentence – which caused the semantic surprise. The usual and fundamental orientation is to meaning and communication, but factors arise that lead even the fluent language user temporarily to attend to the language itself.

The term can still mean different things, however. It is sometimes used to describe *observable external behavior.* For example, a teacher might explicitly attempt to draw students' attention to plural -*s*, having noticed that plural nouns were missing from their speech as they summarized the findings of a library research project on Japanese imports and exports, for example, by writing *cars* and *stereos* on the board, underlining the *s* in each case, pronouncing both words with exaggerated stress on the final sound, and having students repeat the words. The use of such devices to increase the perceptual salience of target items is what Sharwood Smith calls *input enhancement.* What it is hoped that a pedagogical activity will achieve and what it actually achieves are not necessarily the same, however. Studies – for example, Jones, 1992, and Slimani, 1991 – have shown that teachers' intended pedagogical focus and students' actual attentional focus often differ substantially, as does the pedagogical focus perceived by different students, and as do all three in terms of what is retained after a lesson versus what different students may report they have learned. Clearly, a more important sense of focus on form than the teacher's external behavior or its intended result is the learner's internal mental state. That is to say, how focal attention is allocated is something that is negotiated by the teacher and students and not directly observable. The intended outcome of focus on form is what Schmidt (1993b and elsewhere) calls *noticing:*

I use *noticing* to mean registering the simple occurrence of some event, whereas *understanding* implies recognition of a general principle, rule, or pattern. For example, a second language learner might simply notice that a native speaker used a particular form of address on a particular occasion, or at a deeper level the learner might understand the significance of such a form, realizing that the form used was appropriate because of status differences between speaker or hearer. Noticing is crucially related to the question of what linguistic material is stored in memory . . . understanding relates to questions concerning how that material is organized into a linguistic system. (Schmidt, 1993b, p. 26)

Focus on form – in the important sense of how the learner's attentional resources are allocated at a particular moment – *may* (not *will*) be achieved pedagogically by materials designers or teachers in a variety of ways, of which the following are but three illustrations. First, learners may work in pairs on a problem-solving task, the solution of which requires them, for instance, to synthesize information on economic growth in Japan from two or more written sources and use it to graph trends in imports and exports over a 10-year period. Successful completion of the task involves them in reading (and rereading) brief written summaries of sales trends for different sectors of the Japanese economy, each of which uses such terms as *rose, fell, grew, sank, plummeted, increased, decreased, declined, doubled, deteriorated,* and *exceeded.* The frequency of these lexical items in the input, due to their repeated use in the different passages, and/or their being underlined or italicized, makes them more salient, and so increases the likelihood of their being noticed by students. If a subsequent task encourages it, the lexical items are therefore more likely to be incorporated in their speech or writing, as has been demonstrated can occur with written input for such tasks that is "seeded" with grammatical items, with closed tasks more apt to produce the useful "recycling" of the target items than open tasks (Manheimer, 1993).

Alternatively, a teacher circulating among small groups of low-proficiency learners working on a problem-solving task may notice that several of them are repeatedly making the same word order error, saying things like "Red big triangle beside circle" and "Put green small circle above square." Having found the error to be pervasive and systematic, and (from the SLA literature and/or prior teaching experience) knowing the problem to be *remediable* for learners at this stage of development, the teacher is usually justified in briefly interrupting the group work in order to draw attention to the problem, using pedagogical devices appropriate for students of the age, literacy level, and metalinguistic sophistication concerned (for details, see Long, in press). Explicit negative feedback of various kinds has been evaluated in some of the studies reviewed in Part II of this volume.

Another way that focus on form may be attempted is through the provision of implicit negative feedback (see Figure 1). Work in child L1A suggests that grammatical information contained in corrective reformulations of children's utterances that preserve the child's intended meaning, known as *recasts,* is more likely to be noticed. The evidence for this is the higher frequency with which the children repeat those utterances compared with others, and the fact that recasts are more likely to facilitate acquisition than *models* containing the same grammatical information as evidenced, for example, by the rate of development of structures contained in recasts compared with models (see, e.g., Baker & Nelson, 1984; Farrar, 1992). Recent research on implicit negative feedback in child and adult L2A (e.g., Oliver, 1995; Ortega & Long, 1997; Richardson, 1995) has begun to produce similar findings, with adults thus far appearing to be even more sensitive to recasts than children, and to use the information the recasts contain more often – as evidenced by immediate incorporation during task-based conversation or by posttest gains in experimental studies – than children in the L1A studies (for review, see Long, 1996). If these early results are confirmed – and that is all they are as yet, *early results* – they will be especially useful for syllabus designers, materials writers, and classroom teachers interested in task-based language teaching, immersion education, Breen and Candlin's process syllabus, and related content-based language teaching programs, among others. Increased learner control over topic and topic-initiating moves in classroom discourse is a feature of some (but not all) types of task-based language teaching and facilitates a focus on meaning. Rather than such control obstructing attention to language as object, the findings suggest that it facilitates use of a particularly salient procedure, recasting, through which teachers and materials designers can deliver focus on form without interrupting a lesson's predominant focus on meaning, a goal of all such analytic approaches.

Research findings

As indicated earlier, the initial rationale for a focus on form, not formS (see Long, 1988a, pp. 133–136), was partly theoretical and partly based on inferences from the findings of early comparisons of naturalistic and instructed interlanguage development. However, a growing amount of more direct evidence for the utility of a focus on form is to be found in three more recent lines of research: experimental studies of implicit and explicit learning, experimental studies of primary attention to formS or meaning, and quasi-experimental studies of the effects of focus on form, to which we now turn.

Experimental studies of implicit and explicit learning

A number of recent experimental studies of SLA have been motivated by claims in cognitive psychology regarding the role of attention in learning, particularly differences in implicit versus explicit learning that Reber (1989, 1993) claims to have demonstrated in artificial grammar learning experiments (see Schmidt, 1994a, for review). Reber claims that his studies reveal evidence of implicit learning following instructions simply to memorize strings of letters generated by an artificial finite state grammar, with no conscious attention directed toward the rule-governed nature of the stimuli. Reber also claims that implicit learning is often superior to explicit learning following instructions to search consciously for rules. Like Krashen (1982, 1985, 1994), Reber concedes that when the stimulus domain is simple, and learner attention is focused on relevant aspects of the structures to be learned, then explicit conscious rule search and conscious application of rules following instruction can be more effective than implicit learning. However, the artificial grammars used by Reber are much less complex than the grammars of natural languages, for they lack a semantic component and many of the structure-dependent features of natural languages, such as recursion and phrasal embedding (see Braine, 1965; Pinker, 1994). Consequently, in designing computerized implicit and explicit learning conditions based on the work of Reber, experimental studies of SLA have used natural L2s (N. Ellis, 1993; Robinson, 1995a, 1996b, 1997a) or theoretically grounded artificial and semiartificial languages (De Graaff, 1997; DeKeyser, 1995, 1997; Robinson, 1997b) to generate the forms that are the focus of instruction.

Two studies in this area (DeKeyser, 1995; Robinson, 1995a, 1996b) support the conclusion that explicit FonF instruction leads to significantly greater short-term learning than does implicit learning for simple L2 rules, with no advantage for implicit learners over instructed learners for complex rules. One study (N. Ellis, 1993) demonstrates a short-term advantage for learners receiving instruction in complex rules, together with structured exposure to examples. These results provide insight into the microprocesses of SLA and establish comparability with findings and theoretical constructs in cognitive psychology that can thereby contribute to a theory of SLA mechanisms. For reasons described in Long and Crookes (1992), the results do *not* necessarily bear the interpretation that simple rules should invariably be presented prior to complex rules, in line with the focus-on-formS approach implied by proponents of structural syllabuses.

N. Ellis (1993) studied the learning of rules of Welsh morphology by native speakers of English under three conditions. A *random* group was exposed to a randomly ordered series of instances during training – Ellis's operationalization of an "implicit" learning condition. A *grammar* group was taught the rules to a criterion of success before those instances seen by the random group were presented. A *structured* group was taught a blend of rules and examples organized to make the structural alterations described by the rule salient, before being exposed to the same instances as the random and grammar groups. The training task performed in each condition required subjects to learn the English translation equivalents of Welsh phrases containing examples of "soft mutation," in which certain word-initial consonants change (e.g., from *c* to *g*, and from *p* to *b*) in specific contexts, such as following the personal pronoun for *his,* and in more general contexts where the change is triggered, for example, by the occurrence of feminine singular nouns following certain article forms. The rule system describing soft mutation is, therefore, a highly complex one. Despite extensive amounts of training (a total of 71,000 trials), Ellis's research failed to demonstrate implicit learning by the random group, which performed poorly on well-formedness tests and demonstrated little explicit knowledge of the rules in postexperimental debriefing sessions. The group instructed in the rules alone demonstrated explicit knowledge of the rules but was unable to transfer this to successful performance on the well-formedness test. Subjects in the structured group performed best on the well-formedness test and also demonstrated explicit knowledge of the rules.

Ellis's study demonstrates the insufficiency of what Sharwood Smith (1993) terms *elaborate* kinds of input enhancement, such as explicit rule statement, at least in the area of complex rules. The findings of successful performance by subjects in the structured exposure condition, who received both the rule *and* a less elaborate type of input enhancement, imply that the latter was responsible for the superior performance of this group. Ellis argues that both kinds of input enhancement in this condition established knowledge bases that were mutually influential, and that this synergy of rule knowledge and knowledge gained from structured exposure to examples contributed to successful performance. This is not a necessary conclusion, however. The results could have been due to structured exposure alone, in the sense of carefully sequenced presentation of examples. Unfortunately, no laboratory studies to date have isolated the effects of structured exposure on SLA from the effects of explicit rule statement or visual input enhancement, although see VanPatten and Oikkennon (1996) for results of a classroom study comparing a structured exposure group to a rule instruction group that showed advantages for the structured exposure group. (For extensive discussion of the utility of rule explanation as a pedagogical option for achieving focus on form, see DeKeyser, this volume; Doughty & Williams, this volume.)

DeKeyser (1995) examined the interaction between rule complexity and learning condition directly, using two dialects of an artificial language, Implexan, as the stimulus domain. *Implexan* is an agglutinative SVO language, marked for number and case on nouns, and for number and gender on verbs. Some of the agreement rules for the use of morphemes denoting case, number, and gender are categorical; for example, in one dialect, plural marking on nouns is always *-on*. Some Implexan rules, on the other hand, are prototypical in the sense that, for example, there is a choice between two possible morphemes for plural agreement on verbs, *-at* or *-it*, and the choice of the correct allomorph is probabilistically determined by features of the verb stem. If the stem is the prototype containing *-ust* as the last three letters, the plural morpheme is always *-at*. However, if the stem differs in one letter from the prototype, for example, *-usk*, there is only an 80% chance that the plural morpheme will be *-at*, and a 20% chance that it will be *-it*. If the stem differs by two letters from the prototype, for example, *-ufg*, there is only a 60% chance that the correct morpheme will be *-at*, and so on. Prototypical rules are therefore harder than categorical rules, in the sense that they are probabilistic, and impossible to reduce to economical rule statements that apply without exception to the morphological forms concerned.

In twenty learning sessions of 25 minutes each, subjects assigned to two conditions studied pairs of sentences and pictures and were subsequently asked, at the end of the training session, to identify whether certain sentences accurately described various pictures. Subjects in the implicit-inductive (I-I) condition received no instruction on rules of morphology and simply viewed the sentence-picture pairs, whereas subjects in the explicit-deductive (E-D) condition were additionally instructed in the rules for 5-minute periods before the start of the second, third, and eleventh training sessions. Following training, subjects performed a production task during which they wrote sentences describing pictures they had previously seen, as well as new pictures. Analyzing these data, DeKeyser found that E-D and I-I subjects performed at similar high levels of accuracy on the categorical rule (90% and 89%, respectively) in supplying the morphemes in sentences for previously viewed pictures. However, E-D subjects were significantly more accurate than I-I learners (57% and 33%, respectively) in generalizing instruction on categorical rules to the production of novel sentences describing new pictures, suggesting that any implicit learning that had been occurring on categorical rules was more item-dependent and memory-based than the explicit learning following rule presentation. In contrast, there was no difference between the conditions in production of prototypically determined morphemes on sentences describing old and new pictures, although the implicit learners appeared to be more sensitive to the probabilistic nature of those rules.

DeKeyser's results, therefore, partially confirm Reber's and Krashen's claims about the interaction of stimulus complexity and learning condition: Explicit learning was better for the simpler categorical rules. However, in contrast to Reber and Krashen, implicit learning was not superior to explicit learning on the complex prototypical rules. Other dimensions of rule complexity have been suggested, in addition to DeKeyser's proposal, that may interact in similar ways with learning condition, such as the learnability and markedness of structures described by rules, the interactions of L2 rules and L1 knowledge, and the interactions of structural complexity and the transparency (or lack thereof) of pedagogical explanations (for discussion, see DeKeyser, this volume; Doughty & Williams, this volume; Hulstijn, 1995; Robinson, 1996a).

Similar results to those of DeKeyser were obtained by Robinson (1995a, 1996b) with respect to the interaction of attention to form and the complexity of pedagogical rules of English. Robinson matched conditions motivated by Reber's research (an implicit condition, in which learners were instructed to memorize sentences, and a rule-search condition, in which learners were instructed to find rules regulating the sentences) with conditions motivated by Krashen's distinction between acquisition and learning (an incidental condition, in which learners were instructed to read sentences for meaning, and an instructed condition, in which learners were taught the rules and were instructed to apply them to sentences) in order to examine the comparability of learning in the unconscious implicit and incidental conditions, and in the conscious instructed and rule-search conditions. The easy and hard pedagogical rules that formed the basis of the sentences viewed by learners in each condition were identified empirically by asking experienced ESL teachers to rate the complexity of various pedagogical rule formats and, separately, to rate the complexity of structures described by those rules. These ratings clearly identified two rules, previously established to be unfamiliar to the targeted group of subjects for the study: an easy rule describing the constraints on subject-verb inversion following fronting of adverbials of time versus location ("Into the house John ran – ran John"/"On Tuesday Mary arrived – *arrived Mary"), and a hard rule describing how to form pseudoclefts of location ("Where Mary works is in Chicago, not in New York"/"Where the books are is on the table, not in the bag").

The subjects, 104 predominantly Japanese learners of ESL, viewed sentences generated by the rules in each condition. Results showed significantly more accurate performance on a transfer grammaticality judgment test of new sentences generated by the rules for subjects in the instructed condition. There was a significant difference between the more accurate instructed learners versus all others on the easy rule, and a significant difference between the more accurate instructed learners and rule-search learners on the hard rule. There were no significant differences between instructed and implicit or incidental learners on the hard rule. Instructed learners performed most poorly on ungrammatical examples of hard rule sentences, tending, wrongly, to accept them as grammatical. This overgeneralization of instruction is likely to be attributable to the fact that training in all conditions took place via positive evidence of grammatical examples. The learning that took place in the implicit and incidental conditions, though reaching lower overall levels of accuracy, resulted in more accurate performance on hard rule ungrammatical sentence types. These results, therefore, partially support Reber's and Krashen's claims regarding the interaction between rule learning and the complexity of rules, and are in line with findings by both N. Ellis and DeKeyser for the small-scale incremental evidence of implicit learning, suggesting a slow process that nonetheless avoids the excessive overgeneralization that can result from conscious rule application following training on positive examples of grammatical sentences alone.

Experimental studies of primary attention to formS versus primary attention to meaning

The laboratory studies described in the previous section were motivated by a concern for comparability with studies of implicit learning outside the field of SLA, and this has tended to weaken the external, pedagogical validity of the learning conditions operationalized. Other experimental studies not specifically addressing the implicit/explicit learning issue have contrasted performance on learning tasks of more direct consequence for L2 instruction. Doughty (1988, 1991) is one such example. Doughty studied the acquisition of relative clauses at different points on the Noun Phrase Accessibility Hierarchy (NPAH) (Keenan & Comrie, 1977) by twenty adult learners of ESL as a function of exposure under three conditions. A pretest-posttest design was used. Subjects were randomly assigned to one of three conditions, in each of which they read one of three versions of a text in order to perform skimming and scanning activities and answer comprehension questions. Embedded within the instructional materials were relative clauses of the object-of-a-preposition type ("I found the book that John was talking about"). One of the aims of the study was to see whether exposure to this relatively marked relative clause type would result in learning that generalized to other, less marked forms of relative clause, such as relativization of indirect objects ("The girl who I gave the present to was absent"), which the subjects had not yet acquired. Exposure to the relative clauses embedded in the texts was the focus of the instructional manipulation. A control group (COG) simply read the texts containing relative clauses, whereas a meaning-oriented group (MOG) received lexical and semantic rephrasings of the relative clauses that were highlighted and capitalized to make aspects of the structure visually salient; and the rule-oriented group (ROG) read the texts and received additional instruction implemented as rule statements appearing below an animated version of the sentences that also made the structural correlates of the rules visually salient to learners. Results showed that the meaning-oriented group outperformed both the others in transfer comprehension tests. Both the rule- and meaning-oriented groups outperformed the control group in posttest measures of relativization ability. That is, the meaning-oriented group, which processed sentences for meaning, demonstrated better comprehension than the other groups, and a gain equivalent to that of the rule-oriented group in relativization knowledge.

This result conflicts with the findings of VanPatten (1990) regarding the trade-off between attention to meaning and forms. Using a limited-capacity model of learner attentional resources, VanPatten showed that instructions to attend to form while listening in order to comprehend (as opposed to reading in the Doughty study) led to decrements in recall compared with a group instructed to listen only for meaning; performance was worst for learners instructed to attend simultaneously to grammatical morphology, as opposed to lexical items. There are obvious differences between the meaning and forms groups in VanPatten's and Doughty's studies, however, since VanPatten's methodology (asking subjects simply to check the occurrence of formal features when they heard them) involves "dual-task" performance for the meaning and forms groups, in contrast to less-resource-demanding "single-task" performance for the meaning-only group. Although this is true of the contrast between the control and rule-oriented groups in Doughty's study, too, it is clear that Doughty's meaning-oriented condition was not a dual task of the same order of difficulty as VanPatten's. In fact, limited-capacity, single-resource models of attention, which are seemingly adopted, implicitly or explicitly, by almost all L2 researchers, may be less appropriate than multiple-resource models, such as that described in Wickens (1989), which allow greater sensitivity to the modality and processing differences of L2 tasks (see Robinson, 1995b, pp. 293–295, for discussion).

It is important to note that it is not clear what caused the successful performance of Doughty's meaning-oriented group, since two possible causal variables were operating in that condition: the presence both of attention-drawing devices and meaning-oriented instructions to answer comprehension questions on the stimuli. Performance resulting from the treatment, that is, may have been either the result simply of attending to the meaning of the presented sentences containing relative clauses or the result of a conscious search for rules prompted by the salience-inducing highlighting of structural points in the examples. The confound is clear from the instructions to the meaning-oriented group, which required the subjects to read sentences in order to understand the meaning *and* the grammar (Doughty, 1988, p. 85). No debriefing sessions were used to identify the differential extent to which subjects were searching for, or aware of, rules during the meaning-oriented treatment. Consequently, as Schmidt (1994b, p. 2) comments, in both the unsuccessful control condition and the meaning-oriented condition, learners could have been actively pursuing hypotheses about the formal characteristics of stimulus sentences.[1] Comparing the results of Robinson's study, which demons-

---

1 Doughty (personal communication) points out that her study was not designed to examine the issues that are currently of interest to focus-on-form researchers, even though it is often discussed in this way in the literature. At the time of the relativization study, very few effects-of-instruction studies of any kind had been successfully carried out. Thus, the primary aim of Doughty's study was to establish empirically that L2 instruction (of either the meaning-oriented or the rule-oriented variety) was superior to mere exposure to marked relative clauses. In this light, several, more detailed points should be noted:
1. Since the overall aim of the computer-assisted instruction was to read and write about continuing stories, with the treatments appearing on the screen during this activity, all three conditions would currently be considered focus-on-form treatments of varying degrees of explicitness (i.e., the control group received an input flood – see Doughty & Williams, this volume). Interestingly, all three groups improved in relativization ability, although the two instructed groups improved significantly more than did the control group. Furthermore, with the exception of the input-flood (control) group, there were, indeed, several attention-drawing

trated lower acquisition (though in a different grammatical domain) for an incidental meaning-focused condition than for a rule-focused condition, and Doughty's study, which demonstrated equivalent learning for a focus-on-form condition (i.e., what she called, at the time, the meaning-oriented group) and a rule-focused condition, does, however, allow the inference that attention to meaning plus attention to formal features facilitated by the input enhancement techniques used by Doughty has advantages over attention to meaning alone.

This interpretation receives some support from a study by Alanen (1992, 1995) that examined the learning of two aspects of a semiartificial language, based on Finnish, by ESL learners randomly assigned to four conditions. In a classroom setting, subjects took part in two study sessions of 15 minutes each, during which they read texts containing examples of the two target structures: (1) locative suffixes -*lla*, meaning "on," -*ssa*, meaning "in," and -*ssa*, also meaning "on"; and (2) examples of a rule of consonant gradation that involved the change from double to single consonants (e.g., from -*ssa* to -*sa*) when the following syllable was open, that is, CV(V) as opposed to closed, that is, CV(V)C. Subjects were instructed to read the texts for meaning and were given two tasks after each reading to ensure that they had been reading for meaning – a reading comprehension test and a word-translation task. There were two meaning-based conditions, a control group that read an unmodified text (C), and a group that read the text with the target structures enhanced by italicization to promote noticing (E). There were also two FonF conditions, a group that read the unenhanced texts and was instructed in the rules for using locative suffixes and consonant gradation (R), and a group that received both the rule explanation and the enhanced texts (RE).

Analyses of the results of a postexperimental sentence-completion task, during which subjects were required to supply missing locatives and consonants, revealed superior performance on both structures by the rule-based versus the meaning-based treatments. With respect to production of consonants, both the R and the RE groups were significantly more accurate than the C and E groups. There was no significant difference between the two meaning-based and the two FonF groups. In production of locatives, the R group was significantly more accurate than the C and

devices in the instructional treatments. Any focus-on-form study designed now would likely aim to separate out (or determine the necessity of the combination of) these devices with respect to effectiveness for SLA.

2. The instructions to the two groups were intentionally the same so as not to bias one type of instruction over the other (in case one did prove to be more effective – although no directional hypotheses were entertained).

3. The meaning-oriented condition must be considered overall the most effective because not only did the subjects in that group improve in relativization but they also understood 70% of the text, whereas the control- and rule-oriented groups comprehended only about 35%.

E groups, whereas the RE group was significantly better than the C group alone. Further, analyses did reveal some differences between the group receiving enhancement alone versus the purely meaning-oriented control group, since the C group avoided the use of locative suffixes, producing many zero forms, whereas the E group – like the R and RE groups – produced a greater variety of suffixes, albeit incorrect forms. This suggests that the noticing facilitated by the textual enhancement led to a greater awareness of the suffixes, and thereby to hypothesis testing about correct forms, in the E group. It is possible, given the brief nature of the treatment, that over the longer term the E group's awareness might have led to greater accuracy. Interestingly, the meaning-based groups seemed more sensitive than the rule-based groups to the frequency of locatives in the input and tended to overgeneralize the use of the more frequent -*ssa* ending, in line with the findings for the item and frequency sensitivity of subjects in the implicit conditions of DeKeyser's and Robinson's studies. In contrast, the rule-based groups tended to overgeneralize the less frequent -*lla* suffix, meaning "on," using it in contexts properly occupied by the -*ssa* suffix, also meaning "on," perhaps in a conscious attempt to differentiate the functional uses of these two forms.

Alanen's study, then, while revealing local evidence of differences in learning processes under each condition, produced global findings similar to those of Doughty, since the rule-based R and RE groups outperformed the exposure-alone C group in learning locative suffixes and consonant gradation rules, in the same way that Doughty's instructed meaning- and rule-oriented groups outperformed the control group in learning relative clauses. Alanen's E group did not perform similarly to Doughty's meaning-oriented group, despite the fact that they both received similar forms of input enhancement, since the E group did not outperform the C group in learning either locative suffixes or consonant gradation rules. Possibly this was due to the fact, previously mentioned, that Doughty's meaning-oriented group was instructed to attend to meaning *and* grammar, in contrast to Alanen's E group, which was not so instructed. Possibly it was due also to the briefer exposure time in Alanen's study.

Global results similar to those of Doughty and Alanen, demonstrating the superiority of conditions facilitating attention to meaning and forms over exposure to meaning or forms alone, were also obtained by Hulstijn (1989) in a laboratory setting more controlled than either of the previously discussed studies. Hulstijn studied the effects of two primary conditions, focus on formS (Hulstijn's Form group) and focus on meaning (Hulstijn's Meaning Group 1), on measures of recall and retention of a structure by L2 learners of Dutch. The structure was a sentence containing a subordinate clause and a passive modal auxiliary. It was chosen because "intermediate learners of Dutch were unlikely to be familiar with all its grammatical properties" (1989, p. 55). The study thus lacked the elaborate pretesting which Doughty used to measure the extent of an equivalent group of learners' current knowledge of the instructional target or the control over prior knowledge achieved by Alanen's use of a language unknown to the subjects (Finnish). Hulstijn's research questions were whether attention to meaning alone would incidentally facilitate the acquisition of formal knowledge and whether the attention-to-meaning group would outperform the attention-to-form group on measures of both formal knowledge and knowledge of the content of target sentences.

Two sentence-copying pretests of knowledge of the target structure were administered, during which subjects were briefly shown sentences that they subsequently had to copy. Since exposure to the sentences was brief, accurate copying was taken to indicate the use of prior knowledge of the structure. The treatment for the formS group was a series of sentence fragment–ordering (anagram) tasks, in which subjects had to match eight sentence fragments with the order illustrated by a sentence appearing on a computer screen. In contrast, the meaning-oriented group was asked to read the sentences appearing on the computer screen and then were directed to provide their level of agreement with the idea of the sentence (for example, yes agree, agree somewhat, agree not at all). The posttest involved a cued recall task in which subjects were required to remember all the target sentences presented during training. This was scored for accuracy of structure and content. A second posttest measure followed; this was a retention test, identical to the sentence-copying pretest. Because of unequal periods of exposure required during the formS and the meaning treatments, a second meaning-oriented group (Hulstijn's meaning group 2) that had a much shorter exposure time and a formS and meaning group (Hulstijn's form and meaning group) were both added to the primary conditions as controls. The formS and meaning group subjects were simply directed to pay attention to both grammar and meaning and were not given any task to do. Subjects were adult learners of Dutch from a variety of non-Indo-Germanic L1 backgrounds. Results showed that recall of structure was better for the formS group and formS plus meaning groups, with the latter performing the best of all. There were no differences between groups on the second measure of learning, that of retention. These studies, therefore, have produced results suggesting that learning (of complex syntax) is better in subjects instructed to attend to meaning and forms than it is in groups instructed to attend to either forms or meaning alone.[2]

---

2 *Editor's note:* Hulstijn (1989) provides a different explanation for the greater success of the formS plus meaning control group. Since this group did not have to perform any task, subjects could view and process the sentences for twice the amount of time than could subjects in the other three groups. In addition, although there was no true control group in experiment 1 in Hulstijn (1989), this report also includes the findings of a second experiment that utilized the same tasks and procedures but

Quasi-experimental studies of the effects of focus on form

A series of classroom-based studies using intact group designs have investigated the effects of FonF instruction in intensive communicative language programs in Quebec. In an exploratory study, Lightbown and Spada (1990) investigated the influence of differences in the amount of FonF activity in four intact classes of French learners of English, in grades 5 and 6 (aged 10 to 12). Analyses of the classroom data using the Communicative Orientation of Language Teaching (COLT) observation scheme revealed that FonF activities "were almost always reactions to learners' errors or to student requests for assistance with some aspect of language use" (1990, p. 437) and rarely involved explicit grammar teaching.[3] The four teachers observed differed with respect to the amount of time spent focusing on form via corrective feedback (29% in one class, and between 10% and 13% in the other three classes) and also in the forms they chose to focus on. Using a suppliance in obligatory context analysis of production data obtained from a picture-description task, Lightbown and Spada found that learners in the class who received the most focus on form were most accurate in their use of progressive *-ing*, and at a higher developmental level in their use of the possessive determiners *his* and *her*. Other analyses suggested that individual teachers' sensitivity to, and reactions to, particular types of error – when accompanied by feedback making the errors salient to learners (by the use of grimaces or raised eyebrows) – were related to greater group accuracy on those features.

In a two-phase study using beginner-level subjects from the same program and at the same grade levels, L. White (1991) compared performance by two intact classes receiving formal instruction in question formation with three uninstructed classes. Instruction took place over 2 weeks, during which a week of explicit rule presentation was provided on the use of the auxiliaries *can, be,* and *do,* and question words *what, where,* and *when,* followed by corrective feedback on subsequent learner errors in the use of questions during class activities. Posttest scores on a sentence-correction activity immediately following the 2-week treatment showed significantly higher accuracy for instructed learners, with uninstructed learners tending to form questions with subject-verb inversion

substituted artificial grammatical forms (retaining natural language lexical items) and included a true control group that took the pretest, read some unrelated texts, and then took the posttest. Results of the second experiment largely paralleled those of the first; however, the advantage of the formS and meaning group was much smaller this time, and the control group exhibited a test effect. Hulstijn, therefore, attributes the gains reported to a combination of the treatment and the test effect.

3 *Editors' note:* In this study, focus on form and focus on formS (i.e., explicit grammar teaching) were not separated. The authors suggest, however, that the majority of activities were of the FonF type.

wrongly. A similar advantage for instructed learners was found in phase 2 of the study, which extended the range of testing procedures and examined the longer-term effects of instruction using a follow-up test 5 weeks after the period of instruction ended. After 2 weeks of instruction, the three treatment classes and the control class performed two written tasks and an oral communication task. On the first task, subjects corrected scrambled sentences and matched them with cartoon pictures. Instructed subjects, in contrast to the control group, made significant pretest to posttest gains in accuracy. These gains were maintained on the follow-up test. A similar pretest to posttest gain, maintained on the follow-up test, was made by the instructed group in performance accuracy on a preference-rating task of grammatical-ungrammatical pairs of questions and also in accuracy on the oral production task requiring them to use questions to match one of three sets of four pictures with pictures held by the researcher.

Spada and Lightbown (1993) provided further evidence of the long-term effects of instruction on question formation. Using similar groups of subjects to those in the previously described studies, and again following a 2-week period of explicit instruction and corrective feedback, Spada and Lightbown found that subjects in two classes demonstrated pretest to posttest gains in accuracy on the oral production task, and maintained this gain on the follow-up test 5 weeks later. Subjects continued to improve after entry into regular content classes, during which they received no ESL instruction, increasing in accuracy relative to the posttest on a final test administered 5 months later. Unfortunately, no comparison with a control group was possible in this study, since analyses of the classroom data revealed that the supposedly meaning-focused control group teacher had in fact been delivering extensive focus on form, with corrective feedback, on the targeted question forms. In an analysis of the use of questions according to developmental stage, using the Pienemann and Johnston (1986) six-stage model for the acquisition of word order, Lightbown and Spada also showed that greater numbers of subjects in the instructed conditions shifted developmental stages between the period from pretest to posttest, that is, the 2-week period of instruction, than between the posttest and the follow-up 5-week test or long-term 5-month test, suggesting the powerful influence of FonF instruction in accelerating development.

Conflicting findings regarding the long-term effects of focus on form emerge from three studies of the effect of functional-analytic teaching on the L2 acquisition of French in Canadian immersion programs. With intact groups and a pretest, posttest design to study the effect of materials that highlighted functional distinctions between the *imparfait* and the *passé composé*, used for 12 hours over an 8-week period, Harley (1989) found immediate posttest advantages for the instructed groups on cloze tests and oral interview tasks. However, this advantage was not maintained on a delayed posttest 3 months later. In contrast, using materials that focused on the use of the French conditional mood for a total of 17 hours over a 6-week period, Day and Shapson (1991) found immediate posttest gains for instructed learners on a cloze test and on accuracy in written compositions. They also found that the instructed group continued to outperform the control group on a delayed posttest administered 11 weeks later.

In a third study, Lyster (1994a) used materials that focused on *tu* and *vous* as markers of contextually appropriate language for 12 hours over a 5-week period and found immediate posttest advantages for the instructed groups over comparison groups in the use of *tu* and *vous* in a written production test and on a multiple-choice test – an advantage maintained on a delayed posttest 1 month later. However, functional-analytic teaching, as operationalized by Lyster, consisted of a variety of techniques, such as explicit comparison of speech acts containing the target forms, structural exercises highlighting verb inflections resulting from the use of *tu* and *vous*, and intensive reading activities focused on the use of *tu* and *vous* in dialogues (1994a). Consequently, as Lyster notes, it remains difficult to determine which aspects of the instruction contributed to learning (1994a). This is a problem affecting each of the previously mentioned claims for the effectiveness of focus on form during functional-analytic teaching.

In a quasi-experimental study isolating just one of the instructional features subsumed by functional-analytic teaching, the use of visual input enhancement, Leeman, Arteagoitia, Fridman, and Doughty (1995) examined the effects of focus on form on the learning of preterit and imperfect tenses in Spanish during content-based instruction. They contrasted performance by a group receiving a purely communicative treatment and a group receiving an integrated focus on form. The treatment was delivered in two 50-minute periods of instruction. Before the first period, both groups were assigned the same reading and questions on a topic in Spanish history. The target forms were highlighted, underlined, and color-coded for the treatment group. Subjects were instructed to read and answer questions in preparation for a discussion. In addition to input enhancement, the treatment group was also told to pay special attention to how temporal relations were expressed in the materials. During the first class discussion session, the treatment group, in contrast to the communicative controls, received corrective feedback targeted at the use of preterit and imperfect tenses. This varied from recasts, through presentation of models, to the use of gestures and expressions to indicate errors. The second class session consisted of a debate, during which the treatment group was again told to be careful when expressing temporal relations and was given corrective feedback. The communicative group was not so instructed or corrected. This treatment was, therefore, brief (two class sessions and homework periods) and administered outside the classroom (reading texts for homework), as well as inside the classroom (receiving corrective feedback). Comparing pretest and posttest scores on three measures, a cloze completion task, a written essay, and an analysis of production during two in-class debates, Leeman et al. found a significant pretest to posttest gain only for accuracy and suppliance (amount of use) of preterit and imperfect forms during the debates. No significant pretest to posttest differences were found for performance on the other measures for either group (although there was some evidence of interlanguage change in the FonF group, such as increased attempts at expressing past and a shift away from reliance on preterit for all contexts). Further, the slight advantage for the FonF treatment group (although perhaps understandable, given the brief nature of the treatment) must also be interpreted with caution, since it was based on scores for only half of the treatment group, that is, five subjects, for five others were absent during one of the pretest or posttest debates.

Conclusion

Although numerous issues have been left untreated here because they are considered elsewhere in this volume, some brief final comments are in order on the issue of the explanation of the effect of focus on form and the limitations of some of the studies reviewed in this chapter as well as on methodological considerations for future work in this area.

The causal variable to which Leeman et al. attribute the gains for instruction is learner *noticing*. Following Tomlin and Villa (1994), they equate noticing with the process of detection. However, it is likely that subjects in both conditions detected the target forms in the reading materials, since very low levels of attention are necessary for detection, and detection is not necessarily accompanied by awareness – the distinguishing feature of noticing identified by Schmidt (1990). Further, detection alone may not be sufficient for registering in short-term and, subsequently, long-term memory (see Robinson, 1995b). The further processing necessary for encoding detected material in short-term memory may well have been facilitated by the instructional treatment, but only memory measures could establish that. Studies of the short- and long-term effects of focus on form may benefit from the sophisticated methodologies for distinguishing implicit and explicit memory used in cognitive psychology, since these may be differentially sensitive to implicit and explicit learning (for review, see Robinson, 1995b). This is an option so far not adopted in SLA research.

Where models of attention are concerned, most studies appear to assume a limited-capacity model of the learner (e.g., Foster & Skehan, 1996; Leeman et al., 1995; VanPatten, 1990) in which attention is considered to be a single, undifferentiated resource. But other models of attention exist which argue that multiple resources are available, drawing on distinct pools, relative to different aspects of task demands. According to these models, simply put, forms and meaning are not necessarily always in competition for attention (Wickens, 1989). The implications of multiple resource theory are therefore important to predictions about the effects of focus on form during L2 task performance but have not been considered by SLA researchers so far.

With respect to measures of memory, all current studies of the short- and long-term effects of focus on form assess memory using what have been termed *explicit* or *direct* tests of conscious recall (e.g., Lightbown & Spada, 1990; Spada & Lightbown, 1993; L. White, 1991). However, other implicit or indirect measures of memory exist (Schacter, 1987) that may be equally sensitive to the learning occurring in instructed or incidental conditions. In fact, these measures have been claimed to be particularly sensitive to incidental learning resulting from a focus on meaning, which is an important reason why they should be used in FonF research in SLA.

With regard to measures of awareness, as pointed out earlier in this chapter, in an important sense, focus on form is learner-initiated, and it results in noticing. Examining the causal relationship between focus on form, noticing, and learning requires the use of sensitive measures of learner awareness (see Schmidt, 1993a; Shanks & St. John, 1994). At the very least, these measures should include debriefing questionnaires to probe the extent to which learners were focused on form during the instructional treatments, rather than assuming that the instructional treatment translated directly into the quality of learner attention and awareness. However, many of the studies reported in this chapter do not use such measures (e.g., Doughty, 1991; Leeman et al., 1995), and consequently there may be doubts about whether different treatments were actually delivered.

Finally, effects for instruction of any kind may be, and probably almost always are, gradual and cumulative rather than instantaneous and categorical, and they draw on memory for noticed features at subsequent points in development as learners process linguistic material at higher levels. Consequently, effects of instruction attributable to noticing may not be immediate and may result from the delayed interaction of materials noticed and available for recall (rather than simply detected), with developmental processes occurring along other dimensions of language ability than those specifically targeted by the instructional treatment. With these considerations in mind, and given the generally slow, non-linear, and partial nature of much L2 learning, using production measures, especially those demanding nativelike performance of target items, as immediate posttests in studies of the relative effectiveness of focus on formS, meaning, and form, is likely to underestimate the effectiveness of all three treatments. Ideally, future studies should allow for longer periods of exposure than has often been the case to date, despite the difficulty of controlling extraneous variables that longer exposure causes. Short-term studies are likely to underestimate the impact of all three treatments, but especially that of focus on meaning and focus on form, since these two conditions are effective with complex learning problems – problems whose solutions take time.

3 Beyond focus on form

Cognitive perspectives on learning and practicing second language grammar

Robert M. DeKeyser

Introduction

Although the applied linguistics literature of the 1980s was characterized by a debate over whether or not second language instruction should make students attend to form (e.g., Krashen, 1982; Long, 1988a), the vast majority of publications since the early 1990s support the idea that some kind of focus on form is useful to some extent, for some forms, for some students, at some point in the learning process (see, e.g., DeKeyser, 1995; N. Ellis, 1993; R. Ellis, 1993; Robinson, 1996b; Spada & Lightbown, 1993; VanPatten & Cadierno, 1993a, 1993b). Beyond that basic, tentative agreement, however, uncertainty looms large. What forms should students be made to focus on – and how and when? And how much difference is this focus on form expected to make on what kinds of outcome measures for what kinds of students?

These questions constitute a daunting research agenda, but a number of hypotheses and tentative answers can already be found, sometimes in the second language literature (see Long & Robinson, this volume), sometimes in the cognitive psychology literature. Within the length constraints of this chapter, I will concentrate on the psychological literature. I will start with the question of *what* forms are amenable to focus on form, first giving a brief overview of the variables that are likely to play a role. After that I will discuss the *how* and *when* of focus on form, again on the basis of the psychological literature.

Focus on what kind of form?

The question of what elements of language are most amenable to focus on form has been dealt with mostly from a linguistic point of view. It is

I thank Catherine Doughty, Barry McLaughlin, Lionel Menasche, Christina Bratt Paulston, Dorolyn Smith, and Jessica Williams for their comments on earlier drafts of parts of this chapter.

rather uncontroversial that pronunciation is relatively immune to all but the most intensive formS-focused treatments, whereas large amounts of vocabulary can be acquired with very little focus on form. According to N. Ellis (1994b), it is the formal aspect of vocabulary (as opposed to meaning) that is learned the most implicitly (without the learner consciously focusing on it). Even immigrants who have had very little schooling in general and no formal second language training at all, and who have made little progress toward the second language phonology, morphology, or syntax, normally acquire a fairly wide range of functional vocabulary. However, although focus on form may not be necessary for vocabulary and may not be sufficient for pronunciation, the issue is more complex in the area of morphosyntax.

The linguistic variables that have been discussed most frequently in terms of their significance for the question of focus on form are the relevance of Universal Grammar (UG), the need for negative evidence, and the degree of complexity of the target language feature. The first two of these variables have clear implications for instruction. If a structure is part of UG, and UG is accessible to the second language learner, then all that is needed is sufficient input to trigger acquisition, unless L2 is a subset of L1. In the latter case, negative evidence is required; examples in English L2 are adverb placement or interrogative structures for native speakers of French (L. White, 1991; L. White, Spada, Lightbown, & Ranta, 1991). If a structure is not part of UG or cannot be acquired without negative evidence, then a rather strong variant of focus on form, including rule teaching and error correction, will be required. These two ways of reasoning have become widely accepted; the only controversial aspect is finding out what exactly is part of UG, how accessible it is in SLA, and consequently, what structures cannot be learned without negative evidence. The tendency on this point seems to be to see more and more parts of grammar as falling within the domain of UG; even morpheme acquisition orders have received explanatory support from recent developments in syntactic theory (Zobl, 1995).

The variable of complexity is, perhaps appropriately, more difficult to conceptualize. Krashen (1982) made a distinction, which has become widely known, between rules that are easy to acquire but hard to learn, and rules that are easy to learn but hard to acquire. Clearly, rules of the latter type are prime candidates for focus-on-form (FonF) teaching, unless of course one does not consider (initially) monitored knowledge to be useful at all. Again, the implication of this distinction is clear; the problem lies with agreeing on what makes a rule easy to learn but hard to acquire. For Krashen (1982, pp. 97–98), it is the combination of formal and functional simplicity, the typical example being third person -*s*. R. Ellis (1990, p. 167) has made a similar pair of distinctions between simple versus complex processing operations and between transparent versus

opaque form-function relationships, the former apparently corresponding to Krashen's dimension of formal complexity and the latter to his
dimension of functional complexity. Third person -*s*, however, is classified by Ellis as formally complex, instead of formally simple, as Krashen
would have it. Ellis (1990, p. 173, footnote 14) justifies this by referring
to Pienemann, who pointed out that third person -*s* involves a long-
distance relationship with the grammatical number of the subject.
Krashen and Ellis agree, nonetheless, that lack of formal complexity
benefits learnability, and, as a result, Krashen classifies third person -*s* as
easy to learn, because it is formally simple (cf. also Bialystok, 1979; Green
& Hecht, 1992, pp. 179–180), whereas Ellis classifies it as eventually
learnable, but only when the learner is developmentally ready to acquire
the new feature, because it is formally complex.

Functional complexity is equally hard to define. Although Krashen and
Ellis seem to agree that third person -*s* is functionally simple, one could
certainly argue that its form-function relationship is far from transparent,
because one morpheme expresses several semantic concepts at the same
time (present tense, singular, third person), and the rule has a number of
high-frequency exceptions (modals). Many inflectional morphemes (at
least in inflectional as opposed to agglutinative languages) show such
complexity in their form-function relationship. Furthermore, it is hard to
see how a rule could be formally simple if it is functionally complex,
except in the very superficial sense that a rule can be regarded as formally
simple if it involves nothing but presence versus absence of a single morpheme. Again, the third person -*s* is an example: Although presence
versus absence of -*s* may seem like a simple phenomenon, the statement
of the rule must reflect the functional complexity if it is to be correct, and
it is the complexity of the rule and not its surface realization that will
determine how hard it is to learn (cf. Hulstijn & De Graaff, 1994).

Other researchers, for example, Hulstijn and De Graaff (1994), do not
even agree that simple rules are the best candidates for teaching, because
they assume that the easier rules are precisely the ones that students can
discover for themselves. This does not imply that easy rules should not be
the subject of focus on form; some kind of input enhancement may help
to make students find the easy rules. The point is that, instead of giving up
on more difficult rules, teachers may have to put the most emphasis on
them. Ultimately, the answer to this question is likely to depend on the
nature of the student population: Although an academic population may
indeed fit the pattern described by Hulstijn and De Graaff, the average
learner is probably unlikely to induce explicitly any rules at all, and
unlikely to induce implicitly any but the most semantically transparent
and formally simple rules. Thus, although rule complexity is a likely
criterion for focus on form, complexity is hard to define; consequently,

researchers do not always agree on whether some of the most frequently taught rules are simple or complex. Even the very question of whether complexity of a rule makes it a good or bad candidate for focus on form may have different answers, depending on the student population and the degree of focus on form envisaged.

Other linguistic criteria for the desirability of focus on form include reliability of the rule, that is, the extent to which the rule holds true in all the cases to which it applies; scope of the rule, that is, the number of cases in which it applies; and semantic redundancy. Hulstijn and De Graaff (1994) hypothesize that instruction is especially useful for rules with high reliability and wide scope and for rules with semantic redundancy where production is concerned, but also for rules without such redundancy in comprehension.

A different set of criteria comes from research in cognitive psychology, more specifically from the plethora of recent studies on the learning of artificial grammars and other forms of sequence learning (for recent overviews, see Carr & Curran, 1994; Reber, 1993; Shanks & St. John, 1994; for recent discussions of the implications for second language acquisition, see DeKeyser, 1995; Schmidt, 1994b; VanPatten, 1994a). Research in this area has yielded two main findings. First, subjects tend to learn better under conditions of implicit induction (i.e., mere exposure to a very large set of instances or memorization of a set of exemplars) than under conditions of explicit induction (i.e., where they are asked to figure out the rules), in the sense that subjects in the implicit condition are subsequently better at making grammaticality judgments than are their explicit counterparts. Second, even though subjects in the implicit condition perform well, they are unable to state rules about what letter sequences are allowed in the artificial grammar or what regularities they are observing in other kinds of sequence learning.

These findings have led Arthur Reber and a number of other researchers (see, e.g., Mathews et al., 1989; Reber, 1989, 1993; Seger, 1994; Winter & Reber, 1994) to conclude that subjects can learn abstract rules implicitly and can subsequently draw on these rules without being able to state them. The crux of the matter is, however, that it is unclear whether subjects induce rules or memorize exemplars and then later judge new instances on the basis of their similarity with the exemplars. Some researchers have claimed that subjects do not learn abstract rules implicitly but, rather, learn exemplars or parts of exemplars (bigrams or trigrams) explicitly (see, esp., Dulany, Carlson, & Dewey, 1984, 1985; Perruchet & Pacteau, 1990, 1991). Several recent literature reviews (e.g., Carr & Curran, 1994; Shanks & St. John, 1994) favor the view that, although implicit learning of similarity patterns is possible, implicit learning of abstract rules is not. (This conclusion follows from using strict definitions of the terms *implicit* and *rule* and from empirical studies that experimentally dissociate abstract patterns without surface similarity from surface similarities that do not conform to clear rules).

It is important, therefore, to reflect on what makes a structural pattern in natural language an abstract rule or a similarity, and then to assess to what extent these different kinds of structure can be learned with different degrees of focus on form (cf. Bialystok, 1979; Green & Hecht, 1992; Hulstijn & De Graaff, 1994). Two factors conspire to determine whether a structure is most easily learned as a similarity pattern or whether the learner must induce an abstract rule, in which case the structure is harder to notice without explicit focus on form. The first factor is surface variation that tends to conceal the rule: A simple agreement rule, for instance, stating that the verb has to be marked as plural whenever the subject is plural, can be hard to notice for the learner, because both the plural on the verb and the plural on the noun can be realized by different morphemes in an inflectional language, depending on the tense of the verb or the case of the noun. In addition, the different morphemes may present allomorphy, depending on what noun or verb classes the lexical items belong to, or what the phonological characteristics of the stem are. The second factor that makes the structure a rather abstract rule is the distance between the co-occurring elements. To continue with the example of subject-verb agreement, the plural noun and the plural marking on the verb can be separated by noun phrase complements or adverbs, for instance. These two factors make the structural regularity difficult to notice perceptually, and yet it is very simple to state abstractly: Whenever the subject is plural, mark the verb as plural.

A similarity pattern, on the other hand, such as the prototypicality patterns in irregular past tenses in English (cf. Bybee & Moder, 1983; Bybee & Slobin, 1982; Marcus et al., 1992), can be impossible to fully state abstractly, because the pattern may be a probabilistic, prototypical system in which a number of phonological or semantic characteristics determine only the likelihood that a certain morpheme or allomorph will appear. But if the factors that influence these formal alternations are in the immediate proximity, then regardless of how complicated and probabilistic the similarity pattern may be, noticing these co-occurrences at some level can actually be easier than noticing the more regular abstract rules, which, as mentioned before, are concealed because of the surface variations and the distance of co-occurring elements.

Empirical evidence for the differential impact of explicit focus on form in the learning of abstract rules versus probabilistic patterns in a second language can be found in DeKeyser (1995). Subjects in that study learned simple abstract morphosyntactic rules in a miniature linguistic system significantly better under conditions of explicit-deductive learning (traditional rule teaching followed by thousands of illustrative picture and sentence combinations) than under implicit-inductive conditions (mere exposure even to thousands of combinations of pictures and sentences), but they learned the probabilistic patterns in the noun and verb endings somewhat better under implicit-inductive conditions than they did under explicit-deductive conditions. Knowledge was measured by having subjects type sentences they had never encountered before in response to color pictures they had never seen before. In the same vein, N. Ellis (1993) found that explicit grammar presentation, followed by systematic examples and ample practice, yielded better results than several alternatives; his study dealt with initial consonant mutation in Welsh. Robinson (1996b) likewise found that explicitly instructed learners outperformed all others (in implicit, incidental, and rule-search conditions) on simple morphosyntactic (ESL) rules. This was not the case for more complex rules, which seem to be too much to handle for most learners, and therefore, even if they can be stated as abstract rules that always apply, are of no more use than explicit teaching of prototypicality patterns was in DeKeyser (1995).

These three studies were all computerized and highly controlled. In most cases, the learners probably had enough time to monitor their responses to some extent, which means that no strong claims can be made about subjects having any knowledge that would allow for fast, spontaneous performance. The remainder of this chapter is largely devoted to the question of what can be done to improve subjects' performance in that sense, once they have acquired explicit knowledge of abstract rules.

What kind of focus on form?

It is clear that focus on form would not be very useful if it led only to monitored knowledge. The crucial question, therefore, is whether the explicit knowledge that results from sequential models of FonF instruction (see Doughty & Williams, this volume) can eventually be fully automatized. This question immediately brings to mind the interface controversy, but it is not quite the same issue. Krashen's noninterface position (see esp. 1982, p. 83, 1994, p. 47) conflates two issues when he states that the traditional concept of automatization of consciously learned rules is wrong because it implies that "learned knowledge" can become "acquired knowledge." The two distinctions are the explicit (conscious) versus the implicit (unconscious) and the controlled versus the automatic. Both Bialystok (e.g., 1981, 1990, 1994b) and R. Ellis (e.g., 1993, 1994b) have argued repeatedly that these dimensions are distinct, in the sense that both explicit (largely conscious) and implicit (largely unconscious)

48   *Robert M. DeKeyser*

knowledge can vary in their degree of automatization. John Anderson's Adaptive Control Theory (ACT) model of cognitive skill acquisition (1982, 1983, 1993; cf. also Anderson & Fincham, 1994), on the other hand, although not conflating the two dimensions as Krashen does, certainly implies that automatization is dependent on knowledge being implicit (or *procedural* in Anderson's terminology),[1] and that the implicit/ explicit and controlled/automatic dimensions are not completely independent, as Bialystok and Ellis contend. Because Anderson's is the most widely accepted model in the cognitive psychology of skill acquisition, although by no means the only one, I will present it in some detail in the next section and then explore its implications for second language teaching.

Some concepts from skill acquisition theory

The literature on skill acquisition usually distinguishes three stages. In the terminology of Fitts and Posner (1967), for example, there is a cognitive, an associative, and an autonomous stage. In John Anderson's (e.g., 1982, 1983, 1987, 1990, 1993, 1995) terminology of declarative versus procedural knowledge, this corresponds to the three stages of (1) declarative knowledge, (2) proceduralization of knowledge, and (3) automatizing or fine-tuning procedural knowledge, as Anderson explicitly points out (1982, p. 369, 1995, pp. 319–340). It should be noted that, in his more recent writings, Anderson has acknowledged that not all knowledge is initially declarative. Anderson and Fincham (1994), for instance, state: "It is too strong to argue that procedural knowledge can never be acquired without a declarative representation or that the declarative representation always has to be in the form of an example that is used in an analogy process. Nonetheless, the research does indicate that this is a major avenue for the acquisition of procedural knowledge" (p. 1323).

Declarative knowledge is factual knowledge, for example, knowing that Napoleon was defeated in 1815 or knowing that most English verbs take an -s in the third person of the present tense when the subject is singular. Proceduralized knowledge encodes behavior. It consists of condition-action pairs that state what is to be done under certain circum-

---

1 Although they do not have exactly the same meanings, the terms *explicit/implicit* and *declarative/procedural* are often used interchangeably. Anderson (1993, pp. 22–25), for instance, discusses a variety of strands of the literature on explicit/implicit learning and memory using the term *declarative/procedural*; Anderson (1995, p. 308) states that declarative knowledge is explicit, and procedural knowledge is "often implicit." A discussion of the fine distinctions between these two pairs of terms is not relevant to this chapter. The reader is referred to Shanks & St. John (1994, p. 368).

stances or with certain data. Fully automatized procedural knowledge means, for instance, that one uses a third person -*s* for singular verbs without having to think about it.

Learners in this final stage of skill acquisition may lose the declarative knowledge of the rule, although this is not necessarily the case. I was confronted with a striking example of losing declarative, but not procedural, knowledge recently when our departmental secretary asked me what the combination of my office door lock was. I could not answer his question, even though I had opened my office door many times. The secretaries, of course, have procedural knowledge of how to open the combination locks on their doors; further, they do not lose the corresponding declarative knowledge, because they rehearse the knowledge in declarative form each time they give somebody in the department the combination to the main office. This is analogous to the situation of the foreign language teacher who is fluent in the target language, having spoken it daily for many years, but still remembers the rules, because he or she teaches them to students. The teacher's friends, however, who took the same language courses and also used the language for many years, but whose professions have nothing to do with the language, have proceduralized their knowledge but have lost its declarative form (cf. Furey, 1987).

The crucial point in all of this, of course, is not whether one eventually loses declarative knowledge, but how one moves from exclusively declarative knowledge to at least partially procedural knowledge. The essential notion to bear in mind here is that proceduralization is achieved by engaging in the target behavior – or procedure – while temporarily leaning on declarative crutches (Anderson, 1987, pp. 204–205; Anderson & Fincham, 1994, p. 1323), in other words, as in the previous examples, pushing the buttons to open the door while thinking of the digits or conveying a message in the second language while thinking of the rules. Repeated behaviors of this kind allow the restructuring (cf. Cheng, 1985; McLaughlin, 1990) of declarative knowledge in ways that make it easier to proceduralize and allow the combination of co-occurring elements into larger chunks that reduce the working memory load. Once this crucial stage in skill acquisition has been reached, strengthening, fine-tuning, and automatization of the newly acquired procedural knowledge are then a function of the amount of practice, which increases speed and reduces the error rate and the demand on cognitive resources (Anderson, 1987, 1990, 1995; Logan, 1988; Schneider & Shiffrin, 1977). (For an excellent overview of theories of automatization, see Schmidt, 1992; for empirical evidence pertaining to the broader issue of a three-stage model of skill acquisition, see esp. Anderson, 1995; Anderson & Fincham, 1994.) The next section provides a brief sketch of how practice, the crucial element in the acquisition of skill, has been dealt with in second language teaching methodology.

A short history of the concept of practice in second language learning

The term *practice* is used here in the sense of engaging in an activity with the goal of becoming better at it. A brief history of the concept of practice in second language learning should help to bring this notion into focus. As always, a history of this sort is oversimplified, since what most teachers end up doing in the classroom is not exactly a stereotypical implementation of any method.

For *Grammar Translation* teachers, teacher-student interaction typically meant two things: checking and improving the students' memory of rules and vocabulary items, and checking and improving their comprehension of the grammar rules that had been taught. In other words, for these teachers, there was no practice in the sense of striving for more fluency or more spontaneous use of the language, given that productive fluency was normally not an objective of foreign language teaching at the time. To the extent that students gradually became able to use the basic structures with increasing ease, this was a happy side effect of the fact that the same forms-meaning correspondences tended to occur over and over again in translation practice, which was really meant to ensure comprehension and memorization of more advanced rules. Drilling, in this method, was limited to reciting paradigms for verb conjugation or noun declension; it did not involve the kind of sentence manipulation that would be so typical of some later methods.

Teachers following the *Direct Method* made extensive use of highly contrived but contextualized teacher monologues, and student practice consisted largely of meaningful drills involving the structures presented in these monologues (cf. Howatt, 1984, pp. 192 ff.). (I am using the term *meaningful drill* with the meaning it has in the three-way distinction that Paulston [e.g., 1971] made between mechanical, meaningful, and communicative drills.) Mechanical drills are exclusively formS-focused; one can usually perform them without paying any attention to meaning whatsoever, for example, the transformation from "I ate an apple. What did I eat?" to "You ate an apple" and from "I bought a book. What did I buy?" to "You bought a book." Meaningful drills require the student to process meaning, but do not require a student to communicate anything the hearer did not already know, for example: "Is this a pen or a pencil?" "It's a pencil." Communicative drills do require conveying actual content unknown to the hearer, for example, "What did you do this weekend?" "I went fishing." "Did you go fishing too, Kevin?" "No." "No? What did you do then?" "I went swimming with my brother." Direct Method teachers, then, relied heavily on meaningful drills, because learning activities were less structurally controlled and more situationally controlled than was going to be the case in later methods.

The *Audiolingual Method,* of course, has become almost synonymous with the use and abuse of mechanical drills, even though, in practice, quite a few Audiolingual teachers possibly used meaningful and communicative drills rather frequently. Be that as it may, it is probably fair to say that, for most teachers using this method, most time was (and is) spent on a variety of mechanical drills, from repetition and substitution to transformation drills, following theoreticians such as Rivers (1964). When the same author cautions against excessive amounts of drill (1964, p. 150), it is because of the danger of boredom and fatigue, not for psycholinguistic reasons. And, when the possibility of an occasional spontaneous conversation is evoked (1964, p. 158), it is argued that this is good for motivation, not that it is necessary because of the cognitive psychology of skill acquisition.

Cognitive Code was very much a compromise between Grammar Translation and Audiolingualism. John Carroll (1974) and Kenneth Chastain (1971), among others, argued for concept attainment prior to practice, as in Grammar Translation, but for lots of practice, as in Audiolingualism. At that time, that is, the late 1960s and early 1970s, there was an increasing awareness of the importance of communication in second language teaching, for both theoretical and practical reasons. At first, this meant that methodologists like Paulston and Bruder (1976) or Rivers and Temperley (1978) argued for the importance of the communicative stage in the sequence of going from mechanical via meaningful to communicative (MMC). But quickly, communicative language teaching took on a variety of meanings, stressing sociolinguistic competence, the importance of function over structure as an organizing principle, and the importance of fluency over accuracy, or learning through communication rather than through focus on form. All of this led teachers and learners away, in various directions, from the systematic practice of form.

The *Natural Approach* went even further, not only doing away with the structural syllabus but explicitly rejecting the notion of practice in production. Practice does not make perfect, Krashen says (e.g., 1982, p. 60). For him, speaking skills are improved more from getting comprehensible input when reading a book than from practice in speaking. This follows, of course, from his idea that forms are acquired via comprehensible input only, and that once acquired, a form is fully available for production, except for the effect of the "output filter" (Krashen, 1985). It follows logically that drills of any kind have no principled place in this method. As was the case for the Audiolingual Method, however, practitioners took a less extreme point of view; some of the activities suggested in Krashen and Terrell (1983, pp. 78 ff.) look like meaningful drills and are reminiscent of the contextualized practice of the Direct Method.

After this brief overview of the main methodologies from the point of view of what they have to say about practice, I would like to show next that not a single one of these methods, as I have just described them, conforms to the basic concepts of the cognitive theory of skill acquisition.

Skill acquisition theory and second language grammar learning

This section deals exclusively with the acquisition of L2 grammar and focuses on the trichotomy of mechanical, meaningful, and communicative activities to see what cognitive theory can contribute on this point. (For an application of skill acquisition theory to L2 vocabulary learning, see Kirsner, 1994; for more wide-ranging cognitive perspectives on second language acquisition, see Bialystok & Bouchard Ryan, 1985; Faerch & Kasper, 1987; McLaughlin, 1987; O'Malley & Chamot, 1990; Schmidt, 1992.) If we want our students to achieve fluency in the second language (in the sense of automatic procedural skill; cf. Schmidt, 1992), then, according to cognitive theory, we must enable them to engage in the practice of using that language, in the sense of communicating something in that language, while they keep the relevant declarative knowledge in working memory. The most typical second language classroom activity that does this is the use of communicative drills.

Communicative drills require the student to use the language to convey real meaning, while some recently taught rules, the focus of the drill, can be kept in mind. This availability of declarative knowledge during actual practice of the skill to be proceduralized is essential to skill acquisition.[2] Communicative drills are also a prime example of how one can choose the units of activity as large and varied as possible (in this case, whole sentences) while keeping the error rate low, a combination that is essential for skill acquisition (Levelt, 1976, p. 58). The reason why such large units of activity are essential for skill acquisition in the sense of automatization is that "an important feature of an automated plan is its potential to be called by higher-level plans" (Levelt, 1976, p. 58). In the case of communicative drills, the higher-level plan for the sentence calls on the lower-level plans being automatized, for example, procedures for past tense marking or subject-verb agreement. Communicative drills provide the learner with the opportunity to practice these larger units of activity in the sheltered environment set up by the teacher's questions,

---

2 The availability of declarative knowledge during actual practice of the skill is also one of the main strengths of intelligent tutoring (Anderson, 1987, p. 205).

which are meant to elicit grammar structures and lexical items that the student has learned declaratively. I do not think, therefore, that communicative drills are a contradiction in terms, as I have heard some people argue at conferences. On the contrary, they make sense from the point of view of cognitive skill theory.

What *does* constitute a contradiction in terms, from the point of view of skill theory, is the concept of mechanical drills. What are mechanical drills supposed to achieve? If we assume that the student has no declarative knowledge of the teaching point yet, how could he or she practice it? One can only practice something one knows already in some (usually declarative) form (cf. Sharwood Smith, 1994, pp. 182–184). If we assume that the student does already have the relevant declarative knowledge, what are mechanical drills for? They are not what is needed to proceduralize this knowledge (except at the most basic phonological and morphological level – see the discussion on choice of form), because they do not engage the learner in the target behavior of conveying meaning through language. Instead, they provide practice in a very peculiar behavior, a "language-like behavior," which consists of linking forms with other forms, of shuffling forms around, according to a pattern held in working memory, without ever linking those forms with meaning, that is, without the student ever engaging in the target behavior of using language. As a result, no link between forms and meaning is established in long-term memory, and no proceduralization of declarative knowledge takes place, because the student is not engaged in a behavior that would allow proceduralizing knowledge by drawing on it. The student does not draw on declarative knowledge at all, except, possibly, for the first couple of items in the drill. After that, all reference to any rule relating meaning to forms is dropped, for the easiest way to do the exercise is through formal analogy between the items, an analogy that can be drawn without taking meaning into account (and sometimes even without using anything resembling a rule of language).

This, of course, is exactly what the Audiolingualists had in mind as the goal of a mechanical drill: making the student induce formal analogies. The irony is that those who tried to justify Audiolingual methodology with *behaviorist* principles after the fact[3] forgot to define the *behaviors* they wanted to establish. For instance, even though Politzer and Staubach (1961) say that "linguists emphasize that language is 'behavior' and that behavior can be learned only by inducing the student to 'behave' – in other words, to perform in the language" (p. 2), and that "performing in

---

3 See, for instance, the introduction to Fries (1945), which contains terms such as *unconscious habits* (p. 9) and references to structuralist linguistics, but no references to the writings of behaviorist psychologists. See also Bowen, Madsen, and Hilferty (1985, p. 35).

the language" has to be distinguished from "the learning of rules and grammatical terminology" (p. 2), they never see performance as conveying personal meanings, and the sequencing of tasks is purely linguistic, not psycholinguistic: "Linguistically oriented materials are thus apt to form a continuum of drills and exercises" (1961, p. 30). Implicitly, of course, the Audiolingualists' stimulus-reaction chains were supposed to be meaning-forms chains, but what they established in the students' minds, because of the nature of the drills, was mere forms-forms chains. And this is why mechanical drills, in my opinion, are a contradiction in terms: Drills make sense only if they are defined in terms of *behaviors* to be drilled, but the so-called mechanical drills are defined in terms of *structures*, not behaviors. Declarative knowledge of these structures is useful for the development of procedural knowledge, but only if it is kept in working memory during the actual behaviors to be automatized (cf. Gatbonton & Segalowitz, 1988). The behavior actually engaged in by students in most mechanical drills is not even a psycholinguistic behavior in the sense of linking forms with meaning. In conclusion, the only thing that can be drilled is a behavior (based on procedural knowledge), and therefore drills that target a behavior that involves meaning (e.g., how to mark the element of meaning we call *past tense*) are useful only if they make students draw on procedural rules that involve meaning (cf. Chastain, 1987). Some behaviors to be learned, of course, do not involve meaning: Some phonological and morphological rules pertain to mere forms-forms relationships, such as consonant assimilation rules or variation in verb endings as a function of verb classes; in such cases mechanical drills can be useful.

Looking back now to the overview of methods discussed earlier, it should be clear that none of the methods, with the possible exception of Cognitive Code (see later in this section), conceived of practice in a way compatible with contemporary skill theory. Practitioners of Grammar Translation were not even interested in bringing about automatization of productive skills, even though there probably was a certain amount of proceduralization involved in becoming a more fluent translator from one language into another. Followers of the Direct Method tried to instill behaviors (proceduralize knowledge) through meaningful drills before the requisite declarative knowledge had been conveyed. And Audiolingualism was the least adequate of all in this respect, a large percentage of the time being spent on mechanical drills that have nothing to do with either the instilling of declarative knowledge of rules or proceduralizing it.

Cognitive Code, on the other hand, came much closer to the idea of first instilling declarative knowledge of rules and then practicing (proceduralizing and automatizing) the rules in meaningful and communicative activities.[4] The sequence of mechanical, meaningful, and communicative activities advocated by Paulston and Bruder (1976) certainly makes sense from the point of view of skill theory, as long as the mechanical stage in this sequence does not mean drills. It is quite all right to have completely formS-focused activities at the beginning, but their goal is to develop, test, and refine declarative knowledge, which means that the student should have ample time to think, and should never be rushed or put through activities that are so repetitive as to preempt all conscious rule application. Errors are expected to be common at this stage, and correcting them should aim to develop declarative knowledge. It is also quite all right to have drills in order to proceduralize the newly acquired declarative knowledge, but they should be defined in terms of communicative behavior (e.g., telling people what you did this weekend through the use of the simple past tense), not just structures.

Unfortunately, both in theory (cf. Chastain, 1971, esp. pp. 207–213) and in practice, the Cognitive Code Method often relied heavily on mechanical drills. And although some teachers began moving away from mechanical drills in favor of more authentic communicative exchanges (with or without inspiration from Cognitive Code theorists), the profession was confronted with a barrage of methodological innovations, such as individualization of instruction, the various avatars of the Communicative Movement, the "fringe" methods, for lack of a better word (the Silent Way, Suggestopedia, Community Language Learning, Total Physical Response), and last but not least the Natural Approach and its more extreme variants such as the Listening Approach, which largely deny the value of focus-on-form teaching and production practice.

Because none of the mainstream pre-1970 methods was based on an adequate model of skill acquisition, none could be entirely successful, and therefore it is not surprising that most methods comparisons did not find a significant difference between them (Levin, 1972; Scherer & Wertheimer, 1964; Smith, 1970). Although there may be other explanations for this lack of difference, for example, the fact that several of these studies were seriously flawed, and that the methods are far too broad a

---

4 Gatbonton and Segalowitz (1988) argue for a more inductive approach to automatization, in which the controlled presentation of items to be learned follows repetitive practice. For the reasons mentioned in the discussion of mechanical drills, however, it seems preferable to have practice follow more controlled presentation (cf. also Bamford, 1989). I also disagree with Gatbonton and Segalowitz when they state that the automatization of specific utterances rather than abstract structures should be the goal of classroom activities, because, in their opinion, practicing a structure leads to producing semantically unrelated sentences. As my earlier discussion of a communicative drill shows, the sentences in such a drill are hardly semantically unrelated. Moreover, Gatbonton and Segalowitz themselves give an example ("describing past activities") that requires repetitive use of a structure rather than an utterance (1988, p. 479; cf. also Bamford, 1989).

construct to be research variables at all, *if* one can give a meaningful interpretation to this finding of no difference between methods, it may be the inadequacy of all of these methods from the point of view of skill theory.

Competing points of view?

At this point, the reader may wonder how what has been said in the preceding sections fits in with the literature on implicit learning. Some studies on implicit learning, gleaned from the field of cognitive psychology, were mentioned earlier in this chapter; and the applied linguistics literature contains numerous references to the implicit/explicit issue, in particular in discussions of the role of grammar teaching in second language learning. Some theoreticians, most notably Krashen (1981, 1982, 1985, 1994), have argued that the explicit teaching of grammar is fruitless, because the learner cannot use explicit rules efficiently during communication, except for the best learners and simplest rules. Instead of teaching students rules, Krashen argues, the teacher should provide students with large amounts of language input that is just easy enough for them to understand; they will then induce the rules from this "comprehensible input" without any conscious learning, just as is the case for first language learning. Krashen's arguments in favor of implicit learning are mostly indirect, however: They are not based on direct tests, through controlled experimentation, of the hypothesis that implicit learning is better. Therefore, his theories have remained very controversial (cf. e.g., Long, 1988b; McLaughlin, 1987; Stern, 1990, 1992). Empirical studies on the relationship between implicit and explicit knowledge in second language *speakers* (e.g., Bialystok, 1979; Furey, 1987; Green & Hecht 1992) have shown that implicit knowledge is what is used in grammaticality judgments by these speakers, and that it is largely independent of explicit knowledge. These studies do not shed any direct light, however, on the relationship between the two types of knowledge at the time a specific rule is *learned*. Recent empirical studies on classroom second language learning have tended to show that focusing students on form, mainly by teaching them rules and correcting errors, is superior to implicit learning (e.g., Lightbown & Spada, 1990; Spada & Lightbown, 1993; L. White et al. 1991). The matter remains unresolved, however, because the applied linguistics literature typically fails to address the usefulness of explicit teaching for different types of rules, and because it is virtually impossible, in one classroom experiment, to vary independently factors such as linguistic and psycholinguistic characteristics of the structures at issue, individual learning differences, general focus on form, attention to rules, error correction, and other methodological options.

In my opinion, the automatization viewpoint and the implicit learning viewpoint are not incompatible, as long as one realizes two points:

1. The degree to which structures are most easily learned explicitly through the gradual automatization of conscious declarative knowledge – as opposed to completely implicitly – depends on the nature of the rule. Some rules have not been satisfactorily described by linguists and, therefore, are too difficult to teach and practice explicitly. Furthermore, as argued earlier, even within morphosyntax, the efficacy of implicit versus explicit learning can vary according to the nature of the rule: Is the rule a categorical one that applies across the board, or is it more like a prototype, one that applies probabilistically, and whose likelihood of application depends on a number of factors? Is it an abstract rule or a concrete co-occurrence pattern?
2. Different things are meant by the term *automatization.* Sometimes it is used only in the sense of fine-tuning (even more specifically, strengthening), sometimes in a much wider sense including restructuring, proceduralization, and fine-tuning. Although restructuring can affect implicit as well as explicit knowledge (cf. Marcus et al., 1992; McLaughlin, 1987, 1990), and although fine-tuning applies to essentially procedural knowledge (regardless of whether its origin is implicit or explicit), the concept of proceduralization itself implies that rules are acquired in a learning process that starts out as explicit. Only in one aspect of one of its senses, then, namely the proceduralization of explicit declarative knowledge, is the concept of automatization incompatible with implicit learning.

In summary, then, implicit second language learning and learning as it takes place according to contemporary cognitive-psychological views on skill acquisition are not incompatible.

The second obvious objection to the view on language learning implied by skill theory is the existence of acquisition orders, which is well established in the literature (see, e.g., Burt, Dulay, & Krashen, 1982; Meisel, Clahsen, & Pienemann, 1981; Pienemann, 1989; for a review, see Larsen-Freeman & Long, 1991, sec. 4.3; Zobl, 1995). If elements of grammar are acquired in a largely invariable order by children and adults from a range of native languages, regardless of instruction, then how is this compatible with the view that learners think about, remember, proceduralize, and automatize the rules they are taught? After all, there is widespread agreement that, although instruction may affect rate of acquisition, ultimate attainment, and type of errors committed most frequently, it does not have a substantial impact on route (order) of acquisition (see, e.g., R. Ellis, 1994a; Larsen-Freeman & Long, 1991).

I would like to argue that this last finding, though based on a variety of research evidence, has been vastly overgeneralized. First of all, many of the studies confirming a "natural order" were conducted on non-instructed learners; thus it is obviously impossible to tell whether these learners would have acquired structures in the same order had they had instruction. Second, although we do not always have detailed information about the nature of the instruction that students received in the studies that did deal with instructed learners, it is safe to assume (given what was said earlier about all major methods) that none received instruction along the lines of what skill acquisition theory seems to imply: explicit teaching of grammar, followed by FonF activities to develop declarative knowledge, and then gradually less focused communicative exercises to foster proceduralization and automatization. As these conditions were not met, learners could not be expected to acquire as a function of what they were taught, and all they could do was fall back on naturalistic acquisition of the elements present in the input. Finally, it has to be acknowledged that no structural syllabus so far has been based on psycholinguistic considerations of learnability; the knowledge base that the design of such a syllabus could draw on is only now being developed through the work of Pienemann, Long, and others. If we had much more extensive knowledge of this kind, the systematic teaching of productive skill according to a structural syllabus would obviously stand a better chance than it does now. Once more, the findings on acquisition orders or learnability hierarchies appear far from incompatible with the view that explicit knowledge can be automatized through and for production.

Implications for the sequencing of learning activities

A formS-focused lesson often takes the shape of reading a short text, and then explaining one or more grammar points, doing some structural exercises and some communicative exercises, and finally, in the case of a foreign as opposed to a second language class, translating a few sentences. But what does skill theory have to say that is relevant to planning a teaching unit? It says that declarative knowledge should be developed first, before it can be proceduralized. This means that, if grammar is taught, it should be taught explicitly, to achieve a maximum of understanding, and then should be followed by some exercises to anchor it solidly in the student's consciousness, in declarative form, so that it is easy to keep in mind during communicative exercises.[5] Examples of such exercises are sentence-combining tasks or fill-in-the-blank tasks (or even simple translation exercises in the foreign language class), but not of a rushed or repetitive nature; otherwise there is no opportunity to develop and restructure declarative knowledge, and we are back to mechanical

---

5 Note that retrieving declarative knowledge in this type of activity can be seen as a form of practice: practice in remembering that declarative knowledge (cf. Anderson, 1983, p. 182).

drills, a repetitive behavior that is far from ideal for the development of either declarative or procedural knowledge. The purpose of these initial exercises is to use declarative knowledge repeatedly in order to improve its accessibility and to start the process of proceduralization; this use of declarative knowledge is incompatible with rushed output.

Declarative knowledge needs to be proceduralized carefully before automatization can begin. Therefore, at this point, the student may need to go home and study, or at least have some extra individual time to proceduralize the declarative knowledge conveyed (i.e., essentially until no further errors are made without time pressure), because it is important that procedural knowledge be well established before automatization begins. This is a second point that is very different from what is commonly done: Not only do we usually leave challenging tasks like translation for last, but we also tend to move right on from teaching a grammar point to having the students drill it a few minutes later, before they have really had a chance to let it sink in. A third implication is that the unit's reading should probably be done last, instead of first. At that point, when students have had a chance to proceduralize their knowledge to some extent, reading a text that contains many instances of the new structure can contribute to further automatization. Or, to use a very different conceptual framework, the text can become comprehensible input. Because the new structure in the text is now salient and fully understood, thanks to the explicit teaching, students can notice it and process its forms-meaning link, and thereby meaningfully integrate it into long-term memory, in other words, acquire it. This is close, not to Krashen's, but to Swain's (1985; this volume) concept of comprehensible input, because it is fully understood without effort; thanks to the explicit teaching that preceded, the student has sufficient mental resources left to be aware enough of the forms-meaning links in order to process them (cf. also R. Ellis, 1993; VanPatten & Cadierno, 1993a, 1993b, for the argument that explicit teaching improves intake and, therefore, indirectly, production). Comprehensible input as such has an important role to play, but not as a sufficient condition for acquisition, certainly not without any awareness of form.

The main point here is that one should not jump back and forth between exclusively formS-focused activities such as mechanical drills and exclusively meaning-focused activities such as free conversation without error correction, and then think that one has covered the spectrum of practice activities. As Singley and Anderson (1989, p. 8) say in their review of the literature on transfer between tasks (mainly in the domains of algebra, computer programming, and text editing), "transfer depends on whether a common representation of the tasks can be found and communicated to [the learners]." If this has any implication for the second language classroom, it seems to be that learners should be encouraged to use in more open-ended activities what they have practiced in the more structured activities such as communicative drills.

Perspectives for research

Having argued for a skill acquisition perspective on task sequencing and curriculum design, I readily admit that several matters were left rather vague, especially the part about curriculum design. We certainly need more research, first to test the hypotheses formulated in this chapter about the applicability of skill acquisition theory to second language grammar learning, and eventually to make our recommendations for lesson planning and curriculum design more specific. It is really surprising that so little research from the point of view of cognitive psychology has been done on issues so essential to language teaching as task sequencing at the level of the teaching unit or at the curricular level.

One reason for that certainly is that applied linguists and second language researchers are most commonly trained in linguistics departments, language departments, or schools of education rather than in psychology departments. Another reason for this lack of relevant research, however, is that the study of transfer between learning tasks is logically a third step after the study of what performance of a certain skill entails and of how its learning proceeds in a specific task (Newell & Simon, 1972; Singley & Anderson, 1989). As a result, the study of transfer of elements of skill between learning tasks has only recently received close attention from cognitive psychologists themselves.

Be that as it may, there are good recent studies of transfer available in areas such as algebra, computer programming, and text editing. Singley and Anderson's book (1989) reviews this work and can provide inspiration for those who want to do research on how skill acquired by practice in one second language task transfers to a different task – from the conceptual framework and the design of transfer studies to problems of quantification and interpretation.

More generally, hardly any literature is available that combines the degree of control of a psycholinguistic experiment with the validity of research on real second language learning, and certainly not literature that, on top of that, takes a process, that is, a developmental, longitudinal, perspective. Fine-grained, hypothesis-testing experimental research on the basic cognitive processes of second language learning should prove to be more fruitful and of more interest to practitioners than the exchange of often very indirect arguments for and against the possibility of automatization that have been around since the mid-1980s, from the debate about Krashen's distinction between learning and acquisition to debates among cognitive scientists about the modularity of the mind. If we can document, in detail, how restructuring of knowledge, proceduralization, and automatization proceed, we will not only have shown *how* they work, but at the same time have proven *that* they work.

At this point, a variety of studies document to what extent people have explicit or implicit knowledge after a certain amount of input, teaching, and practice in the classroom (cf. DeKeyser, 1994; Harley, 1994), but they present neither a sufficiently fine-grained implementation of different kinds of practice nor a sufficiently fine-grained set of measurements to document how automatization of knowledge proceeds in an individual over time as a function of certain kinds and amounts of practice. The studies that come closest to doing that are perhaps those by VanPatten and Cadierno (1993a, 1993b), which looked at the role of production practice versus comprehension practice in two groups of students that had both received formal training. Even these studies do not provide anything comparable to the level of detail about treatment and outcome that one would see in a study conducted in the cognitive psychology laboratory.

Future research should make all possible efforts to be fine-grained, highly controlled, and longitudinal. Above all, it should probably proceed in modest steps, first showing what structures are best learned implicitly or explicitly, then documenting to what extent automatization of explicitly learned knowledge is possible, and finally investigating what sequencing of tasks is most effective at bringing this automatization process about. Tentative answers from such highly controlled research can and must then be tested in real classrooms to ensure ecological validity.

Summary and conclusions

Cognitive psychologists have documented how people use explicit knowledge to help them acquire a wide variety of skills, from making cigars to programming computers, by going through several stages. The most critical of the three stages is that in which knowledge about a skill leads to the ability to use the skill or its subskills in a more direct fashion, without necessarily having to refer to this initial knowledge. This transition is brought about by trying one's best at the skill to be performed, while keeping the relevant knowledge about it in mind.

This seems to imply a view on language learning that encourages performing the relevant skill, namely rendering certain meanings through certain forms, while thinking of the relevant knowledge about links between forms and meanings. This, in turn, implies that this knowledge has to be solidly anchored in the student's mind, so that it can be drawn on easily during the behavior that should lead to its automatization. None of the traditional methods of second language teaching fully meets these basic requirements for the acquisition of cognitive skill.

If we want to implement a teaching methodology that is consistent with this view, we need to think carefully about what the goal of each teaching/learning activity is: instilling knowledge about rules, turning this knowledge into something qualitatively different through practice, or automatizing such knowledge further in the sense that it can be done ever faster with fewer errors and less mental effort. Whichever of these three goals for specific learners and specific structures might be at a specific time, mechanical drills seldom have anything to offer. If we have our students perform entirely formS-focused exercises, they should not be drills but should stimulate reflection that will shape knowledge about the rules; drills make sense only once this knowledge has undergone a certain extent of qualitative change. This means that all practice designed to make the student more skilled at fluent production of the language, throughout the curriculum, should avoid being exclusively formS-focused or exclusively meaning-focused; otherwise it cannot contribute to transformation of knowledge into a behavioral pattern that consists of linking forms with meaning.

Four caveats are in order at this point. First, I believe that comprehensible input is important in language acquisition and that it is important to keep the fundamental difference between learning and acquisition in mind. I do not believe, however, that comprehensible input is the one and only necessary and sufficient condition for second language development, but instead agree with Long (1988a; Larsen-Freeman & Long, 1991) that focus on form is at least one of the ways to make instruction useful. This focus on form does not need to imply a return to a structural syllabus but, in my opinion, can, for certain learners, imply the explicit teaching and systematic practicing of certain forms. Second, for certain groups of learners the approach I have described may not be the best one, because it is aimed at efficiency over the middle to long run for academically oriented learners. Therefore, it would not be suited for immigrants who need a crash course in survival skills, for instance. Third, the sociolinguistic dimensions of the learning context have not been dealt with in this chapter; they would certainly need to be taken into account for broader issues of curriculum design. Finally, it would be premature to try to design an entire teaching methodology on the principles outlined here, for there has been virtually no empirical work aimed at testing them in the second language field.

The viewpoints described in this chapter are based on a well-established body of findings in cognitive psychology, have important implications for practice, and, in my opinion, do not contradict what we have learned from second language acquisition or applied linguistics research, provided one is careful about interpreting that research. They do not constitute, however, a blueprint for a new "language teaching method." Instead, they will have served their purpose if they stimulate researchers and teachers to test, in the field of second language acquisition, some implications of contemporary theorizing in cognitive psychology and to make second language teaching methodology more psychologically sound by maximizing the use of theoretically motivated and empirically validated practice activities.

4 Focus on form through conscious reflection

Merrill Swain

Introduction

This chapter describes several classroom-based studies carried out with the pedagogical intention of exploring ways to help adolescent learners in French immersion classes to enhance the accuracy of their target language production. The underlying theoretical motivation of these studies was to investigate possible roles that output (talking and writing) might play in second language learning.

Research to date has provided descriptive evidence of the existence of learning processes stimulated by output (Cumming, 1990; Swain & Lapkin, 1995). However, there is a paucity of research that demonstrates whether these output-oriented processes are facilitative of second language learning. In this chapter, one such pilot study will be described. The study, part of a larger program of research, contributes to the broader debate of the usefulness of explicit focus on form. However, it is perhaps helpful to understand the local language-teaching context in which the debate has emerged. Thus, the chapter begins with a short characterization of French immersion education in Canada, along with a capsule description of the resulting target language proficiency. The nature of this target language proficiency, combined with systematic observation in immersion classrooms, has led to the theoretical proposal of possible roles of output in second language learning (Swain, 1985, 1995) and to a consideration of potential pedagogical solutions. A discussion of these theoretical claims and pedagogical solutions serves as background to the study described in more detail in the section called Pilot Study, later in this chapter.

I wish to thank Alister Cumming, Birgit Harley, Sharon Lapkin, and Miles Turnbull for reading an earlier draft of this chapter. In helping to make this a better paper, they have each contributed to ideas about what the next study in the OISE program of research might be.

Background

The second language teaching context

More than 300,000 children in Canada are enrolled in French immersion programs. Many of these students, few of whom had had any exposure to French before starting school, began their schooling with a teacher who spoke to them only in French. The grade 8 students who participated in the research discussed in this chapter, like many other immersion students, were taught entirely through the medium of French until grade 3. After that, they received some instruction in English. By grade 8, several academic subjects were still taught using French as the language of instruction.

Observations in immersion classes suggest that the overall context of second language learning is communicative and experiential – and thoroughly content-based. However, particularly as students progress through the grades, teachers may engage in formal grammar instruction, often as a lesson separate from content teaching (Swain, 1991b). It is highly likely that, as students enter the intermediate grades, they will have been exposed to an eclectic language teaching approach consisting of learner-centered activities fortified with doses of traditional, prescriptive grammar activities.

More than 2 decades of research in French immersion classes suggests that immersion students are able to understand much of what they hear and read even at early grade levels. And, although they are well able to get their meaning across in their second language, even at intermediate and higher grade levels they often do so with nontargetlike morphology and syntax. (For overviews of this research, see, e.g., Genesee, 1987; Swain, 1984; Swain & Lapkin, 1986. For detailed accounts, see, e.g., Harley, 1986, 1992; Harley & Swain, 1984; Vignola & Wesche, 1991.)

This research, related to the French proficiency of immersion students, makes clear that an input-rich, communicatively oriented classroom does not provide all that is needed for the development of targetlike proficiency (Swain, 1985). It also makes clear that teaching grammar lessons out of context, as paradigms to be rehearsed and memorized, is also insufficient.

What, then, is to be done to move immersion students toward more nativelike proficiency, that is, to further their interlanguage development? Few immersion teachers and researchers would disagree that more attention to grammatical accuracy is needed, but less consensus would be found as to how this might be best accomplished and at what age and proficiency level such a focus might begin.

Several classroom-based experiments have been conducted in immersion classes in which specially developed curriculum materials were used over a period of weeks (Day & Shapson, 1991; Harley, 1989, this volume; Lyster, 1994a). The materials have in common a focus on form through enhanced input, increased opportunities for output, and, in some cases, explicit instruction, particularly in drawing attention to form-function links. Always, the activities in which the students engaged were embedded in a supportive, meaningful context.

These studies, although demonstrating the combined effect of these variables, could not isolate the impact of any one variable in particular. In Ontario Institute for Studies in Education (OISE) research visits to immersion classes, we observed that students were given limited opportunities for extended output where linguistic accuracy was demanded (Allen, Swain, Harley, & Cummins, 1990). We wondered whether this in itself was having an effect on the nature of immersion students' proficiency. Considerable research effort was devoted to addressing issues about input and second language learning. However, what roles output might have in second language learning were not being considered.

Potential roles of output in second language learning

Three functions of output have been proposed that relate more to accuracy than to fluency in second language learning (Swain, 1995).

Noticing

I have hypothesized that, under certain circumstances, output promotes *noticing* (Swain, 1995). This is important if there is a basis to the claim that noticing a form in input must occur in order for it to be acquired (R. Ellis, 1994a; Schmidt, 1990, 1992). The sense in which Swain and Lapkin (1995) have used *noticing* coincides with that of Schmidt and Frota (1986), who state that by *noticed*, they mean "in the normal sense of the word, that is consciously" (p. 311). What is noticed is available for verbal report, as discussed below and illustrated in Example 1.

There are several levels of noticing. Learners may simply notice a form in the target language due to the frequency or salience of the features themselves, for example (Gass, 1988). Or, as proposed by Schmidt and Frota (1986) in their "notice the gap principle," learners may notice not only the target language form itself but also that it is different from their own interlanguage. Or, learners may notice that they cannot say what they want to say precisely in the target language (Swain, 1995), what Doughty and Williams (this volume) in reference to this idea have called noticing a "hole" in one's interlanguage. It is my current conjecture that noticing the hole may be an important stimulus for noticing the gap.

The important issue here, however, is that it is *while attempting to produce* the target language (vocally or subvocally) that learners may notice that they do not know how to say (or write) precisely the meaning they wish to convey. In other words, under some circumstances, the activity of producing the target language may prompt second language learners to recognize consciously some of their linguistic problems: It may bring to their attention something they need to discover about their second language (possibly directing their attention to relevant input). This may trigger cognitive processes that might generate linguistic knowledge that is new for the learner or consolidate the learner's existing knowledge (Swain & Lapkin, 1995). Example 1, taken from a think-aloud session with a grade 8 immersion student while he is composing, is illustrative.

[1]   *La dé . . . truc . . . tion. Et la détruction.* No, that's not a word. *Démolition, démolisson, démolition, démolition, détruction, détruision, détruision, la détruision des arbres au forêt de pluie* (the destruction of trees in the rain forest).

(from Swain & Lapkin, 1995)

In Example 1, the student has just written "*Il y a trop d'utilisation des chemicaux toxiques qui détruissent l'ozone.*" ("There's too much use of toxic chemicals which destroy the ozone layer.") In his think-aloud, we hear him trying to produce a noun form of the verb he has just used. He tries out various possibilities (hypotheses), seeing how each sounds. His final solution, "*la détruision,*" is nontargetlike, but he has made use of his knowledge of French by using the stem of the verb he has just produced and by adding a French-sounding suffix. This example is revealing, because the incorrect solution allows us to conclude that new knowledge has been created through a search of his own existing knowledge. His search began with his own output, which he heard as incorrect.

Hypothesis formulation and testing

A second way in which producing language may serve the language learning process is through hypothesis formulation and testing. As seen in Example 1, the learner used his output as a way of trying out new language forms (hypotheses). Tarone and Liu (1995, pp. 120–121) provide evidence that it is precisely in contexts "where the learner needs to produce output which the current interlanguage system cannot handle . . . [and so] . . . pushes the limits of that interlanguage system to *make* it handle that output" that acquisition is most likely to have occurred.

In Example 1, the learner was in a situation in which feedback from an external source was not available; thus there was nothing to test his hypotheses against except his own internalized knowledge. In more usual circumstances, however, learners are able to obtain useful information for testing their hypotheses from other sources. When external feedback has been available, learners have also modified, or reprocessed (Swain, 1993), their output. For example, Pica, Holliday, Lewis, and Morgenthaler (1989) found that, in response to clarification and confirmation requests, more than one third of the learners' utterances were modified either semantically or morphosyntactically. The fact that learners modify their speech in one third (but not in all) of their utterances suggests that they are testing out only some things and not others. It may be that the modified, or reprocessed, output can be considered to represent the leading edge of a learner's interlanguage.

Thus, learners may use their output as a way of trying out new language forms and structures as they stretch their interlanguage to meet communicative needs; they may use output just to see what works and what does not. That immediate external feedback may not be facilitative or forthcoming does not negate the value of learners having experimented with their language resources.

Metatalk

A third function of output is its metalinguistic function. In this case, the learners' own language indicates an awareness of something about their own, or their interlocutor's, use of language. That is, learners use language to reflect on language use. In doing so, although learners may make use of metalinguistic terminology, it is by no means essential as part of the definition of *metatalk*. In fact, in the case of the data collected from grade 8 immersion students, the majority of our examples illustrate students talking about language without using metalinguistic terminology. The examples demonstrate, however, how students are thinking about their target language, that is, the hypotheses they hold about the target language. Example 2 is illustrative.

[2] S1: *Un bras . . . wait . . . mécanique . . . sort?*
     (An arm . . . wait . . . a mechanical [arm] . . . comes out?)
     S2: *Sort,* yeah.
     (Comes out, yeah.)
     S1: *Se sort?*
     (Comes out?) [reflexive form: *se sort*]
     S2: *No, sort.*
     (No, comes out.) [correct form: *sort*]

                                                        (Swain & Lapkin, 1996)

In Example 2, the first student (S1) is wondering whether the reflexive form of the verb *sortir* should be used in this context. The second student (S2) is able to provide S1 with correct answers to her questions.

This metatalk, happening as it does here – *in the context of "making meaning"* – may well serve the function of deepening the students' awareness of forms and rules, and the relationship of the forms and rules to the meaning they are trying to express; it may also serve the function of helping students to understand the relationship between meaning, forms, and function in a highly context-sensitive situation.

My current working assumption is that metatalk is a surfacing of language used in problem solving; that is, it is language used for cognitive purposes. In metatalk, we are able to observe learners' working hypotheses as they struggle toward solving mathematical problems, scientific problems, or, as we are concerned with in SLA, linguistic problems. If this is the case, then much of what is observed in metatalk when learners are faced with a challenging language production task and are encouraged to talk about the problems they encounter in doing the task should help us to understand language learning processes. It should help us to understand these processes because much of what is observed will be language learning *in progress*. In other words, in metatalk, noticing, hypothesis formulation and testing (cognitive problem solving), and other learning processes (e.g., comprehending) may be made available for inspection. They are available for inspection by researchers, teachers, and, possibly most important, for students themselves as they engage in second language learning.

Thus, by encouraging metatalk among second and foreign language students, we may be helping students to make use of second language acquisition processes. That is, metatalk may be one pedagogical means by which we can ensure that other language acquisition processes operate. It is essential, however, that this metatalk is encouraged in contexts where the learners are engaged in "making meaning," that is, where the language being used and reflected upon through metatalk is serving a communicative function. Otherwise, the critical links between meaning, forms, and function may not be made.

Experimenting with task types

From the perspective of the research reported on in the rest of this chapter, the metalinguistic function of output has been the most important for us in thinking about the types of tasks in which we could engage French immersion students that might help them move beyond their current interlanguage toward more nativelike French. We have sought to utilize tasks that would encourage output (therefore, we used collaborative tasks), but that would also result in students' focusing their attention on forms while in the process of expressing their intended meaning. In other words, we have begun to try out in the classroom different tasks that are communicatively oriented, but in which communication is, in part, at least, about language, that is, tasks in which students will talk about – consciously reflect on – their own output. One task that we feel has been particularly effective in achieving these goals is described in the next section (see Kowal & Swain, 1994, 1997 for details).

The dictogloss

The *dictogloss* is a procedure that encourages students to reflect on their own output (Wajnryb, 1990). With this procedure, a short, dense text is read to the learners at normal speed; while it is being read, students jot down familiar words and phrases; then the learners work together in small groups to reconstruct the text from their shared resources; the final versions are then analyzed and compared. The initial text, either an authentic or a constructed one, is intended to provide practice in the use of particular grammatical constructions. Wajnryb suggests that "Through active learner involvement students come to confront their own strengths and weaknesses. . . . In so doing, they find out what they need to know" (1990, p. 10).

With slightly modified procedures, one class of grade 8 immersion students was given three different dictoglosses during a school term, each of which was related in content to the *geographie* material the students were studying (Kowal & Swain, 1994, 1997). Their teacher (Kowal) had developed the dictoglosses herself and was fully confident that, in terms of content, they would be understood by her students.

The transcribed talk of each pair (occasionally a threesome) of students as they reconstructed the text provided us with the sort of data we hoped the task would elicit: talk about the language of the text they were reconstructing (metatalk). We observed students noticing things they did not know or could not say to their own satisfaction, and we observed these same students formulating hypotheses and testing them out using the tools at their disposal (themselves, each other, their dictionaries, their verb book, their teacher). In addition, students ignored some of the errors they made. They often functioned at a semantic level, wanting to use the right word as well as thinking about correct inflections and relationships between words; and they focused on many other points of grammar than the one the teacher had in mind in developing the particular dictogloss.

We examined the transcripts of each pair of students for language-related episodes (LREs). A *language-related episode* is defined as any part of a dialogue in which students talk about the language they are producing, question their language use, or other- or self-correct (Swain & Lapkin, 1996). The main focus of approximately 30% of the LREs was on lexical meaning, and the main focus of approximately 40% of the

LREs was on form. An orthographic focus accounted for the rest of the LREs (Kowal & Swain, 1994).

We therefore felt assured that the dictogloss had created opportunities for metatalk, which these immersion students took up (some with considerable enthusiasm, others with less!). The question of interest that this raises is, of course, does this metatalk support second language learning? Or, even, is the metatalk, itself, evidence of learning occurring? We speculated also that if the teacher were to have modeled metatalk for her students when introducing the dictogloss procedure, this might have promoted even more of a focus on form on the part of the students as they reconstructed the dictogloss text than had been found in Kowal and Swain (1994).

At this point in our research program then, we began to plan in detail a large-scale study to investigate the issues just raised (Swain & Lapkin, in progress). It was our good fortune that Donna LaPierre, an OISE master's student, was also interested in the issues and offered to pilot, as part of her M.A. thesis research, some of the procedures we had hoped to include in our larger-scale research. In particular, in the LaPierre study two different ways in which teachers might demonstrate (model) for their students ways of talking (metatalking), when reconstructing their dictogloss, were tried out. In addition, the feasibility of developing tailor-made posttests was explored. The idea was to tailor-make posttests based on the substance of the dialogues of pairs of students as they talked about the language they were producing. Aspects of LaPierre's (1994) study and her findings are described in the next section.

The pilot study

Research questions

Two of the research questions that LaPierre addressed in her study are relevant here.

MODELING METATALK

Does a demonstration by the teacher and researcher of the nature of the talk students are being encouraged to use in carrying out a task influence their use of it? In other words, does the modeling of metatalk by the teacher influence students' use of the metatalk? Does it help students to focus their attention on, to reflect about, their language use?

SECOND LANGUAGE LEARNING

Is there a relationship between metatalk and second language learning?

Research design

Two classes of French immersion students were involved. The instructions about how to do the task (dictogloss) were similar for both classes, with one exception. The teacher and the researcher together role-played (modeled) for the whole class how to reconstruct a text ("Vive la compagne," see Appendix A at the end of this chapter). The difference between the two classes lay in what the teacher and researcher said to each other as they reconstructed the text. The metatalk that was modeled for the metalinguistic (M) group included the provision of rules and metalinguistic terminology, whereas the metatalk that was modeled for the comparison (C) group did not make use of rules and metalinguistic terminology. (Details are provided in the following sections.)

Students completed three dictoglosses, one per week for 3 weeks. The first two sessions were given in order to familiarize students with the procedures of the dictogloss. The third session followed the same procedures; however, during this session, the students were tape-recorded as they worked in pairs on the task.

One week after completing the third dictogloss, students were given a tailor-made dyad-specific test, described in the following sections.

Participants

The study's participants consisted of 48 students from two grade 8 classes of an early French immersion program. The two classes consisted of mixed-ability students with lower-middle- to middle-class backgrounds from different schools within the same board of education located in a large urban area. The M class contained 26 students; the C class contained 22 students. The classes were assigned randomly to the two conditions.

These students entered the early French immersion program in kindergarten. In the early grades they were taught entirely in French. In grade 3, English (their native language) was introduced as a language of instruction. By grade 8, the proportion of French-medium to English-medium instruction was approximately 40:60.

The task

The type of task used was a dictogloss. Four different dictoglosses were prepared for this study: two for the modeling and practice session, one for a second practice session, and one for the session during which students were tape-recorded. The first two focused on number (formation of plural nouns and adjectives), the third one focused on gender (formation of masculine and feminine adjectives), and the fourth one focused on the *passé composé* (compound past) and the *imparfait* (imperfect). The grammatical areas of focus were the areas in which immersion students continued to make errors, even at the grade 8 level.

Procedures

The procedures adopted for all students are described in the following sections. Next, the procedures followed according to session and group are given.

MINI-LESSON AND DICTOGLOSS

Prior to hearing each dictogloss, students were given a short (5–10-minute) review lesson by the researcher. During that time, the meaning of vocabulary in the dictogloss that the students' teacher had thought might be difficult for her students was explained. Also, the researcher reviewed a set of rules relevant to the grammatical point in focus. The purpose of this explicit teaching and reviewing of forms was to heighten students' awareness about an aspect of language that would be useful to them in carrying out the dictogloss. (See also Lightbown, this volume.)[1]

The dictogloss passage was read twice. The first time it was read, students were asked to listen to the passage. The second time it was read, students were encouraged to take notes to help them reconstruct the passage. Students then worked in pairs for approximately 25 minutes to reconstruct the passage. Following this, the reconstructed passage of one pair of students was compared to the original dictogloss passage in a whole-class context.

SESSION AND GROUP PROCEDURES

As mentioned before, there were three sessions in which a dictogloss was given. The sessions were a week apart.

SESSION I (MODELING AND PRACTICE)

The researcher read the dictogloss "Vive la campagne" twice (see Appendix A). The researcher then displayed on the overhead a set of notes that two students might have written in listening to this dictogloss. Using these, the classroom teacher (previously "trained" by the researcher) and

---

1 We did not expect that students would "learn" from this brief review of rules. Our expectation was that, by heightening their awareness of the grammatical point, the likelihood of their talking about it would be enhanced. Although we have not studied this issue quantitatively, we would likely find that the consequences of the mini-lesson are highly dependent on both what the lesson was about (e.g., gender versus verb formation) and the developmental stage of the learner. I have become convinced, by examining the substance of learners' metatalk, that learners talk about what they *need* to talk about, that is, those aspects of language about which they are not sure. And that, in turn, will depend on their own current, internalized state of knowledge about language and its use.

the researcher modeled the reconstruction process. The way in which this was done is described for each of the metalinguistic (M) and comparison (C) groups in the next sections.

Following this, students heard another dictogloss (*"Les erables en automne"*) twice, taking notes during the second reading. Pairs of students then tried to reconstruct the passage. Finally, as a whole-class activity, the researcher reviewed the work of one pair of students, comparing the students' work against the original, modeling the M or C format whenever possible, and, as appropriate, to the group.

Metalinguistic (M) group.   When the teacher and the researcher modeled the reconstruction process for the metalinguistic group, their goal was to give the students a way of seeing how to deploy explicit linguistic knowledge to solve a problem caused by a "hole" in their interlanguage. In other words, they were trying to provide students with a demonstration of rules in action, in a very specific linguistic context. To do this, the teacher (T) and researcher (R) drew attention to grammatical form *and* provided an explanation for it. Examples 3 and 4 show their reconstruction of "Vive la campagne."

[3]   R: *OK, alors la première phrase commence avec "Les rues étroites."*
        (OK, so the first sentence begins with "The narrow streets.")
       T: *Oui "les rues étroites." N'oublie pas le "s" sur "rue" parce que c'est pluriel.*
        (Yes, "the narrow streets." Don't forget the "s" on "street" because it's plural.)
       R: *Oh, c'est vrai, alors, il doit avoir un "s" sur* "étroite" *aussi.*
        (Oh, that's right, so there must be an "s" on "narrow" too.)

[4]   T: *Est-ce que c'est les "rues" qui avaient, ou la "ville" qui avait?*
        (Is it the "streets" that had [plural form] or the "town" that had [singular form]?)
       R: *C'est les "rues" qui avaient. C'est les "rues" qui est le sujet, alors on doit faire l'accord avec les "rues." Donc, ça doit être avec e-n-t à la fin.*
        (It's the "streets" that had [plural form]. It's the "streets" that is the subject [of the sentence], so we have to make the verb agree with "streets." So, it must be written with e-n-t [plural form] at the end.)

Comparison (C) group.   When the teacher and the researcher modeled the reconstruction process for the students in the comparison group, they drew attention to grammatical form. However, no explicit rules were invoked. In this sense, the students were not specifically provided with a demonstration of at least one possible way to solve an encountered linguistic problem. Examples 5 and 6, parallel to Examples 3 and 4, respectively, follow.

[5] R: *OK, alors la première phrase commence avec les rues étroites.*
         (OK, so the first sentence begins with "The narrow streets.")
     T: *Oui, "les rues étroites." N'oublie pas le "s" sur "rue."*
         (Yes, "the narrow streets." Don't forget the "s" on "street.")
     R: *Oh, c'est vrai. Sur "étroite" aussi.*
         (Oh, that's right. On "narrow" as well.)

[6] T: *Est-ce que c'est les "rues" qui avaient, ou la "ville" qui avait?*
         (Is it the "streets" that had [plural form], or the "town" that had
         [singular form]?)
     R: *C'est les "rues" qui avaient.*
         (It's the "streets" that had [plural form].)

SESSION 2 (PRACTICE)

During this session, 1 week after the first session, the full dictogloss
procedure was implemented in order to make sure that the students
understood the nature of the task and to provide them with another
opportunity to practice reconstructing a text. First, difficult or possibly
unknown vocabulary that appeared in the dictogloss ("La vieille femme")
was reviewed (e.g., *cire, serre, drue, moutonnante*). This was followed by
a short (3–5-minute) lesson on how to form feminine adjectives from
masculine ones. "La vieille femme" was read twice to the students. During the second reading, students jotted down notes. Then, in pairs, students worked to reconstruct the dictogloss. Students in each group were
reminded that they should try to write their text so that it would be as
close to the original as possible in grammar and content. After the students had finished their text, the researcher selected the work of one pair
and corrected it, modeling the format appropriate to each group.

SESSION 3 (DATA COLLECTION)

The procedure used in the second session was repeated 1 week later:
Difficult vocabulary from the dictogloss "Cauchemar" (see Appendix B
at the end of the chapter) was reviewed; a short (3–5-minute) lesson on
the *passé composé* and *imparfait* was given; the text was read twice, with
students taking notes the second time; then, working collaboratively in
pairs, students reconstructed the passage. Each pair was recorded as they
worked to reconstruct the dictogloss.

THE TAILOR-MADE DYAD-SPECIFIC POSTTEST

This test represented our first attempt to measure linguistic knowledge
that appeared to be co-constructed through the metatalk of individual
pairs. The process of test development involved transcribing the talk of
each pair of students as they reconstructed the dictogloss passage. The
transcripts were then examined for LREs. The definition of LREs was the
same as that used by Swain and Lapkin (1996) and provided earlier in
this chapter, except that self-correction was not included. From these

LREs, tailor-made dyad-specific questions, designed to assess the target language point discussed, were created.

The questions on this posttest were of several formats: dual- or multiple-choice, fill-in-the-blank, translation, and open-ended. With the exception of the open-ended format, the test item types were of a discrete nature. The reason for using discrete item types was straightforward: We hoped to measure the learning of the *exact aspect of language* about which students had metatalked. We felt that the use of more integrative item types might have led to problematic interpretations. Of course, in further research of this sort, it will be important to develop tests that measure the transfer of linguistic knowledge to new forms, the ability to use them in a variety of formats, and so on. But at this early stage in our research program, we are most interested in seeing whether we can document, at all, the learning that our theoretical account suggests would be occurring in the LREs.

An example of an LRE that appeared in the dialogue of two students and the question that was given to that pair of students 1 week after having engaged in the discussion follows.

[7]   S1: *J'ai fait un rêve effrayant la nuit dernière.*
        (I had a frightening dream last night.)
      S2: *La nuit dernière.*
        (Last night.)
      S1: *Puis je sais le début de la seconde phrase.*
        (And I know the beginning of the second sentence.)
      S2: *Attends. Attends. Attends. Il y a quelque chose de mal avec cette phrase. Est-ce que c'est "une rêve" ou "un rêve"?*
        (Wait. Wait. Wait. There is something wrong with this sentence. Is it "dream" [feminine] or "dream" [masculine?])
      S1: *Je pense que c'est "un rêve."*
        (I think it's "dream" [masculine]).
      S2: *Le rêve, la rêve, le rêve?*
        [Testing whether *dream* is masculine or feminine; seeing which sounds better.]
      S1: *On va le laisser comme ça.*
        (We're going to leave it like that.)
      S2: *J'ai fait un rêve. . . . OK.*
        (I had a dream [masculine]. . . . OK.)

Test Question:

Indicate whether *"rêve"* is masculine or feminine: F   M

The number of dyad-specific questions varied from pair to pair depending on the number of LREs that occurred in each transcript. Thus a "percentage correct" score was calculated for each student.

Results

The first research question is concerned with whether a demonstration of metatalk for the students might influence their use of it. Because the theoretical argument being developed here is that metatalk may engage language learning processes, increased use of metatalk would be seen as positive. The second research question asks whether there is evidence of a relationship between metatalk and second language learning.

To examine the first research question, we counted the LREs produced by pairs of students. The average number of LREs produced by the M group was 14.8, and by the C group was 5.8. In other words, group M produced approximately 2½ times more LREs than group C. Although the LREs of group M did not contain frequent use of metalinguistic terminology or of the statement of rules, this use was nevertheless evident to a greater degree than in the LREs of group C. The difference in the average number of LREs between the two groups suggests, furthermore, that the demonstration of metatalk that included the explicit statement of rules and the use of metalinguistic terminology succeeded to a greater extent in capturing students' attention and focusing it on their own language use.

In examining the second research question, we combined the data from both M and C groups. We did this because the question relates equally to both groups rather than entailing a comparison between groups. To examine the question of the relationships between metatalk and second language learning, we might have conducted a number of analyses. For example, we might have examined the learning outcomes of the intended focus versus the feature actually focused upon. The intended focus in "Cauchemar" was the *passé composé* and *imparfait;* however, students rarely focused on that aspect of grammar. The students were much more likely to talk about gender and number issues that had been reviewed in the dictoglosses they had done in the previous 2 weeks. We suspect, however, that what they focused their attention on had less to do with the minilessons than it had to do with the needs of the students; that is, students talked about what they needed to talk about according to the state of their own internalized knowledge.

As it was, we took several steps to examine the second research question. The first step was to analyze the responses on the dyad-specific tests in relationship to the LREs that led to their generation. In order to do this, the LREs were first categorized into four types: Type I: problem solved correctly (see Example 7); Type II: problem not solved or disagreement about problem solution (see Example 8); Type III: problem solved incorrectly or disagreement about problem solution (see Example 9); and Type IV: other.

[8]   (problem not solved or disagreement about problem solution)

S1: *Un passage étroit, à la métro?*
(A narrow passage, at the subway?)

S2: *C'est "dans" la chose.*
(It's "in" the thing.)

S1: *Dans la métro ou à la métro?*
(In the subway or at the subway?)

S2: *Non, c'était quelque chose comme à l'endroit, ou à la métro.*
(No, it was something like at the place, or at the subway.)

S1: *Je pensais que c'était, je marchais dans un passage étroit a la métro.*
(I thought it was, I was walking in a narrow passage at the subway.)

S2: *Un passage étroit dans le métro . . . in the . . . in the subway.*
(A narrow passage in the subway . . . in the . . . in the subway.)

S1: *À la métro.* I just don't know.
(At the subway. I just don't know.)

S2: *Mais, c'est comme "dans."*
(But, it's like "in.")

S1: OK, anyway, *on va continuer.*
(OK, anyway, let's continue.)

[9]   (problem solved incorrectly or disagreement about problem solution)

S1: *La nuit dernière je marchais dans un long passage étroit.*
(Last night I was walking in a long narrow passage.)

S2: *Non, étroite.*
(No, narrow [feminine form].)

S1: *Avec un "e"?*
(With an "e"?)

S2: *Oui.*
(Yes.)

There was a total of 256 LREs in the two groups: 140 (54.7%) were of Type I; 50 (19.5%) were of Type II; 21 (8.2%) were of Type III; and 45 (17.6%) were of Type IV.

The second step was to calculate, for each type of LRE, the percentage of correct responses on the dyad-specific questions. The results were as follows: On average, 79% of students' responses were correct for Type I; 40% for Type II; and 29% for Type III.[2] (This figure was not calculated for Type IV.)

This means that when students, through dialogue, reached a correct solution (Type I), there was a strong tendency for them to perform accurately on the relevant posttest item 1 week later. Furthermore, and equally as telling, when students co-constructed an incorrect solution

2 Comparisons of observed frequencies with expected frequencies using a chi-square model were conducted to determine whether significant differences existed. Expected frequencies were derived from the whole sample. For Type I, observed correct responses were 110, and expected were 90; for Type II, observed correct responses were 20, and expected were 28; and for Type III, observed correct responses were 6, and expected were 14. All differences between observed and expected frequencies were statistically significant.

(Type III), they tended to be inaccurate in their responses on the relevant posttest items 1 week later. In other words, the students tended to "stick with" the knowledge they had constructed collaboratively the previous week. Finally, the correct response rate of 40% attained when no solution was agreed upon (Type II) might be thought of as a baseline against which Types I and III can be compared, with Type I being considerably higher and Type III being somewhat lower. These results suggest rather forcefully that these LREs, during which students reflect consciously on the language they are producing, may be a source of language learning. Thus, increasing the frequency of LREs in pedagogical contexts through appropriate modeling, and through opportunities for use, may be useful in promoting second language learning.

Discussion

The collection of studies discussed in this chapter (Kowal & Swain, 1994, 1997; LaPierre, 1994; Swain & Lapkin, 1995, 1996, in progress) shows evidence of learners noticing the "gap" in their interlanguage, that is, noticing the difference between what they want to say and what they are able to say. As proposed by the output hypothesis, this happens as the students try to produce the target language. Equally as important, sometimes noticing the hole triggers a search for a solution: Students engaged in a language production task alone or together work to solve their linguistic difficulties, making forms and meaning the focus of their attention. The students formed hypotheses and tested them against available resources. Vocabulary, morphology, and complex syntactic structures each became the focus of their attention, and in turn, their attention became focused by talking about the problem. Verbalization of the problem allowed them the opportunity to reflect on it and, apparently, served as one source of their linguistic knowledge.

The collection of studies has implications for both pedagogy and further research. Pedagogically, the results point to the potential usefulness of collaborative work in promoting output and second language learning. They make clear that the value of collaborative work for second language learning can be enhanced in at least three ways. First, careful consideration must be given to task characteristics; that is, not just any task will elicit metatalk. Furthermore, a task that elicits metatalk from one group of learners may not do so from another group of learners. This may be due to the level of learners' proficiency, the age of the learners, and any of a host of other factors. Although this was not discussed in the present chapter, we observed considerable variation in how the French immersion students carried out the dictogloss task, particularly concerning the amount of metatalk they produced.

Second, the results seem to suggest that the value of collaborative work can be enhanced through the thorough preparation of students for task performance. For example, familiarity with task procedures is important. Accompanying instructions by, for example, teacher modeling and role-playing of the activity can be useful.

Third, the results point to the potential value of feedback to students. Although the overall percentage of LREs during which the students believed that they had solved their linguistic problem, but did so incorrectly, was small, the outcomes were consequential. Students tended to remember their incorrect solutions. They learned, but they learned the wrong thing. Teachers' availability during collaborative activities and their attention to the accuracy of the "final" product subsequent to the completion of collaborative activities are potentially critical aspects of student learning.

From a research perspective, one point I wish to emphasize here is that we must continue to explore ways to document the ongoing learning of students as they work collaboratively. We believe that we have demonstrated, at this point using rather simple and crude measures, that some learning was taking place in the metatalk we observed. We are fully aware, however, that we have not identified all that was learned, having scraped only the surface of linguistic forms and meaning.

The second point is that it seems essential in research to test what learners *actually do,* not what the researcher assumes instructions and task demands will lead learners to focus on. Not testing what learners do means that we are missing opportunities to identify some of the sources of second language learning. Although the tasks we used did encourage students to pay attention to accuracy and form-function links, the students established their own goals and agenda as to what they focused on. As Coughlan and Duff (1994) point out, "any event that generates communicative language is unique – [it is] an activity born from a particular constellation of actors, settings, tasks, motivations, and histories" (p. 190). Given this, why would we expect consistent learning outcomes from the activities our research tasks generate? Thus, it would seem crucial, if we are to measure the learning that occurs as a result of task involvement, that we tailor our tests to the contents of actual task performance. This content can be seen in the dialogue of the interactions themselves. The preparation of learner-specific tests may seem like a daunting task for the researcher, but it may be essential if we are to capture the language learning that occurs as learners co-construct linguistic knowledge through their metatalk.

Appendix A: Dictogloss used for modeling

Vive la campagne

Les rues étroites de la ville sont remplies de tricycles, d'autobus impitoy-
ables et de motocyclistes imprudents. Heureusement, à cinq minutes du
centre-ville, nous reprenons la grande route et nous retrouvons avec joie
la campagne.

Appendix B: Dictogloss used for recorded session

Cauchemar

J'ai fait un rêve effrayant la nuit dernière. Je marchais dans un long
passage étroit du métro. Soudain, j'ai entendu des pas derrière moi. Je me
suis retourné(e) et j'ai vu un homme aux cheveux couleur de carotte striés
de mèches violettes, et en costume d'Adam. Il tenait un énorme oreiller
noir. L'expression de ses yeux était diabolique.

PART II:
FOCUS ON FORM IN THE CLASSROOM

5 Getting the learners' attention
A typographical input enhancement study

Joanna White

Introduction

Recently, researchers have begun to investigate the effects of manipulating and enhancing input, implicitly and explicitly, with the aim of increasing the usefulness for second language (L2) acquisition of the input available in the classroom. The central question of this chapter concerns the relationship between input in which a linguistic feature has been enhanced and the acquisition of that linguistic feature by learners who are known to have problems acquiring it.

The study described in this chapter was carried out within the framework of a program of classroom-based research that has investigated the effectiveness of focus-on-form (FonF) instruction involving different types of input enhancement provided within a communicative context (Lightbown & Spada, 1990, 1994; Spada & Lightbown, 1993; L. White, 1991; L. White, Spada, Lightbown, & Ranta, 1991; Trahey & L. White, 1993). These studies were carried out in Quebec, where English as a second language (ESL) instruction is provided to all school children from grade 4 to the end of secondary school. This instruction, in accordance with guidelines set out by the Ministry of Education of Quebec, tends not to focus on formal aspects of language other than vocabulary.

There is a growing body of evidence in Quebec and elsewhere, however, that when instruction focuses on meaning to the virtual exclusion of formal aspects of language, learners may fail to reach high levels of linguistic knowledge and performance despite extensive exposure to target language input (see, e.g., Harley & Swain, 1984; Lightbown & Spada, 1990; Swain & Lapkin, 1982, 1986). A number of explanations have been offered for the low accuracy levels attained by learners in meaning-focused classrooms. One concerns the limited number of opportunities that learners have to produce language that goes beyond simply getting their messages across (Swain, 1985, 1993). Another explanation concerns the quality of the input available for acquisition, much of which is the linguistic output of other learners (Lightbown, 1992).

The explanation that this study addresses is that learners may fail to

detect a number of linguistic features that are present, but not perceptually salient, in the input. As a number of second language acquisition
(SLA) researchers have pointed out, learners must attend to linguistic
features in the input as well as to messages (e.g., Sharwood Smith, 1986;
VanPatten & Cadierno, 1993a). Hulstijn (1989) proposed that attention
to form at the point of input encoding is the necessary and sufficient
condition for learning to take place (see also Alanen, 1995; Berry, 1994;
Schmidt, 1990; for a different perspective, see Krashen, 1982, and
elsewhere).

The study described here was designed to increase the perceptual salience of a set of linguistic features without placing excessive demands on
learners' attentional resources (see VanPatten, 1990). Typographical enhancement, which involved the manipulation of italics, bolding, enlargement, and underlining, was selected for investigation because it was expected to direct the learner's attention to the target forms more explicitly
than input flooding but less explicitly than rule explanation, two input
enhancement techniques that had previously been investigated with comparable groups of learners (for rule explanation, see L. White, 1991; L.
White et al., 1991; for input flooding, see Trahey, 1992, 1996; Trahey &
L. White, 1993).

The selection of third person singular possessive determiners (PDs) as
the target features for this study was motivated by the following considerations: They have been examined within the context of ESL classes and
are known to present particular difficulties for francophone learners of
English (Lightbown & Spada, 1990; Martens, 1988; Zobl, 1985). Furthermore, Zobl's theoretical and empirical work has provided a useful
framework for the analysis of PDs.[1]

The L2 acquisition of possessive determiners

Francophone learners of English find *his* and *her* to be particularly
difficult and often continue to have problems with these forms after many
years of ESL instruction. Their problems may be due, at least in part, to
differences between the English and French rules for establishing the
gender of third person singular PDs. English uses an agreement rule
referring to the *natural* gender of the possessor: The masculine form *his* is
used when the possessor is masculine; the feminine form *her* is used when
the possessor is feminine. French, on the other hand, requires agreement
between the *grammatical* gender of the noun naming the possessed entity
(person or thing) and the PD: The masculine form *son* is used when the

---

1 Although PDs were the target forms in this study, third person singular subject and
  object pronouns were also enhanced. For more information, see J. White (1996).

possessed noun is masculine; the feminine form *sa* is used when the possessed noun is feminine.[2]

The English and French agreement rules for PDs are illustrated in the four pairs of sentences that follow, where capital letters represent the gender required in English, and lowercase letters represent the gender required in French. The examples all involve kinship terms (e.g., mother, father), which have natural, as well as grammatical, gender.

Mf 1a Robert sees his mother.

    1b *Robert voit sa mère.*

Fm 2a Alice sees her father.

    2b *Alice voit son père.*

When the natural gender of the possessor and the grammatical/natural gender of the possessed entity are different, as in the preceding pairs of sentences, the difference between the English and French rules is more transparent than when the natural gender of the possessor and that of the possessed entity are the same. When they are the same, it is not possible to know whether the learner is using the L1 French rule or the L2 English rule, because grammatically correct English PDs would be produced in either case.

Mm 3a Robert sees his father.

    3b *Robert voit son père.*

Ff 4a Alice sees her mother.

    4b *Alice voit sa mère.*

English and French also differ with respect to possession of body parts. In French, body parts are normally referred to using the definite article, and possession is marked with a reflexive pronoun. In English, possession of body parts is normally marked with a possessive form.[3] Compare the following English and French sentences:

[1]   Alice is washing her hair. [feminine PD]

[2]   *Alice se lave les cheveux.* [feminine subject; third person singular reflexive pronoun; definite article]

---

2 Gender distinctions disappear in French when the possessed object is plural. The plural form *ses* is used with both masculine and feminine possessed nouns.

3 Note, however, that in English, the definite article is used with possessed body parts in prepositional phrases concerned with the object (e.g., "She took me by the hand") or, in passive constructions, with the subject (e.g., "I was hit on the head with a baseball") (Quirk, Greenbaum, Leech, & Svartvik, 1972). Although input containing the definite article with possessed body parts may be infrequent, it would seem that any input at all of this type would serve to reinforce the French rule.

SLA research suggests that learners in naturalistic as well as classroom contexts pass through a series of stages as they attempt to make sense of the personal and possessive pronoun subsystems of the target language. There is evidence that learners begin by avoiding pronouns and PDs and using nouns (Felix, 1981) or the definite article (Martens, 1988; Zobl, 1985) instead. Once they begin to use pronominal forms, they may substitute one for another in apparently free variation (Felix & Hahn, 1985; Nicholas, 1986), or they may overgeneralize one all-purpose pronoun to all contexts (Butterworth, 1972; Wong-Fillmore, 1976).

The systematicity underlying avoidance, substitution, and overgeneralization has been demonstrated in a number of studies. Felix (Felix, 1981; Felix & Hahn, 1985) inferred the following acquisition order for the semantic features of English pronouns and PDs from the errors made by German high school learners: case before number, then person, and finally gender.

Zobl (1984) proposed that classroom-instructed francophone learners break down the English agreement rule for gender marking of PDs into subrules that they apply in the following sequence, moving from the most general to the most specific:

1. definite article
2. person/possessive marking, for example, *your*
3. third person marking, for example, *his* overgeneralized
4. French agreement rule
5. mature English rule

Zobl predicted that beginning learners of English would not transfer grammatical gender from French to inanimate entities (see Kellerman, 1978) but might retain natural gender for some time, since it is both meaningful and grounded in perception. Because kinship terms conflate grammatical and natural gender in French, Zobl predicted that learners would have more difficulty discarding the French agreement rule in the human domain than in the nonhuman (inanimate and body parts) domains.

In his pedagogical studies, Zobl found evidence to support his predictions; that is, learners applied each of the subrules systematically, first in the nonhuman domain and then in the human domain (1984, 1985). Since learners also tended to overgeneralize the masculine form within each domain, there was considerable intralearner variability in rule application across domains.

In addition, Zobl observed interlearner variability in the extent to which individuals applied the French agreement rule. This was particularly evident with regard to the use of the definite article with body parts. Some learners held on to their L1 rule even though they had reached high levels of accuracy in their use of Fm and Mf forms (1984).

Lightbown and Spada's (1990) descriptive classroom-based study suggests the possibility of a role for focus-on-form instruction. They analyzed instances of *his* and *her* in the speech of francophone learners in four intensive ESL classes in grades 5 and 6. Although their data did not permit a full-stage analysis using the developmental framework they had inferred from Zobl (1985), the researchers suggested that learners in the lowest accuracy group may have "been at a different level of development from the others" (p. 442), since they made fewer attempts to use PDs and since those attempts were less successful. They concluded that the observed differences between the classes may have been due to variations in the amount and type of formal instruction and corrective feedback offered by the four teachers within similar communicative language teaching contexts. These differences suggested that some types of instruction may be more effective than others in contributing to the acquisition of PDs and other forms.

The quasi-experimental study described here built on that descriptive research by investigating the effects of instruction on the acquisition of PDs. It provided opportunities for learners to focus on these forms by drawing their attention to them through typographical enhancement. The specific research question that the study addressed was: Would typographically enhanced input promote acquisition, which has been said to require the learner's focused attention?

Context of the study

Subjects

The study was carried out over a 5-month period in a French elementary school near Montreal. Three intensive grade 6 ESL intact classes provided the subjects for the investigation. The learners were francophone Quebecois, and all said that they spoke French at home.

Teachers

The three teachers were trained ESL specialists with many years of experience and were fluently bilingual in English and French. Classroom observations established that, at the time of the study, they had in common a high tolerance for student errors and gave little corrective feedback.

Intensive ESL

Intensive ESL is an innovative approach to second language teaching that is adapted to the political context in which ESL is taught in Quebec. It expands the communicatively oriented ESL curriculum set by the Ministry of Education of Quebec for use in the regular, 2-hour-per-week instructional settings. In the intensive model under investigation in this study, elementary school learners study only English for 5 months of 1 academic year, either grade 5 or grade 6. The other 5 months of that year are devoted to intensive study, in French, of the academic subjects that are required to complete the grade level (see Lightbown & Spada, 1994, for a full description of these programs).

Instructional treatments

There were three treatment conditions, a different one for each group. Group E+ (N = 27) received a typographically enhanced input flood in addition to extensive reading and listening; Group E (N = 30) received a typographically enhanced input flood; Group U (N = 29) received a typographically unenhanced input flood. These treatment conditions are described in more detail in the next sections.

Enhanced/unenhanced input

Two versions of a 10-hour instructional package of reading activities were designed for the study. (A sample of the instructional materials can be found in the Appendix at the end of this chapter.) Group E+ and Group E received a set of materials in which all third person singular pronouns and PDs were enhanced visually on the page. In addition, they completed tasks that required them to understand these forms in context. For example, after reading a story entitled "The Frog Prince," learners read a series of statements and decided whether the underlined pronouns and PDs referred to the frog, the princess, or her father.

The target forms were typographically enhanced through enlargement and different combinations of the following techniques: bolding, italics, and underlining. Since PDs were the target linguistic feature, they were enlarged more than subject and object pronouns to increase their visual salience. The type of enhancement was varied from activity to activity to maximize the novelty of the technique and to increase the likelihood that students would attend to the forms. However, care was taken not to make the enhancement so salient that it would cause students to become irritated or distracted while reading.

Group U received the same set of texts, but third person singular pronouns and PDs were not enhanced. The students did parallel tasks that provided general comprehension practice but did not focus their attention on pronouns and PDs. For example, after reading "The Frog Prince," learners answered a set of factual questions about the events in the story. To account for the possibly distracting effect of enhancement, all past tense *-ed* endings were typographically enhanced for Group U.

All enhanced and unenhanced texts were adapted versions of stories, fables, and poems written for English L1 children.[4] Several short texts were grouped, along with accompanying tasks, to make a unit of theme-based activities. A total of six instructional units were taught to the three groups over a period of 2 weeks, amounting to 10 hours of class time. Although all three groups had an input flood with many examples of third person singular pronouns and PDs, only Groups E+ and E had typographical and task enhancement.

In addition to the 10 hours of enhanced input, Group E+ was exposed to a supplemental book program extending over the entire 5-month intensive ESL session. The book program consisted of 2 to 3 hours per week of in-class pleasure reading and listening to stories read aloud by the teacher above and beyond the baseline reading activities that all three teachers included in the regular, ongoing intensive ESL program. Thus, the E+ group's exposure to written input containing naturally occurring, correct instances of the target forms, which they read and had read to them, was considerably greater than that of the other two groups, both in duration (5 months versus 2 weeks) and total number of hours (about 50 additional hours of book-related activities were done with Group E+).

To ensure that the treatment did not include explicit rule explanations, all three teachers were asked before the beginning of the intensive session not to "teach the rule" about third person singular PDs at any time during the 5-month study, and not to correct students' errors involving these forms any more than they normally did. They were told, however, that they were free to answer learners' questions about the target forms if questions arose.

Hypotheses

The study was designed to investigate the effects of typographical enhancement on the acquisition of PDs. Typographical enhancement, proposed by Sharwood Smith (1981, 1991) and investigated by Doughty (1988, 1991), is considered to be the "visual equivalent of stress and emphasis" in spoken input (Doughty, 1988, pp. 87–88). It was expected that the learners' attention would be directed to the typographically enhanced forms, for some learners a necessary condition for the conversion

---

4 Adaptations primarily involved shortening the stories so that they would fit into a task sequence taking between 60 and 90 minutes of class time, but some nouns in the original stories were replaced with third person singular pronouns and possessive determiners.

of input to intake (Hulstijn, 1989; Tomlin & Villa, 1994). Thus the first hypothesis of the study was the following:

H1:   Learners exposed to typographical input enhancement of third person singular pronouns and PDs would progress further in the acquisition of these forms than would learners who did not get enhanced input.

It was expected that if typographical enhancement increased the likelihood that learners would detect the target structures in the input, then learners in the extensive reading and listening group would have more opportunities to detect them than would learners in the other two groups. Accordingly, the second hypothesis of the study was the following:

H2:   Learners exposed to typographical input enhancement of third person singular pronouns and PDs in combination with extensive reading and listening would progress further in the acquisition of these forms than would learners who got enhancement without extensive reading and listening.

Findings from previous SLA research carried out in instructional contexts indicate that follow-up posttests sometimes portray a different picture for the effects of instruction than do immediate posttests. This may be because the comparison groups have "caught up" with the experimental groups (Harley, 1989) or because the learners appear to have "forgotten" (L. White, 1991). Although it is difficult to specify the amount of time that should elapse between the immediate and delayed posttests, a minimum of a month would seem to be both reasonable and practical, given the constraints of school-based research.

In this study, it was expected that the effects of instruction would be powerful enough for differences among groups to be statistically significant 1 month later. First, if enhanced input was successful in getting learners to notice the target forms, the regular classroom input in which pronouns and PDs occurred frequently would sustain the effects of instruction for Groups E+ and E. Second, the sustained high-quality input available to Group E+ through their continuing extensive reading and listening program was expected to maintain the predicted advantage for this group. For these reasons, the third hypothesis was formulated:

H3:   The effectiveness of typographical input enhancement with and without extensive reading and listening would still be evident 1 month after the 2-week treatment period had ended.

Schedule and instruments

The research schedule appears in Figure 1. Initial baseline listening comprehension and multiple-choice pronoun tests that were administered to the three groups on the second day of their 5-month intensive program

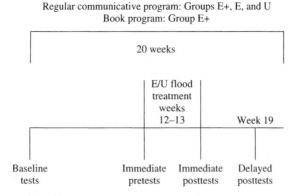

Figure 1   Research schedule.

established that there were no significant differences among them at the outset. The day after the baseline tests, the extensive reading and listening treatment began for Group E+.

Several other tests were administered at three different points in the study to measure learners' developing knowledge and ability to use third person singular pronouns and PDs. They included a passage correction task, a multiple-choice test, and an individually administered oral picture description task (see J. White, 1996, for details). Immediate pretesting was done the day before the 2-week treatment period began, when the learners in all three groups had had 11 weeks of intensive communicatively based ESL instruction, and the learners in Group E+ had also had 11 weeks of the extensive reading and listening program. The immediate posttests were administered the day after the 2-week enhanced/unenhanced input treatment ended. The second set of posttests was administered 5 weeks after that, in the nineteenth week of the 20-week intensive program.

Only the PD data collected during the picture description task will be discussed in this chapter. This task was designed to provide contexts in which learners would be likely to use the target forms in their oral production. The pictures depicted familiar, often humorous, family situations involving one or two parents and one or two children. The task was administered to each student individually, and the interviews were tape-recorded and transcribed.

The analyses of the oral data took into account the contexts that each student established for the use of third person singular PDs. Each context was coded for whether a PD was supplied and, if so, whether it was used correctly or incorrectly. In addition, each context requiring *his* or *her* was coded according to whether the possessed entity was animate, inanimate, or a body part. Two subcategories were established for coding animate entities: kinship terms, same gender (e.g., *his* father, *her* mother), and kinship terms, different gender (e.g., *his* mother, *her* father).[5]

Quantitative and qualitative analyses were carried out on the oral production data for the three test administrations. For the quantitative analyses, frequency counts and accuracy ratios were calculated. The qualitative analyses involved a stage analysis of the learners' development.

Results of quantitative analyses

Frequency of use

The first analysis compared the number of correct and incorrect third person singular PDs that learners in all three groups used to describe a set of pictures immediately before and after the 2-week enhanced/unenhanced input treatment period.[6] Figure 2 shows that learners in all groups used more PDs at the immediate posttest and that the increase in grammatical forms was greater than the increase in ungrammatical forms. Group E+ showed the greatest increase in grammatical forms. An analysis of covariance (ANCOVA), using pretest frequencies as the covariate, revealed that, at the immediate posttest, the difference in the number of grammatical forms used by Groups E+ and E was statistically significant ($p = .03$). Although familiarity with the task could be expected to account for a modest increase in all three groups, the extent of the increase suggests that all the treatment materials, and especially those used with Group E+, served to draw the learners' attention to *his* and *her* in a way that led them to try to use the forms in their oral picture descriptions.

Intralearner variability

The most striking characteristic of the oral production data was the enormous variability in the use of *his* and *her*. Grammatical and ungrammatical uses of these forms frequently co-occurred in the same utterance, and learners used *his* and *her* along with developmentally earlier forms like *your* and *the* to describe a single picture. The following examples, from the immediate posttest, illustrate this phenomenon. Each PD context established by the learner is underscored.

[3]   This learner used *his* and *her* in a context for *his*.

Learner: The boy have *his* first bicycle and he go in the street and he have a rock and he fell with *her* bicycle a lot of time.

---

5 The body parts category was kept separate from the inanimate category, although Zobl (1985) combined the two.
6 Incorrect possessive determiners include zero forms, articles, and all possessive forms used in a context for *his* or *her*.

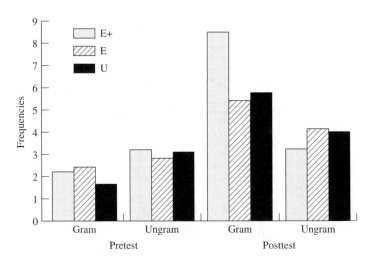

Figure 2   Mean number of grammatical or ungrammatical third person singular PDs.

[4]   This learner used both *your* and *her* in the same sentence in a context for *her*.

Learner: Ok, the, the girl ah make up ah in *her* face and ah not just in *your* face and ah all *her* body.

[5]   Sometimes learners revealed that their hypotheses about *his* and *her* were exactly reversed, as in this example. Note that the learner did not pick up on the interviewer's unintended cue:

Interviewer: So what is the girl doing to celebrate *her* birthday?

Learner: Go at the zoo with *his* big sister and *his* father and they look the giraffe.

Interviewer: Okay, good. And what does the boy do?

Learner: Uh, in *her* hand he has a balloon and he go uh at the stadium with the Expo.

Interviewer: Who is he with?

Learner: With *her* little brother and *the* mother.

Accuracy

Accuracy ratios offered one way to describe this variability. They were calculated by dividing the number of correct uses by the total number of contexts that an individual established during the task (i.e., the sum of the total number of correct, incorrect, and zero uses). In this study, only those

Domain 1: Inanimate possession

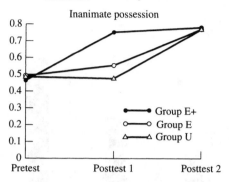

Domain 2: Human kinship possession

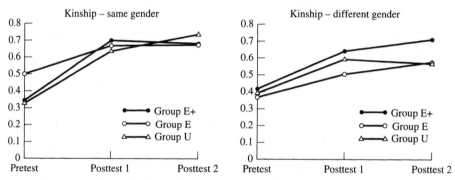

Domain 3: Human body part possession

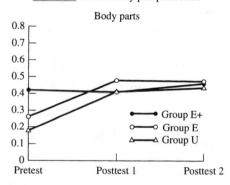

Figure 3   Accuracy percentages for third person singular PDs in three domains.

learners who established one or more contexts for the third person singular PD were included in the group accuracy ratio calculations.

Accuracy ratios were determined for the three domains into which the data had been coded: possession involving inanimate entities, kinship terms referring to same and different gender, and body parts. Figure 3 shows an overall pattern of increased accuracy for all groups in all domains across the three test administrations. ANOVA measures calculated within domains revealed no statistically significant differences among the groups at any of the test administrations.

Within the human domain, kinship different gender (Mf and Fm) appears to have been more difficult than kinship same gender (Mm and Ff). Recall that the kinship different gender domain is the one that provides the most information about the learner's control of the English agreement rule. The finding that, at the delayed posttest, Group E+ was considerably more accurate in the kinship different domain than Groups E and U were suggests a developmental advantage for Group E+. However, the differences are not statistically significant. Accuracy ratios were the lowest in the body parts domain. Many learners continued to use the definite article with body parts after they had begun to mark gender in other domains. This finding lends support to Zobl's (1985) claim that the body parts domain shows the most enduring effects of transfer from French.

Although accuracy ratios permitted a number of comparisons, they were inadequate to describe the variability that was such a salient feature of the oral data. One limitation is that accuracy calculations did not capture the developmental difference between using *the, your,* or the wrong gender-marked form in a context requiring a PD. Equally important, accuracy ratios camouflaged learners' interlanguage rules; this led them to use the right gender-marked forms for the wrong reasons, as when they overgeneralized one form or used the L1 rule in Mm and Ff contexts.

Results of qualitative analyses

To investigate whether there were qualitative differences between the groups, a stage analysis was carried out on the oral production data. The framework for the stage analysis was based on the developmental sequence inferred from accuracy ratios by Zobl (1984, 1985) and Lightbown and Spada (1990). It consisted of the eight stages shown in Table 1.

The following assumptions applied to the developmental framework: (1) Stages are based on emergence criteria, and behavior characteristic of earlier stages may be present in later stages; (2) the criterion in Stages 3 to 8 is four correct uses in different utterances regardless of the number of

TABLE 1. DEVELOPMENTAL SEQUENCE IN THE ACQUISITION OF THE
AGREEMENT RULE FOR POSSESSIVE DETERMINERS BY FRANCOPHONE LEARNERS
OF ENGLISH

Stage 1	Preemergence: avoidance of *his* and *her* and/or use of definite article
Stage 2	Preemergence: use of *your* for all persons, genders, and numbers
Stage 3	Emergence of either or both *his* and *her*
Stage 4	Preference for *his* or *her* (accompanied by overgeneralization to contexts for the other form)
Stage 5	Differentiated use of *his* and *her* (not with kin-different gender)
Stage 6	Agreement rule applied to *either his or her* (kin-different gender)
Stage 7	Agreement rule applied to *both his and her* (kin-different gender)
Stage 8	Error-free application of agreement rule to *his* and *her* (all domains, including body parts)

Adapted from Zobl (1984); Lightbown and Spada (1990).

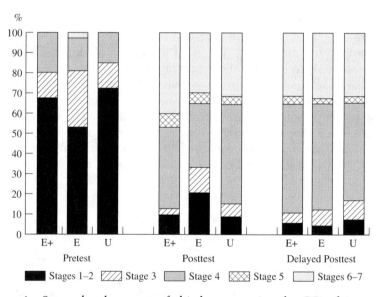

Figure 4   Stage development of third person singular PDs for experimental groups at three test sessions.

incorrect utterances that may also be present; (3) acquisition of the English rule for possessed body parts is not considered in Stages 1 to 7.[7]

Figure 4 shows that many learners in all three groups made considerable developmental progress over the period of 2 weeks. Whereas the majority were at preemergence stages (Stages 1 and 2) at the immediate pretest, 80% or more of all learners were using gender-marked forms (Stages 3 to 7) at the immediate posttest. Although the distribution patterns suggest that Group E+ learners initially benefited more from their instructional treatment than did learners in Groups E and U, the differences were not statistically significant. By the delayed posttest 5 weeks later, the distribution patterns for the three groups were similar: Most learners showed a clear preference for one form, either *his* or *her* (Stage 4); a few remained in the preemergence and emergence stages (Stages 1 to 3); and a third of the learners showed an ability to differentiate between *his* and *her* in some linguistic contexts (Stages 5 to 7). No student in any group demonstrated nativelike control of the English rule for PDs (Stage 8).

Figure 5 shows that learners in this study followed a number of different developmental paths. Some moved forward gradually from the immediate pretest to the immediate and delayed posttests. Others moved forward rapidly; of these, some moved back to developmentally earlier stages at the second posttest, and others maintained their gains. A few students in each group remained at their pretest stages throughout the study.

These differences appear to be related to the learner's developmental stage at the time the enhanced/unenhanced treatment period began. Of the 55 learners who started out at the preemergence stages, 6 (11%) were still at Stage 1 or 2 at the delayed posttest, 38 (69%) were at Stage 3 or 4, and 11 (20%) were at Stages 5 to 7. Of the 30 learners who started out at Stage 3 or 4, 10 (33%) were at Stage 4 at the delayed posttest, and 20 (67%) were at stages Stages 5 to 7. Regardless of the starting point, however, there was considerable variation in the developmental paths that individual learners took.[8]

A particularly interesting finding is that 14 of the 33 learners who were at Stages 5 to 7 at the immediate posttest "regressed" to Stage 4 at the delayed posttest. These learners dropped the gender distinction and over-

---

7 Note that emergence criteria, rather than accuracy calculations, were used at each of the eight stages. The term *emergence* is used with Stages 3 and 4 to make the contrast with Stages 1 and 2, when the learner did not use gender-marked forms.

8 At the pretest, one learner in Group E met the criteria for classification at Stage 7. However, this individual used only *his* (Stage 4) at the first posttest and continued to overgeneralize *his* at the delayed posttest, with instances of *her* below criterion (Stage 4).

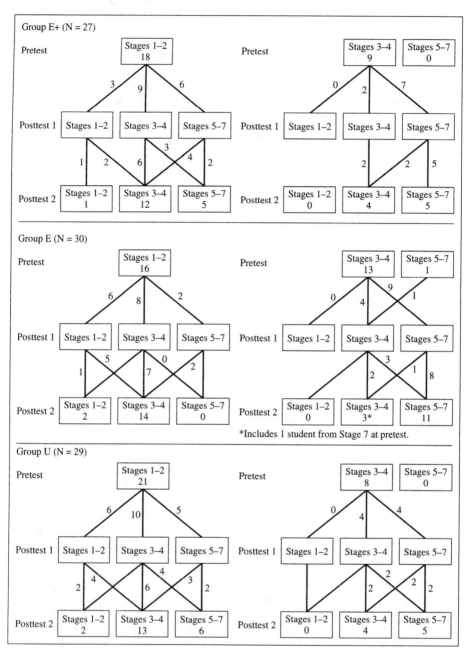

Figure 5 Development paths for third person singular PDs.

generalized one form, usually *his*. Nine (64%) of the learners who did this were at Stages 1 or 2 at the immediate pretest.

Discussion

Even though learners in all three treatment groups improved in their ability to use *his* and *her* in an oral communication task, the findings did not support the hypotheses of this study. Although accuracy ratios overall followed the predicted order, that is, Group E+ >> Group E >> Group U, the within-group variance canceled out most of the predicted between-group effects at the two posttests. This variance was illustrated earlier in this chapter in relation to intralearner variability and individual differences in learning sequence. The next sections examine the factors that may have contributed to reducing the between-group differences in this study.

Salience

Although there is general agreement that attention plays a key role in the conversion of input to intake, the level of attention that is required for L2 acquisition and the role of conscious awareness in facilitating intake processing are currently the topic of debate and empirical investigation. Schmidt's assertion (1990) that no L2 learning takes place without noticing (awareness at the point of intake) was countered by Tomlin and Villa (1994), who claimed that detection is the central component of attention. According to Tomlin and Villa, although awareness may play a role in facilitating detection, it is not essential for detection to occur.

In the study described here, PDs were made visually more salient in order to increase the likelihood that learners would detect them. It was expected that additional salience would result from an increase in the frequency with which learners encountered the forms as they completed a set of learning tasks. The findings presented suggest that PDs may have been equally salient in the input available to learners in all three groups. Although the treatment conditions were designed to provide three different types of enhancement, other factors may have been operating which reduced the between-group differences.

One factor involved the written tests that were administered three times along with the oral production task (see J. White, 1996). In particular, the multiple-choice test created contexts that contrasted *his* and *her* and required the learners to choose among several forms. It is plausible that the process of deliberating over the forms at the three test administrations drew the learners' attention to the gaps in their knowledge and increased the salience of the forms that they encountered in the enhanced/

unenhanced treatment materials, as well as in the regular classroom input. Learners who found the forms puzzling would have formulated
hypotheses about the English rule, and they would have had many opportunities to try out their hypotheses. In this way, the tests may have enhanced the target forms similarly for learners in all three of the treatment
groups, thereby reducing the differences among them.

Familiarity may have been another factor affecting salience in this
study. It is certain that learners had already encountered the target forms
in their regular intensive ESL program. Following Cook's distinction
(1991, 1993), they may have been able to understand (decode) messages
containing PDs, even though most of these learners had not yet worked
out the underlying rule ("broken the code"). Thus, the forms may not
have been novel enough to attract the learners' attention to the extent
that was predicted.

Explicitness

In order to ensure that enhancement was at the implicit end of an im-
plicit/explicit continuum, care was taken to avoid focusing the learners'
attention on the target forms in more explicit ways, such as through the
presentation of pedagogical rules, corrective feedback, discussion of the
typographical enhancement, or direct questioning regarding what the
learners understood to be the specific purpose of the tasks or of the study
itself. There is evidence, however, that the typographically enhanced input, alone or in combination with extensive reading and listening, was
more similar to unenhanced input than anticipated in terms of the information that it did *not* provide to the learners about PD agreement. Specifically, none of the treatments focused the learners' attention on the key
points of interlingual contrast: the agreement rules in English and French
and the forms used with body parts.

Clearly, learners needed more help than the input provided. At the end
of the study, 58% of the learners were at Stage 3 or 4. That is, although
they used gender-marked forms, they showed no evidence of consistently
applying the English rule. A few, 6%, used no gender-marked PDs in any
domain (Stage 1 or 2). Only 36% of the learners demonstrated partial
control of the English rule (Stages 5 to 7), and no one gave evidence of
targetlike use of PDs in all domains, including body parts (Stage 8).

These findings, along with the quantitative analyses, indicate that
many of the learners in this study might have benefited from a more
explicit type of enhancement. For example, a different typographical
technique involving the use of arrows or color coding could have been
used to clarify the relationship between the PD and its referent (see
Doughty, 1991, for another explicit visual technique). An even more
explicit pedagogical technique would have included a brief rule explana-

tion, either at the beginning of the input enhancement period or part of the way through it, to help learners structure the input (see discussions in Berry, 1994; Scott, 1989). VanPatten's work has shown the benefits of rule explanation in combination with input processing instruction in helping learners develop automatic access to the target language rule in comprehension and production tasks (VanPatten & Cadierno, 1993a; VanPatten & Sanz, 1995).

Individual learner characteristics may account for the fact that some learners in all groups reached Stages 5 to 7 without some type of more explicit instruction. These learners may have been more comfortable with the inductive approach used in this study and more able than other individuals to figure out the patterns in the input on their own (see Skehan, 1989, 1991, regarding individual differences in L2 acquisition).

A questionnaire about typographical enhancement that was administered in the learners' L1 at the end of the 2-week treatment period sheds additional light on the salience and explicitness of the typographical enhancement. Learners' responses suggested that typographical enhancement was salient enough to attract their attention to the target forms without distracting them while they read. The majority of the learners in all three groups also reported that enhancement had helped them understand the texts, but only a third of the learners named the enhanced forms when asked why they thought some of the words had been enlarged.[9] Instead, they repeated what their teachers had said at the beginning of the treatment period, that is, "because the words are difficult." It would appear from this that many learners were uncertain about the purpose of the typographical enhancement and that it had not been useful in helping them figure out the English agreement rule.[10]

Density

A different interpretation of the findings is that benefits resulting from the experimental treatment conditions were due to increased exposure through the flood of target forms and not to any other kinds of enhancement. Although this study did not include a control group not exposed to a flood, data were subsequently collected from a cohort of ninety-eight intensive ESL learners from the same school who were not exposed to

9 Recall that regular past tense -*ed* endings were enhanced for Group U.
10 These findings must be interpreted cautiously, however, in light of the difficulty of investigating processes that take place inside the learner's head. To find out about input enhancement after the end of the treatment period, it was necessary to rely on the learner's memory and ability to describe the experience. Asking explicit questions about an ongoing, presumably implicit process during the study, on the other hand, would have risked altering it (Alanen, 1995; Jourdenais, Ota, Stauffer, Boyson, & Doughty, 1995; Swain & Lapkin, 1995).

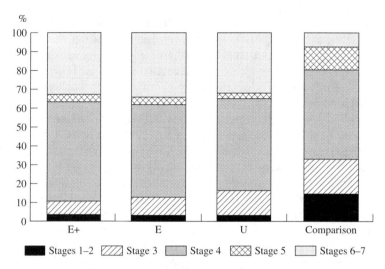

Figure 6   Stage development of third person singular PDs: Experimental versus comparison groups on delayed oral posttest.

either the enhanced or the unenhanced input flood. In every other way, these learners were comparable to those in the study: They had the same teachers, the same meaning-focused program, and the same oral picture description task at the end.

In Figure 6, the results of the stage analysis for this group are compared to the delayed posttest findings for the experimental learners. The figure clearly indicates that the comparison group learners were developmentally less advanced than the learners in Groups E+, E, and U: A larger percentage of comparison group learners were in Stages 1 to 3; a smaller percentage were in Stages 5 to 7; and a similar percentage were in Stage 4. Of particular interest is the contrast between the experimental and comparison groups at Stages 6 and 7, where application of the English rule is required. Although these differences on their own leave unresolved the question of whether it was the input flood, typographical enhancement, or multiple test administrations that was responsible for the developmental advantage of the experimental learners over the comparison group, they suggest that learners in the group that received no enhancement of PDs showed less progress.

Developmental framework

Although the term *stage* is widely used in the SLA literature, the concept of stage is not often discussed (Cook, 1993). The stages used to analyze the oral production data in this study were based on previous theoretical and empirical work by Felix (Felix, 1981; Felix & Hahn, 1985) and Zobl (1984, 1985). They were refined, and stages added beyond those proposed by Lightbown and Spada (1990), to capture the developmental changes evident in the data as learners attempted to apply the English PD rule in different semantic domains.

The stages describe the learners' gradual acquisition of the ability to produce the PDs *his* and *her* during a communicative task. They can be grouped in the following way:

1. Preemergence – learners in Stages 1 and 2 do not use gender-marked PD forms
2. Emergence – learners in Stages 3 and 4 use *his* and/or *her* but show no evidence of applying the English rule
3. Postemergence – learners in Stages 5 to 7 gradually develop the ability to use the English rule
4. Targetlike performance – Stage 8 assumes targetlike use of the English PD rule in all semantic domains (inanimate, kinship, and body parts)

The framework assumes that the four stage clusters are qualitatively different and that together they represent an acquisitional sequence. The evidence clearly supports this claim for the preemergence and emergence stages since, with one exception, learners did not go back to preemergence stages once they had begun to use gender-marked PD forms (Figure 5). Furthermore, the data strongly suggest that the emergence stages are the pivotal ones for learners in all groups: The majority of the learners were at an emergence stage at the end of the study, either because they had advanced to it or because they had gone back to Stage 4 from one of the postemergence stages.

This backward movement does not pose a problem for the developmental framework. In fact, the shift from correct use of a target feature to a developmentally earlier L2 feature and eventually back again to targetlike use is well documented in the SLA literature and has been characterized as U-shaped development (Kellerman, 1985) and as restructuring (McLaughlin, 1990). Zobl (1984) also used the term *restructuring* to describe the phenomenon in which learners simplify their interlanguage PD rule by dropping the gender distinction and overgeneralizing one form. This is precisely the developmental pattern that was found when learners in this study went from a postemergence stage to Stage 4. Thus, restructuring can be viewed as part of the normal acquisition sequence for at least some of the learners.[11]

---

11 It is possible that all learners experienced restructuring of the PD rule even though the researcher was not present at the appropriate developmental moment to detect the occurrence of this phenomenon.

There are several explanations for the restructuring that occurred in this study. One is that learners who met the criteria for Stages 5 to 7 at the immediate posttest were using memorized chunks from the input flood and had not yet analyzed the chunks to find the underlying English agreement rule. At the delayed posttest 5 weeks later, when the memorized chunks were less readily available for use in the oral production task, learners adopted the cognitively less demanding rule simplification strategy and used one PD in all contexts. The learners who did this may have been more memory-oriented than others and more likely to rely on prefabricated chunks and routines (Skehan, 1991).

For others, the backward movement may have been an artifact of the coding procedure. That is, the coding procedure may have overestimated a learner's development at one test administration and underestimated it at the next. Overestimation would have been possible in the case of learners who produced a lot of language because, regardless of the number of PD errors they made, they could still have been assigned to a stage if they met the minimum criterion for correct uses. Underestimation could have occurred if learners had said less and not produced enough target forms to be reassigned to their previous stage.

Conclusion

It would appear that a number of factors, including characteristics of the enhanced/unenhanced input, normal developmental processes leading to restructuring, multiple test administrations, and the coding procedure itself, may have contributed to reducing the differences between the groups. The findings suggest that, although drawing the learners' attention to a linguistic feature may be sufficient to speed up acquisition of that feature, implicit FonF instruction may not be adequate in cases involving L1-L2 contrasts. Furthermore, there may be a ceiling on this development when the L1 and L2 differ in ways that are not evident to the learner on the basis of positive evidence available in the input. In such cases, learners may need somewhat more explicit information about the L1-L2 contrasts in order to progress to more advanced developmental stages. The ways in which this information can be combined with additional exposure and increased salience are in need of further investigation.

Appendix 1   The Frog Prince – Enhanced Version

Once upon a time there was a king. *He* had a beautiful young daughter. For *her* birthday, the king gave *her* a golden ball that *she* played with every day.

The king and *his* daughter lived near a dark forest. There was a deep well near the castle. Sometimes, the princess would sit by the well and play with *her* ball. One day, the princess threw *her* golden ball in the air but it did not fall into *her* hands. It fell into the well. Splash! The well was deep and the princess was sure *she* would never see *her* ball again. So *she* cried and cried and could not stop.

"What is the matter?" said a voice behind *her*. The girl looked around, and *she* saw a frog. *He* was in the well, *his* head sticking out of the water.

"Oh, it's you" said the girl. "My ball fell into the well."

"I can help," said the frog. "I can get your ball. What will you give me if I do?"

"Whatever you want," said the princess. "I'll give you my beautiful gold ring. I'll give you flowers from my garden."

"I do not want your beautiful gold ring or flowers from your garden," said the frog. "But I would like to live with you and be your friend." *He* continued, "I would like to eat from your dish and drink from your cup. I would like to sleep on your bed. If I get your ball, will you promise me all this, Princess?"

"Oh, yes," said the princess. "I'll promise." But *she* thought, "Silly frog! I could never live with *him*!"

When the frog heard *her* promise, *he* went down in the well. *He* soon came up with the golden ball in *his* mouth. *He* put it at *her* feet.

She was happy when *she* saw *her* ball. *She* picked it up and ran away.

"Wait," cried the frog. "Wait for me! Take me with you!"

But *she* did not listen. *She* just ran home. *She* soon forgot the poor frog.

That night, the princess was eating dinner when – plop-plop, plop-plop – something came climbing up the steps. When it reached the door, it knocked. It cried out in a loud voice.

"Daughter of the king
Open the door for me."

The princess ran to the door. There was the frog, wet and green and cold! *She* slammed the door in *his* face.

The king saw that *she* was afraid.

"My daughter, what are you afraid of?" *he* asked.

"It's a fat, old frog," said the princess.

"And what does *he* want from you?" asked the king.

The princess explained what had happened, how *her* ball had fallen into the well and the frog had brought it back to *her*; how *she* had promised *him* *he* could be *her* friend; how *she* said *he* could eat from *her* dish and drink from *her* cup. But *she* never thought *he* would leave his well. *She* said *she* had even promised that *he* could sleep in *her* bed!

The frog knocked again and said,

"Daughter of the King,

Open the door for me.

You promised I could

be your friend.

Open the door for me."

Then the king said, "You know that if you make promises, you must keep them. So you must open the door."

The princess listened to *her* father. *She* knew that *she* had to do what *he* said. *She* opened the door. The frog said, "Pick me up. I want to sit by you at the table." *She* shook *her* head and turned away from *him*. But *her* father looked at *her* and said, "You must keep your promise."

Then the frog said, "Now push your dish close to me." Again the princess looked away. But *she* had to do it. The frog ate and ate, but the princess could not eat a thing.

At last the frog said, "I feel tired. Take me to your room. I want to sleep now."

The princess looked at *her* father. It was bad enough to touch the frog. But *she* did not want *him* in *her* bed. The king said, "The frog helped you when you needed *him*. Now, you must keep your promise to *him*."

The princess was angry. But *she* put the frog at the foot of *her* bed. Then *she* went to sleep. The next day, the frog went away. *She* did not know where. But the next night *he* came back. *He* knocked at the door, and *she* had to let *him* in. Again, *he* ate out of *her* dish, and *he* drank from *her* golden cup. Again *he* went to sleep at the foot of *her* bed. In the morning *he* went away again.

The third night *he* said, "I want to sleep at the head of your bed. I think I would like it better there." The girl thought *she* would never be able to sleep with a cold, wet frog near *her* face. But *she* put *him* there. Then *she* cried herself to sleep again.

In the morning the frog jumped off the bed. But when *his* feet touched the floor, something happened. *He* was no longer a cold, green frog, but a young prince!

He looked at the princess and smiled. "I was not what I seemed to be!," *he* said to the princess. "I was turned into a frog by magic. No one but you could help me. I could only turn back into a prince if you kept your promise."

He smiled. "I waited and waited at the well for you to help me."

The princess was so surprised *she* did not know what to say.

"Will you let me be your friend now?" said the prince, laughing. "You promised."

The princess laughed too. *She* ran to tell the king what had happened. For years they were the best of friends. And when they grew up, they were married and lived happily ever after. The End.

Princess, King, or Frog

Who does the underlined word refer to? Write *P* in the blank if it refers to the princess, write *K* in the blank if it refers to the king, and write *F* in the blank if it refers to the frog. If necessary, look back at the story. The first one is done for you.

1. For *her* birthday, he had given *her* a golden ball.   *K*
2. The princess lived with *him* near a dark forest.   _____
3. *She* played with *her* golden ball.   _____
4. *She* dropped *her* golden ball in the well.   _____
5. *He* was in the well, sticking *his* head out of the water.   _____
6. *She* offered to give *him her* fine golden ring and flowers from *her* garden.   _____
7. The frog said *he* wanted to be *her* friend.   _____
8. *She* thought *she* could never live with *him*.   _____
9. *He* soon came up with the golden ball in *his* mouth.   _____
10. *She* slammed the door in *his* face.   _____
11. *He* saw that *she* was afraid.   _____
12. The princess listened to *him*. *She* knew *she* had to do what *he* said.   _____
13. The king told *her* that *she* must keep *her* promises.   _____
14. The frog ate from *her* plate and drank from *her* cup.   _____
15. The king said, "*He* helped you when you needed *him*. Now, you must keep your promise to *him*."   _____
16. *He* slept at the foot of *her* bed.   _____
17. When *his* feet touched the floor, something happened.   _____
18. The prince looked at *her* and smiled.   _____
19. No one but the princess could help *him*.   _____
20. For years, *he* was *her* best friend.   _____

Appendix 2   The Frog Prince – Unenhanced Version

Once upon a time there was a king. He had a beautiful, young daughter. For her birthday, the king gave her a golden ball that she play*ed* with every day.

The king and his daughter liv*ed* near a dark forest. There was a deep well near the castle. Sometimes, the princess would sit by the well and play with her ball. One day, the princess threw her golden ball in the air but it did not fall into her hands. It fell into the well. Splash! The well was deep and the princess was sure she would never see her ball again. So she cri*ed* and cri*ed* and could not stop.

"What is the matter?" said a voice behind her. The girl look*ed* around, and she saw a frog. He was in the well, his head sticking out of the water.

"Oh, it's you" said the girl. "My ball fell into the well."

"I can help," said the frog. "I can get your ball. What will you give me if I do?"

"Whatever you want," said the princess. "I'll give you my beautiful gold ring. I'll give you flowers from my garden."

"I do not want your beautiful gold ring or flowers from your garden," said the frog. "But I would like to live with you and be your friend."

He continu*ed*, "I would like to eat from your dish and drink from your cup. I would like to sleep on your bed. If I get your ball, will you promise me all this, Princess?"

"Oh, yes," said the princess. "I'll promise." But she thought, "Silly frog! I could never live with him!"

When the frog heard her promise, he went down in the well. He soon came up with the golden ball in his mouth. He put it at her feet.

She was happy when she saw her ball. She pick*ed* it up and ran away.

"Wait," cri*ed* the frog. "Wait for me! Take me with you!"

But, she did not listen. She just ran home. She soon forgot the poor frog.

That night, the princess was eating dinner when – plop-plop, plop-plop – something came climbing up the steps. When it reach*ed* the door, it knock*ed*. It cri*ed* out in a loud voice.

"Daughter of the king
Open the door for me."

The princess ran to the door. There was the frog, wet and green and cold! She slamm*ed* the door in his face.

The king saw that she was afraid.

"My daughter, what are you afraid of? he ask*ed*.

"It's a fat, old frog," said the princess.

"And what does he want from you?" ask*ed* the king.

The princess explain*ed* what had happened, how her ball had fallen into the well and the frog had brought it back to her; how she had promised him he could be her friend; how she said he could eat from her dish and drink from her cup. But she never thought he would leave his well. She said she had even promised that he could sleep in her bed!

The frog knock*ed* again and said,

"Daughter of the King,

Open the door for me.

You promis*ed* I could

be your friend.

Open the door for me."

Then, the king said, "You know that if you make promises, you must keep them. So you must open the door."

The princess listen*ed* to her father. She knew that she had to do what he said. She open*ed* the door. The frog said, "Pick me up. I want to sit by you at the table." She shook her head and turn*ed* away from him. But her father look*ed* at her and said, "You must keep your promise."

Then the frog said, "Now push your dish close to me." Again the princess look*ed* away. But she had to do it. The frog ate and ate, but the princess could not eat a thing.

At last the frog said, "I feel tired. Take me to your room. I want to sleep now."

The princess look*ed* at her father. It was bad enough to touch the frog. But she did not want him in her bed. The king said, "The frog help*ed* you when you need*ed* him. Now, you must keep your promise to him."

The princess was angry. But she put the frog at the foot of her bed. Then she went to sleep. The next day, the frog went away. She did not know where. But the next night he came back. He knock*ed* at the door, and she had to let him in. Again, he ate out of her dish, and he drank from her golden cup. Again he went to sleep at the foot of her bed. In the morning he went away again.

The third night he said, "I want to sleep at the head of your bed. I think I would like it better there." The girl thought she would never be able to sleep with a cold, wet frog near her face. But she put him there. Then she cri*ed* herself to sleep again.

In the morning the frog jump*ed* off the bed. But when his feet touch*ed* the floor, something happen*ed*. He was no longer a cold, green frog, but a young prince!

He look*ed* at the princess and smil*ed*. "I was not what I seemed to be!," he said to the princess. "I was turned into a frog by magic. No one but you could help me. I could only turn back into a prince if you kept your promise."

He smil*ed*. "I wait*ed* and wait*ed* at the well for you to help me."

The princess was so surprised she did not know what to say.

"Will you let me be your friend now?" said the prince, laughing. "You promis*ed*."

The princess laugh*ed* too. She ran to tell the king what had happened. For years they were the best of friends. And when they grew up, they were married and liv*ed* happily ever after. The End.

The Frog Prince Questions

Answer the questions below. The first one is done for you.

1. Who gave the princess a golden ball for her birthday?
   The king

2. Where did the princess live?

3. Who did the princess live with?

4. Where was the princess playing with her golden ball?

5. What happened to the ball?

6. What did the princess offer to give the frog if he return*ed* her ball?

7. What did the frog want?

8. Who brought back her ball?

9. What did the princess do when the frog knock*ed* at the door?

10. What did the king tell the princess?

11. What did the frog do when he went into the castle?

12. Where did the frog sleep?

_____

13. What happen*ed* when the frog's feet touched the floor?

_____

14. How was the prince turn*ed* into a frog?

_____

15. What happen*ed* to the prince and princess?

_____

6 Communicative focus on form

Catherine Doughty
Elizabeth Varela

Introduction

Although there is general agreement that accuracy is an important classroom language acquisition goal, it is by no means clear *how* learners can best be assisted via classroom procedures and tasks in becoming more targetlike. On the contrary, attention to linguistic form in language teaching can be accomplished by using a variety of procedures, ranging from the most explicit metalinguistic rule explanation to the most implicit visual input enhancement (see Doughty & Williams, Chapter 10, this volume). Arguments against explicit procedures center around the likelihood of precluding fluency, which has, after all, been the major advancement of communicative approaches to classroom language acquisition, since in explicit procedures language becomes the object rather than the means of discussion. Therefore, in our view, a quintessential element of the theoretical construct of focus on form is its dual requirement that the focus must occur in conjunction with – but must not interrupt – communicative interaction. Accordingly, implicit focus-on-form (FonF) techniques are potentially effective, since the aim is to *add* attention to form to a primarily communicative task rather than to *depart* from an already communicative goal in order to discuss a linguistic feature.

This chapter discusses classroom research in which focus on form was carefully operationalized and implemented into a content-based ESL class in the United States. The main aim of the study was to determine whether and how learners' attention can be drawn to formal features without distracting them from their original communicative intent. Much of the motivation for the type of focus on form investigated in this study came from the following intriguing pedagogical recommendation:

[W]hereas the content of lessons with a focus on *forms* is the *forms* themselves, a syllabus with a focus on *form* teaches something else – biology, mathematics, workshop practice, automobile repair, the geography of a

We would like to thank Michael Couglan for his participation in the study and Michael Long for his comments on an earlier version of the chapter.

country where the foreign language is spoken, the cultures of its speakers, and so on – and overtly draws students' attention to linguistic elements as they arise incidentally in lessons whose overriding focus is on meaning or communication. (Long, 1991, pp. 45–46)

Although the intent of Long's theoretical construct of focus on form is clear, the procedures and tasks remain to be specified and tested empirically. Nonetheless, three specific criteria for implicit FonF task development may be gleaned from Long's recommendation:

1. The target of the focus on form should arise incidentally in the otherwise content-based lesson.
2. The primary (in Long's terms, "overriding") focus should remain on meaning or communication.
3. The teacher should draw students' attention to form rather than leaving it to chance that students will notice linguistic features without any pedagogical assistance.

These criteria, in turn, raise a number of classroom SLA issues. For instance, can tasks be designed during which problematic forms are likely to arise, providing a natural, contextualized opportunity for teachers to focus on form? If so, can focus on form be incorporated into a content-based class more or less incidentally in such a way that the dynamics of the classroom interaction will remain centered on the learning of content, circumventing any shift to a traditional focus on formS? In the event that it is possible to provide communicative opportunities for focus on form, it becomes important to investigate the details of precisely when and how focus on form is effectively incorporated. For example, when should focus on form occur in individual classrooms (e.g., as planned a priori by the teacher or only when the need arises)? And furthermore, what specific procedures can be used that are both task-natural and more or less incidental to the aims of the content material? Finally, once the FonF task and procedure issues are addressed, it ultimately must be determined whether focus on form contributes effectively to classroom language acquisition. In other words, is the task-natural, incidental focus on form that emerges out of these considerations effective in promoting L2 use and accuracy?

The research team

In order to investigate whether a task-natural and mainly incidental focus on form would be feasible and effective in an overridingly communicative classroom, we formed a researcher–classroom teacher team. The teacher invited to participate in this study (Varela) was known to the researcher to be a dedicated, communicatively oriented language teacher. Her teaching responsibilities at the time of the study were content-based science and math classes for ESL students in grades 6 through 8. Because the primary aim of these classes was the teaching of science and math content, it was assumed that this context would be ideal for the incidental implementation of focus on form.

At the outset of the design of the study, the researcher (Doughty) discussed the theoretical construct of focus on form with the teacher and asked her to reflect upon her own willingness to collaborate and, as well, to consider the feasibility of operationalizing focus on form in her ESL science classroom. After a brief initial reaction of reluctance, not untypical of communicatively trained teachers (see Lightbown, this volume), the teacher agreed to collaborate, provided that the FonF procedure was implicit and would not interfere with the ordinary science curriculum.[1] In designing the materials and procedures for this study, the teacher observed the students in her ESL science content-based class for a period of 2 weeks, in order to make an assessment of their interlanguage so that two steps could be taken: the selection of a feature of English for which the majority of students could potentially benefit from a push to target accuracy, and the development of a task that could be used to embody the FonF research by providing an essential, or at the very least, natural context for the use of the form (Loschky & Bley-Vroman, 1993). In the meantime, the researcher developed the motivation for the design of the FonF technique from some recent advances in the investigation of negative evidence provided to children and the natural occurrence of such evidence to learners in ESL and foreign language classrooms (Doughty, 1994b).

Recasting as focus on form

As is well known in debates in child language acquisition research, there is no consensus as to what constitutes the negative evidence that provides learners with information about what is not possible in the target language. Early, but oft-cited definitions typically limited negative evidence to explicit prohibitions or corrections of child language. Thus defined, there is, of course, very little support for a role for negative evidence in child language acquisition (Brown & Hanlon, 1970). More recently, however, there has been a concerted effort by child language researchers to reconceptualize negative evidence in a manner that is more consistent

---

1 There has been considerable opposition to the notion of focus on form from primarily communicative language teachers who, not without basis, fear a return to purely grammar-based methods.

with the data on child-directed discourse, as well as to investigate any correlations between negative evidence and subsequent language acquisition. These child language acquisition findings vis à vis the provision of negative evidence by adults can be only briefly summarized here.

Three findings are statistically important. First, it has been found that adults are more likely to recast or request clarification of children's ill-formed utterances than of the well-formed ones (Demetras, Post, & Snow, 1986). Next, it was shown that adults are more likely to recast ill-formed utterances with only one error than those with many (Bohannon & Stanowicz, 1988). And finally, adults are quite likely to provide *specific contrastive evidence* by giving exemplars (in their recasts) of the correct syntactic form or pronunciation immediately after the child error has been uttered (Bohannon & Stanowicz, 1988). These findings suggest that parents provide systematic information to children by recasting their errors in a focused way (e.g., they address only one error and provide the targetlike exemplar).

Of course, it has been argued that documenting the provision of negative evidence is not sufficient to establish its usefulness in language acquisition (Grimshaw & Pinker, 1989). In response to this argument, it has been shown that children both *notice* the linguistic information brought into focus by adults and seem to *make use of it*, as indicated by a number of L1 acquisition findings. For example, children show their sensitivity to parental feedback by being more likely to repeat recasts than to repeat adult repetitions[2] (Bohannon & Stanowicz, 1988; Farrar, 1992). As well, children imitate the grammatical morphemes contained in corrective recasts, but they do not imitate the identical information contained in other discourse categories (all constituting positive evidence; Farrar, 1992). And perhaps most important of all, parental feedback has been shown to be correlated with child language acquisition of these specific morphemes (Farrar, 1990).

Taken together, these findings suggest that not only do adults provide negative evidence to children but that children notice this information and make use of it in acquisition. Furthermore, examination of examples of the child-directed discourse reported in the above-mentioned studies shows clearly that the provision of negative evidence via recasting does not halt communication between parent and child but, rather, is relatively incidental to the primary goal of mutual understanding. These findings provided a basis for predicting that recasting would be the ideal FonF procedure to be implemented in our study, provided that such recasting could successfully be accomplished in a classroom setting. In fact, it had

---

2 Adults have also been shown to repeat well-formed child utterances but not to repeat ill-formed child utterances (Demetras, Post, & Snow, 1986).

been shown in an earlier classroom observation study that recasting behaviors arise naturally and frequently during communicative tasks in ESL
and foreign language classes (Doughty, 1994b). Furthermore, it has been
demonstrated that not only is recasting (among other types) a frequent
feature of child native speaker–nonnative speaker task discourse (25%
overall) but that nonnative speakers are able to use the information provided in the recasts in their own subsequent utterances (about 35% of the
time; Oliver, 1995).

Given that recasting seems both frequent and effective in child natural
and classroom L1 and L2 language acquisition, it was decided that the
implicit focus on form in this study would be operationalized as corrective recasting. The teacher piloted the procedure in advance of the study
to ascertain whether she could incorporate recasting in a natural way into
her usual content-teaching style. Indeed, it was feasible for her to recast
learner utterances consistently during the everyday science class activities. The specific procedures she employed in this study aimed to draw
learner attention to problematic linguistic features and subsequently to
provide a specific exemplar so that learners could make a cognitive comparison between their interlanguage utterance and the teacher's recast.
How this was accomplished in the classroom will be discussed later in
this chapter. Thus, with the task and procedures developed, we turned
our attention to the question of what feature of English to target in the
FonF instruction.

Form in focus

The remainder of this chapter is a description of the implementation of a
focus on form in an ESL science class designed to be implicit enough so as
not to alter science learning and communication, and yet salient enough
so as to be potentially effective. In order to arrive at a form on which to
focus, the teacher in the treatment group analyzed students' writing in
their weekly lab reports, in which they were asked to summarize the
problem, steps, hypothesis, results, and conclusion of a science experiment performed earlier that day or on the preceding day. The results of
this period of observation showed that many of the students had difficulty with past time reference, even though past time reference is both
natural and, at times, essential to the reporting of previously completed
experiments. Since experiments already comprised a major portion of the
science curriculum, it was decided that past time reference would be the
targeted feature in the FonF investigation. Although students were having
difficulty with other forms as well (comparatives and superlatives, third
person singular -*s*, noun-adjective inversion), simple past and conditional
were selected as the form in focus because the science lab report elicited

such past time reference naturally, for the students needed to report on what they had just completed. In addition, numerous errors of time reference tended to result in oral and written reports that were less than successful with regard to communicating the predictions and outcomes of the science lab experiments.

Context of the study

The subjects in the experiment were thirty-four middle school students from two different intact classes studying science at an intermediate ESL level in a suburban east coast school district. Nonnative speakers in the district make up approximately 30% of the total school population, and the ESL population countywide is 17%. The content drives the curriculum in the science program, for the students study earth, space, physical, life, and health sciences in a program that reflects mainstream objectives for grades 6, 7, and 8. The subjects ranged in age from 11 to 14, because the ESL students are grouped by English ability and not by grade level. The majority of subjects came from Spanish-speaking countries in Central and South America, but a few subjects represented other languages and cultures (two Portuguese native speakers, one from Portugal and one from Brazil, one student from China, one from Ethiopia, one from Albania, two from Vietnam, and one from Thailand).

Prior to the study, both teachers of these students admitted to spending little if any time on grammar instruction or correction in their science classes, either orally or in writing. However, the students received some focus on formS in their language arts classes, although even that portion of the curriculum embraces a "whole language" approach in which instruction emphasizes integrating reading and writing skills for communication, and grammar instruction is minimal. As with most ESL classes, the students within and between the two classes ranged quite a bit in their academic backgrounds and English-speaking abilities. They had, however, several things in common. The students all would be placed in mainstream science classes at their grade level in the following school year. At the time of the study, they remained nontargetlike in their use of many features of English despite their language arts teachers' attempts to focus on forms, which, as noted by Varela, was unfortunate, given that their achievement in mainstream classes could be hindered until they were able to reach a level of precision in their oral and written grammar that would be acceptable to the mainstream teachers. Nonetheless, prior to their participation in the study, both of the ESL science teachers routinely rejected the inclusion of explicit grammatical instruction in their lessons for fear that it might manipulate, take away from, or hinder science learning or communication about science.

The science report task

As can be seen in Figure 1, after students performed a simple science experiment, it was important for them to be able to report past events and to explain a prediction that was made prior to conducting the experiment that the lab report documented. In particular, students needed to use past and conditional past for time reference, as can be seen in Examples 1 and 2 (from Subject 3, Posttest).

[1] Relating the experiment:

I took a cup with three six and nine pennies and twelve and I blew from fifteen centimeters away from my chin and then I measured and get the average.

[2] Relating the prediction:

I thought the cup with three pennies would go the farthest.

The science report was carried out in both written and oral modes, with written reports always completed first and the teacher later interviewing the students individually, audiotaping their responses to the same questions asked in the written lab report. The students were not permitted to read their written responses but, rather, were encouraged to change or add thoughts to what they had previously written. In addition to the five questions posed on the report, the teacher asked them: "What did I (the teacher) think would happen before we did the experiment?" This question (asked just after the students answered question 3 in Figure 1) was task-natural, because at the start of the experiment the teacher hypothesized along with the students about the possible outcomes. The additional question was included because it gave the teacher the opportunity to elicit a second instance of the conditional past time reference in the form of responses such as "You thought X would happen." It is interesting to note that the experiments were set up so that the outcome most likely to be predicted was rarely the actual outcome, thereby allowing students to make a scientific "discovery." This state of affairs was particularly motivating to the students when they reported on the science labs.

Questions 1, 2, and 3 were generally successful at eliciting contexts for the simple past. Question 3 and the subsequent additional oral question about the teacher prediction were successful at eliciting contexts for the conditional. Question 5 did not work well to elicit past time reference of any kind, because subjects often either did not understand what a scientific conclusion was (favoring personal or storylike conclusions) or reported their conclusion with present reference, which was pragmatically appropriate, since any conclusion stands as true at the time the report is

SCIENCE LAB REPORT

Directions: Fill out this paper *after* you do the experiment. Use *complete sentences.*

1. **Problem:**
   What problem did you try to solve with this experiment?

   _____

   _____

   _____

2. **Steps:**
   What steps did you follow for this experiment?

   _____

   _____

   _____

3. **Hypothesis:**
   What did you think would happen?

   _____

   _____

   _____

4. **Results:**
   What happened in this experiment?

   _____

   _____

   _____

5. **Conclusions:**
   What can you conclude from this experiment?

   _____

   _____

   _____

Figure 1   The science report format.

given. Ultimately, responses to question 5 were not included in the corpus.

The design

In order to determine the effectiveness of incidental focus on form in the context of the content-based ESL science class, it was necessary to employ a pretest–posttest control group design (see Figure 2). As noted earlier,

Pretest and Posttests (embodied the data collection)

Pretest (Week 1)	**WonderScience construction challenge** What is the effect of folding on the strength of a paper bridge? *Predict which of three types of paper bridges (flat, arched, and accordion) would be the strongest.*
Posttest (Week 6)	**Huff, puff, and slide** What is the effect of weight on the distance a cup can be blown across a desk? *Predict which would go farthest across a desk when blown: a plastic cup with three pennies, one with six pennies, one with nine pennies, or one with twelve pennies.*
Delayed posttest (2 months later)	**Heads or tails** What is the effect of surface contours on volume? *Predict which side of a penny – heads or tails – holds more drops of water.*

Pedagogical Labs (embodied the focus on form)

Lab 1 (~ Weeks 2 and 3)	**How will the earthworm respond?** What is the effect of light, vinegar, and touch on an earthworm? *Predict how the earthworm would react to each of these.*
Lab 2 (~ Weeks 3 and 4)	**The ball bounce** What is the effect of the type of ball on the distance it will bounce? *Predict which ball (basketball, soccer ball, rubber ball) would bounce the highest.*
Lab 3 (~ Weeks 4 and 5)	**Paper airplanes** What is the effect of different types of paper on the distance a paper airplane will fly? *Predict which plane – one made of construction paper, one of folder paper, and one of typing paper – would fly the farthest.*

Figure 2   The science experiments.

the subjects were already in intact classes, with both classes following the same content curriculum and attending the same kind of language arts class. No instruction on past time reference was given in language arts for the duration of the study. All students in both classes completed and reported on six science experiments, each taking 1 or 2 weeks to complete. The first, the fifth, and the sixth (oral and written) reports served as the pretest, posttest, and delayed (after 2 months) posttests, respectively.

The three experiments that the classes carried out in between the pretest and the immediate posttest were the pedagogical labs during which the treatment group (FonF) received focus-on-form instruction in addition to science content instruction, whereas the control group (Control) received only the science content instruction. Both teachers returned to the content-only regular science instruction during the 2-month interval between the two posttests. Figure 2 shows the pedagogical content as well as the empirical design of the five science labs that comprised the pretest and posttest corpora and also embodied the instructional treatment.

Twenty-one students comprised the FonF group, taught by Varela; thirteen students were in the control group, taught by a colleague whose teaching style was known to be similar to Varela's in terms of commitment to the teaching of science content to the exclusion of the teaching of linguistic forms. The control classes, which were audiotaped to ensure that no attention to past time reference was given, confirmed that the control teacher followed the district science curriculum and paid no attention to grammar.

FonF tasks and techniques

The instructional tasks were designed to elicit spontaneous and planned production of all aspects of the past tense, both orally and in writing. For oral production, the students, upon completion of a science experiment, reported on the procedure in several ways. For one task, they worked in groups of four. For this task, the students divided up the sections of the lab report and practiced presenting the steps before their peers. They were familiar with this type of activity because they had done it in class before. What differed was that, when the teacher walked around the classroom assisting the groups, she gave them feedback not only on the science content but also on the forms of the past tense. In fact, throughout the period during which the pedagogical labs were carried out, whenever past or conditional errors occurred in speaking or writing, Varela drew attention to the problem and then immediately provided corrective feedback in the form of a recast. No other errors were addressed, and there was no metalinguistic discussion. Thus, all procedures were consistent in that each focused on only one learner error (of past time reference) and each constituted some kind of attentional focus – typically via repetition of the learner utterance with rising intonation – plus a recast providing the necessary target exemplar, either in contrast to a learner error or as a model for a missing past morpheme, with recasts always delivered with a falling intonation curve.

As shown in more detail in Example 3, the negative evidence was often provided in two phases, which we term *corrective recasting:* (1) repetitions to draw attention followed by (2) recasts to provide the contrastive L2 forms. Although slightly more explicit than recasts that do not have a preceding attentional focus, corrective recasts nevertheless did not interfere with the flow of the science reports or discussions. In some instances, the teacher would repeat a phrase containing an incorrect past verb, putting the error in focus by using stress and rising intonation to prompt the student to notice the nontargetlike form. Recasts were then used when the student did not attempt any past time reference at all. In such a recast, the teacher provided the exemplar needed, using falling intonation and, once again, emphasizing the verb with added stress. This generally resulted in the student incorporating the recast and then, typically, continuing with the science report.

[3]   Corrective Recasting
      José: I think that the worm will go under the soil.
      Teacher: I *think* that the worm *will* go under the soil?
      José: (no response)
      Teacher: I *thought* that the worm *would* go under the soil.
      José: I *thought* that the worm *would* go under the soil.

In another task, the teacher required the students to respond spontaneously to questions in a class discussion. When she noticed an error of the focused form, she not only used the above procedure, with the student making the error, but also allowed other students in the class to repeat the phrase containing the correct form before moving on quickly with the discussion of the various aspects of the science experiment. Another task required the students to plan and present the labs in front of the entire class, again with each student taking responsibility for one part of the lab report. For this task, the teacher thought it best not to provide any recasts because the students were presenting in a formal way in front of their peers. It was believed that feedback at this time might have caused embarrassment and was certain to impede the flow of communication. Instead, the presentations were videotaped in order to take advantage of the errors during another lesson. The day after the students presented their labs for the class, they watched the videotape. The emphasis for this review of the tape was to look for any improvement that might be made on the content and presentation skills of the speakers. The specific objective was for the class members to come up with two or three components of the report that they thought each group did particularly well, and one or two that might have been done better. As the students watched the tape, the teacher paused it at places where an error of the past was noticed and asked the students in the class to repeat the correct form simultaneously.[3]

---

3 Interestingly, on the final judgments and recommendations, no student offered *better grammar* as a way to improve any presentation. This provides some indication that the implementation of the focus on form was not overly obtrusive.

As noted earlier, students also completed written lab reports. Every effort was made to simulate the oral attention-getting and recasting features in the written focus on form. In addition to her normal comments, the teacher drew students' attention in the written mode by circling all errors of past time reference. She gave negative evidence in the form of a juxtaposed recast. She also offered content-based comments on the written lab report. The students were then asked to redo the lab report taking into account all comments.

Analysis

Coding

The corpus for analysis of the effects of incidental focus on form on the development of past and conditional in the ESL science class included the transcribed oral lab reports and the written lab reports. In order to perform an interlanguage analysis of these data, the framework of coding decisions shown in Figure 3 was developed. Decision 1 examined every context in which a verb was or should have been produced. For Decision 2, it was simply noted whether or not a verb was supplied in this obligatory context. In Decision 3, it was determined whether this verb context required the marking of past time; eventually, all verb contexts that both did not require past marking and (correctly) did not include past marking were categorized as targetlike nonpast forms and were not further analyzed. In other words, only those verb contexts for which it was necessary to mark past, as well as those contexts in which past marking was overused, were retained for analysis.

Once the contexts and verbs were identified, the nature of the past marking was considered: Decision 4 determined whether the past or conditional was marked, and Decision 5 analyzed whether the past marking, if present, was targetlike, was an interlanguage attempt at encoding past reference, or was "inappropriate" in the sense that some kind of time marking was apparent (e.g., present time or future time) but time reference was inappropriate to the context of the verb. Finally, where the marking was inappropriate, the nature of that nonpast marking, for example, "inappropriate use of present for past" or "inappropriate use of future for conditional," was coded.

Coding socialization was carried out on some data that had been discarded from the study because the students were not present for both pretesting and posttesting in either the oral or the written formats. The coding framework was revised based on our experience, and then the data were coded independently.[4]

---

4 Both of us coded all of the pretest and posttest data. Simple agreement on coding

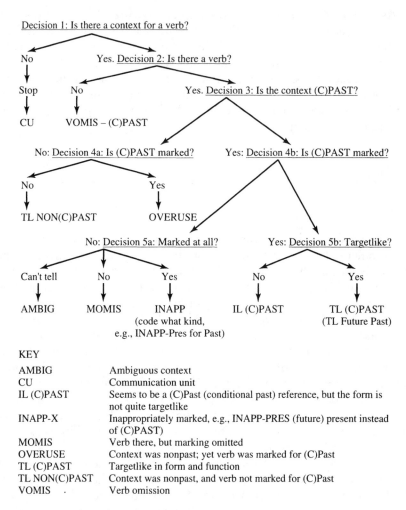

Decision 1: Is there a context for a verb?

No → Stop → CU

Yes. Decision 2: Is there a verb?

No → VOMIS – (C)PAST

Yes. Decision 3: Is the context (C)PAST?

No: Decision 4a: Is (C)PAST marked?

No → TL NON(C)PAST

Yes → OVERUSE

Yes: Decision 4b: Is (C)PAST marked?

No: Decision 5a: Marked at all?

Can't tell → AMBIG

No → MOMIS

Yes → INAPP
(code what kind,
e.g., INAPP-Pres for Past)

Yes: Decision 5b: Targetlike?

No → IL (C)PAST

Yes → TL (C)PAST
(TL Future Past)

KEY

AMBIG	Ambiguous context
CU	Communication unit
IL (C)PAST	Seems to be a (C)Past (conditional past) reference, but the form is not quite targetlike
INAPP-X	Inappropriately marked, e.g., INAPP-PRES (future) present instead of (C)PAST)
MOMIS	Verb there, but marking omitted
OVERUSE	Context was nonpast; yet verb was marked for (C)Past
TL (C)PAST	Targetlike in form and function
TL NON(C)PAST	Context was nonpast, and verb not marked for (C)Past
VOMIS .	Verb omission

Figure 3   Coding decisions.

Interlanguage analysis

The interlanguage analysis was designed to examine the ways in which the subjects linguistically encoded the important meaningful elements of

categories was quite high (95% for oral and 92% for written); therefore, we split up the coding for the delayed posttest data. To check to see that our agreement was still high, we each coded one third of the data and then divided the remaining two thirds. Agreement for the delayed posttests was 90% and 92% for the oral and written categories, respectively.

reporting about an experiment. It should be recalled that questions such as "What problem did you try to solve in this experiment?" and "What steps did you follow in this experiment?" elicited obligatory contexts for past verbs. And the questions "What did you think would happen?" and "What did I think would happen?" elicited essential contexts for conditional past. In terms of the meaning of elements that need to be expressed in these contexts, past verbs encode past time and events that actually happen, which can be represented semantically as shown in Example 4.

[4]   Past   [+past] [+realis]

Past conditional verbs that are used to relate the prediction about the experiment made before conducting the experiment encode past but encode possible outcomes rather than actual events, since they are, as yet, unknown, as shown in Example 5.

[5]   Conditional past   [+past] [+irrealis]

These notions of [+past] and [+realis] or [+irrealis] were sometimes encoded in nontargetlike ways by the subjects. To capture this, we grouped the coded verbs and verb contexts into three major categories (see Figure 4 and compare it with Figure 3 for details). The first group was the completely targetlike (TL) encoding of [+past] and [+realis] or [+past] and [+irrealis]. In other words, both the forms and the function are targetlike. The second group was made up of the emergent interlanguage (IL) encoding as well as the TL encoding plus encode [+past] and [+realis] or [+past] and [+irrealis] in interlanguage ways. In the latter cases, although it was clear to us that the intended reference was either past or past conditional, the forms encoding these meanings were not targetlike. In other words, the function was targetlike, but sometimes the emergent IL forms were not. Thus, the second grouping of the data captures all attempts at past time reference, whether or not they were accurate in a targetlike sense. Finally, we noted nontargetlike (NTL) encoding: These were the cases in which the verbs were either not marked for any time reference or prediction or were marked inappropriately, such as in the frequent uses of present marking for past reference or future marking for past conditional reference. Here the term *inappropriate* refers to the inappropriateness of the time reference. In this category, then, both the forms and the function were nontargetlike in the context being analyzed.

In the groups of verbs shown in Figure 4, as in our analysis, past and conditional past time reference are combined. Although it would be interesting to examine whether the FonF treatment differentially affected these two verb forms, sufficient steps were not taken during the treatment to motivate such an analysis. That is to say, although throughout the treatment, whenever either of the two forms arose in the course of the

---

Form/Function Coding

Accuracy	TL	Emergent IL	NTL
Function	X	X	0
Forms	X	0	0

Group 1   Verbs that reflect some sort of attempt to mark past: Targetlike (TL) encoding: encode [+past] and [+realis] or [+past] and [+irrealis] in targetlike ways. Both the forms and the functions are targetlike.

TL All Past = TL Past
                    TL Past Cont
                    TL CPast
                    TL Fut Past (*I thought it was going to squirm*)

Group 2   All attempts at past or conditional time reference: TL encoding plus emergent interlanguage (IL) encoding: encode [+past] and [+realis] or [+past] and [+irrealis]. The function was targetlike, but sometimes the forms were not.

IL All Past = All of the above categories, plus:
                    IL Past (*toke* for *took*)
                    IA* Past for CPast (*went* for *would go*)
                    IL CPast (*wode go* for *would go*)
                    Overuse

Group 3   Verbs that contain no evidence of past marking: Nontargetlike encoding; these were the cases in which the verbs were either not marked for any time meaning or prediction meaning or were marked inappropriately, such as in the cases of using present marking for past reference or future marking for past conditional reference. Both the forms and the function were nontargetlike for past contexts.

NTL All Past = IA Fut for CPast (*will go* for *would go*)
                    IA Fut for Past/CPast
                    IA Fut for FutPast (*will go* for *was going to go*)
                    IA Pres for Past (*goes* for *went*)
                    IA Pres for CPast (*goes* for *would go*)
                    IA Pres for Past/CPast
                    All types of MOMIS (*go* for *went*)
                    All types of VOMIS

*IA = Inappropriate use.

Figure 4   Framework for interlanguage analysis.

pedagogical labs, attention was consistently drawn to errors or omissions through focused recasting, no attempts were made to document the relative amount of focus given to each form. Furthermore, the forms were selected for their task naturalness rather than on the basis of any known differences in their emergence. (See Williams & Evans, this volume, for a study that does compare the effects of focus on form on different target forms, one already emergent in subjects' production, and the other yet to emerge.)

The effectiveness of communicative focus on form

In this section, we consider the last and perhaps most important issue of our investigation. That is to say: Is task-natural, incidental focus on form effective? Until it can be shown that focus on form, at least as we implemented it in this study, is beneficial to students, it would be premature to discuss the feasibility of its incorporation into communicative language classes. We have looked for the effects of focus on form to appear in the targetlike use of the subjects as well as in the interlanguage versions of past time reference produced by the subjects. Although the primary aim of focus on form is to promote accuracy, it is well known that language learning is not instantaneous and that learners may first exhibit emergent interlanguage forms. This might especially be expected when the majority of the verbs used before the treatment are bare verbs without any morphological marking.

As can be seen in Table 1 and Figures 5 and 7, the group median changes from pretest to posttest in the FonF group are striking.[5] For the FonF group, on all oral and written measures, targetlike and interlanguage past time use showed significant and large gains. The nontargetlike use, which is essentially the use of inappropriate time reference or of bare verbs, decreased significantly on both the written and the oral measures.

Since the sample sizes were fairly small, and the data were not normally distributed, the nonparametric Wilcoxon Matched Pairs Signed Ranks test was used to assess the significance of the differences between treatment and comparison groups (see the right-most column in Table 1 for the detailed results of the statistical testing). This choice is additionally conservative in that the comparison is made between performances on repeated measures. Although the experiments that the subjects carried out on the pretest and immediate and delayed posttests were of differing scientific content, the elicitation measures (i.e., the oral and written science reports) were the same. The matched-pairs analysis takes into account that it would be expected that students would improve their performance on the task by virtue of practice. We believed that this conservative approach was particularly necessary since the subjects had also gained practice on the elicitation measures during the treatment phase.

The pattern of change for the control group can be described essentially as one of no change at all on five of the six oral and written

---

5 Because the data were not normally distributed, the median was selected as the more appropriate measure of central tendency.

TABLE I. THE EFFECT OF FOCUS ON FORM

Group and test	Pretest median*	Posttest median	Delayed posttest median	Nature of change	Significance† (a) Pre → Post (b) Post → DPost (c) Pre → DPost
FonF oral					
TL	11.11	57.14	65.69	Gain, maintained	(a) $p = .01$; $\eta^2 = .79$‡ (b) n.s.
IL	22.22	69.23	72.50	Gain, maintained	(a) $p = .01$; $\eta^2 = .79$ (b) n.s.
NTL	77.78	30.77	27.21	Loss, maintained	(a) $p = .01$; $\eta^2 = .79$ (b) n.s.
Control oral					
TL	33.33	42.86	26.14	No change	(a) n.s. (b) n.s.
IL	44.44	42.86	30.68	No change	(a) n.s. (b) n.s.
NTL	55.56	57.14	69.50	No change	(a) n.s. (b) n.s.

TABLE I. CONTINUED

Group and test	Pretest median*	Posttest median	Delayed posttest median	Nature of change	Significance† (a) Pre → Post (b) Post → DPost (c) Pre → DPost
FonF written					
TL	20.00	60.00	43.65	Gain, not maintained	(a) $p = .01$; $\eta^2 = .74$ (b) $p = .01$; $\eta^2 = .46$ (c) n.s.
IL	41.67	81.82	60.42	Gain, decreased but maintained	(a) $p = .01$; $\eta^2 = .80$ (b) $p = .01$; $\eta^2 = .40$ (c) $p = .01$; $\eta^2 = .83$
NTL	58.63	18.18	39.59	Loss, increased but maintained	(a) $p = .01$; $\eta^2 = .80$ (b) $p = .01$; $\eta^2 = .40$ (c) $p = .01$; $\eta^2 = .41$
Control written					
TL	20.84	18.18	12.50	No change	(a) n.s. (b) n.s.
IL	30.56	50.00	33.33	Gain, not maintained	(a) $p = .05$; $\eta^2 = .27$ (b) n.s. (c) n.s.
NTL	69.45	50.00	66.67	No change	(a) n.s. (b) n.s.

*All medians are reported as percentages of the total number of contexts for past + conditional past verbs to take into account different report lengths.

†(a) = pretest to posttest; (b) = posttest to delayed posttest; (c) = pretest to delayed posttest.

‡η^2 is a measure of the strength of association between the two variables being compared (treatment and L2 ability). The number represents in decimal form the percentage of overlap, that is, the amount of variance that can be explained by the treatment.

measures (see Table 1 and Figures 6 and 8). The control group median improved slightly but significantly on the written measure, where the analysis was of interlanguage past time reference. It is perhaps not unexpected that learners can make some progress on their own without attention to linguistic forms. However, the progress made by the FonF group was much more substantial. In particular, results suggest that verbs that had been expressed in the present time or without any tense marking on the pretest lab reports given by treatment group subjects were increasingly marked with accurate past time reference on the posttests. Furthermore, in addition to this improvement in accuracy on the part of the treatment group subjects, there was an overall increase in their number of attempts to express past as indicated by the category of emergent interlanguage which includes both targetlike and interlanguage past time reference. It should be noted that the fact that the gains made by the treatment group subjects were quite large is important. A rank sums test of the relative ability of the treatment and comparison groups at the outset of the study showed that, whereas there was no difference on any category of the written measure between the two groups, the comparison group had a small but significant advantage over the treatment group on all three categories of the oral measure (TL $z = -18.10$; IL $z = 8.59$; NTL $z = 4.22$). Results indicate strongly, however, that not only did the treatment group subjects catch up to their counterparts, they overtook them substantially, whereas the comparison subjects' use of past time reference changed very little, if at all, from pretest to posttest measurement.

Two months after the immediate posttesting, subjects in both groups carried out another science lab, and delayed posttest data were analyzed as described earlier. Table 1 and Figures 5 through 8 show the results of the delayed posttesting in comparison with the pretests and immediate posttests already discussed. When delayed posttests are not significantly different from the immediate posttest, it can be said that the subjects maintained the ability they exhibited on the immediate posttest. When there are significant differences between the two posttests, a change in ability is evident, but the question remains as to whether the change is a complete reversion to the starting ability as measured by the pretests. When the delayed posttest is still significantly higher (for TL and IL ability) or lower (for NTL ability) than on the counterpart pretest, it can be said that the FonF effects have endured (see the right-most column of Table 1 for these statistical comparisons).

On the oral measure, the FonF treatment group maintained both the TL and IL increases in past time reference as well the NTL decreases. The pattern was similar for the written measure, with the exception that pure gains in accuracy (the TL-only category) were not maintained. Given also that the IL gain decreased and the NTL decrease lessened, the effects of focused recasting in the written mode appear not to have been as robust

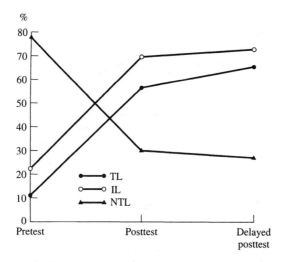

Figure 5   FonF oral.

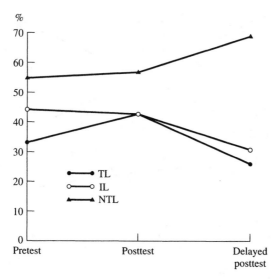

Figure 6   Control oral.

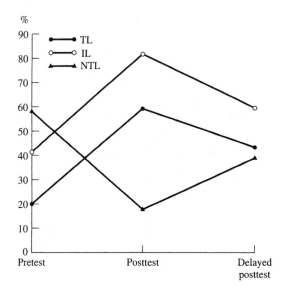

Figure 7   FonF written.

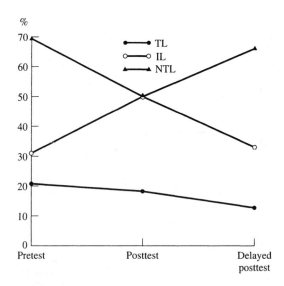

Figure 8   Control written.

as those in the oral mode, even though they did technically endure for both the IL and the NTL categories of verbs. It is important, however, that the control group subjects did not make any progress on their own during these 2 months, indicating that the implementation of the focus on form into the communicative science curriculum was more effective than leaving students to their own devices to develop targetlike ability in past time reference. Next, we will turn to a discussion of the feasibility, from the communicative language teacher's perspective, of the particular tasks and techniques that were employed in this study.

The feasibility of communicative focus on form

Through analysis of tapes of the pedagogical labs as well as reflection in the teacher's journal, it was evident that the science experiment tasks provided many natural opportunities for use of past time reference, and we were satisfied that the focus on form designed for this study was well integrated into the normal activity of a content-based ESL science class. Some interesting occurrences were observed after a week or two of FonF implementation. First, there was evidence of the awareness on the part of learners of the appropriate forms by the time of the second lab. The students were beginning to self-correct before the teacher had the opportunity to recast. In some cases, the students had started to overgeneralize the past tense and were double-marking verbs such as in "the paper airplane *flewed* farther." Perhaps the most interesting observation was that a few students corrected each other in much the same way that the teacher had been correcting them.

Not only were the opportunities for use of past tense task natural and salient, but the focus on form provided by the teacher was reasonably incidental to the overall aim of discussing and reporting science experiments. Although there were a variety of features utilized according to task opportunity for focus on form, rarely did the recasts become the object of the lesson, and when they occurred, they were immediate and brief. The course outline was followed with regard to content to be taught, and, with the exceptions of focused error correction on written lab reports and the swift teacher repetitions and recasts, science learning proceeded as normally for the twenty-one science students in the experimental class as it did for the comparison students.

At the end of each day's lesson, the teacher jotted down notes about individual reactions to corrective feedback as well as a daily analysis of the possibility of implementing focus on form into the daily routine. When these notes were reviewed, several observations were repeated throughout that might be significant for future implementation of focus on form in a communicative classroom. First, the teacher must remember to pay attention to what the student is saying as well as to the formal realization of the message. This is not easy to do: It indeed takes practice for the teacher to focus on content, forms, and classroom management simultaneously. The importance of doing so, however, was illustrated on one occasion early in the study when the teacher gave feedback to a student who asked a question about his own analysis of the science after performing a lab. The teacher neglected to comment on his analysis and simply offered feedback on an incorrect form. It turned out that he knew that his reasoning was faulty, and he was waiting for the teacher to offer a better explanation. Although he repeated the form correctly after the feedback, he seemed disturbed by the fact that his science teacher was ignoring the science. Fortunately, the teacher was able to adapt her behavior immediately to become more sensitive to the content-learning needs of her students. In the same vein, teacher notes emphasized that too many corrections in one turn should be avoided. In one case, a student who was willing to accept the first and second corrections as he reported on a lab, waved his hand upon the third correction as if to say, "All right, already" or "Enough is enough." If the focus on form is to be incidental to the content learning, clearly the intervention must be brief (see also Lightbown, this volume).

Finally, the teacher noted that some opportunities were more appropriate for recasting than others. For instance, individual presentations in front of the class were not the best opportunities to offer correction. Communication was indeed hindered when correction was offered in "panel discussions," for example, because the students stopped speaking for too long in order to repair errors and recover from what appeared to be slight embarrassment. The teacher quickly determined that the best opportunity to offer feedback was when the students were working in pairs or in small groups. After focusing on past time reference for several weeks, the teacher then interviewed the students to obtain their thoughts on the procedures she had developed. In response to a question regarding what he thought about when he reported on a lab, one student replied, "I think about science. I think about what happened." When the teacher asked him whether he thought about anything else he said, "Oh, yeah. I think about how to say it right." The teacher pressed further and asked him whether it was difficult to think about two things at once. "No," he replied. "I have to concentrate, but it's not too hard."

In sum, with regard to the issues pertaining to the implementation of communicative focus on form in our investigation, that is, the feasibility, procedures, and timing of focus on form in a content ESL science class, five observations can be made. First, focus on form should be brief and immediate and should be provided when more than one student is involved in speaking. Second, students believe that they can pay attention to meaning, communication, and form at the same time. Third, some students are not comfortable with receiving more than one or two instances of correction within one exchange. Fourth, teachers should be aware of their students' desire for comments on the meaning of the message as well as on the correctness of the language. And fifth, it *is* possible to incorporate a focus on form with no risk to the content curriculum as long as the tasks are carefully created and incorporated into authentic content lessons already in place.

Conclusion

In this collaborative study, we set out to investigate the feasibility and effectiveness of incorporating a relatively implicit FonF technique into a content-based and, therefore, communicative language classroom. The effects of the intonational focus and corrective recasting during science lab experiments are clearly interpretable from our results. Learners in the treatment group improved in both accuracy and total number of attempts at past time reference, particularly in the oral reporting of the science labs. The evidence for the effectiveness of the analogous focus on form implemented into the written labs, although certainly present, is less convincing, since the gains in pure (target language only) accuracy that were evident on the immediate posttest did not endure – as revealed on the 2-month delayed posttest. This may have been because the FonF techniques that we developed were based on parental recasting, which is a feature of oral child-directed discourse. Although we thought it best to model the written focus on form closely on the oral format, this may not have been appropriate. On the other hand, it is equally possible that the consistency of the focus on form that was provided for nearly all learner errors, and that used virtually the same techniques, may have contributed to its overall effectiveness in both modes. These considerations await further investigation.

Since one of our primary aims was to overcome the current Communicative Language Teaching prohibition against any attention to linguistic forms at all, it was particularly noteworthy that the relatively implicit FonF technique, which we had anticipated would work well in the content-based class, in fact turned out to be task-natural and reasonably incidental to science teaching, as well as comfortable for the teacher. Furthermore – unlike studies that have shown little incorporation of diffuse, unplanned recasting (Lyster & Ranta, 1997) – our study demonstrated the effectiveness of the combination of communicative pressure (i.e., the in-built need to use past in reporting experiments) and narrowly focused, frequent recasting (i.e., in response to only two linguistic features and nearly always provided, unless too intrusive). We believe that our findings bode well for the promotion of ESL learner accuracy to a level that will be acceptable to their future mainstream teachers, who will judge them academically and linguistically in comparison with their native-speaking peers.

7 What kind of focus and on which forms?

Jessica Williams
Jacqueline Evans

Introduction

A renewed interest in focus-on-form (FonF) instruction dates to Long's 1991 article that introduced the term *focus on form,* referring to instruction that draws learners' attention to form in the context of meaningful communication. However, it has not been clear exactly what it means to *draw a learner's attention to form* or how this is to be accomplished.

A number of studies have pointed to the effectiveness of instruction that includes some focus on form, relative to that which does not (Day & Shapson, 1991; Doughty, 1991; Fotos, 1993, 1994; Harley, 1993; Lightbown, 1991, 1992; Lightbown & Spada, 1990; Lyster, 1994a; Trahey, 1996; Trahey & White, 1993; L. White, 1991; White, Spada, Lightbown, & Ranta, 1991; see Harley, 1994; Williams, 1995, for summaries). From these results, it would appear that focus on form is a good idea, but the issue is actually far more complex, as the discussions presented in this volume demonstrate. This chapter is an attempt to answer some preliminary questions about two related aspects of FonF research and instruction: the choice of forms for FonF instruction and the interaction between choice of forms and instructional treatment. The impetus for the investigation was our belief that not every form would be an equal candidate for focus on form, and certainly not for the same kind of FonF treatment. Specifically, the study examined the following general research questions:

1. Do forms differ in terms of how learners will respond to focus on form? Are some forms more amenable to focus on form than others? If so, in what ways do the forms themselves differ?
2. How is focus on form to be operationalized? What is likely to attract learners' attention? Is "drawing their attention" enough?
3. Will the answers to these two questions differ for learners at different stages of development?

The authors would like to thank Rachel Scheiner, who participated in the pilot study for this project and created the illustration for all the pretests and posttests, as well as Michael Long for helpful suggestions on an earlier draft.

Choice of form

A variety of criteria have been used in choosing forms in FonF studies, notably arguments based on linguistic theory (e.g., L. White, 1991), learnability (e.g., Spada & Lightbown, 1993), and likelihood of (either L1- or L2-induced) error (Herron, 1991; Tomasello & Herron, 1989). Studies that have examined the effect of the same kind of instruction on a variety of forms have often yielded disparate results (Herron & Tomasello, 1992; Zhou, 1992), suggesting that learners will not respond equally to the same kind of focus on form on all forms. Harley (1993) has suggested that likely candidates for effective focus on form are those that:

1. Differ in nonobvious ways from the learners' first language, for example, adverb placement for L2 French and English.
2. Are not salient because they are irregular or infrequent in the input, for example, conditionals in L2 French.
3. Are not important for successful communication, for example, third person singular -s in L2 English.
4. Are likely to be misinterpreted or misanalyzed by learners, for example, dative alternation in L2 English.

The choice of forms in this study was pedagogically motivated and based on some of the code-based criteria above but also on learner-based criteria. Each of the two forms that are the focus of this study held a rather different status in the learners' interlanguages (ILs). They were used (or not used) in different ways by the learners, but both posed difficulties for them. These two forms did correspond to at least two of the criteria suggested by Harley. The first set of forms, participial adjectives of emotive verbs, was chosen because the forms were actively used in the speech and writing of these learners but were often used incorrectly. For example, learners often used present and past participial adjectives interchangeably, and in other cases, they used just the bare form:

[1] I'm so boring in school.
     My trip to Niagara Falls was really excited.
     I think computers are really fascinate.

The two forms are closely related and easily misinterpreted by second language learners (SLLs). (See item 4 in the preceding list.) They have the same lexical root and are homophonous with a nonadjectival participle. Continued, though unsystematic, error correction in their written work appeared to have little effect. Yet the forms-meaning relationship of participial adjectives is fairly straightforward for this set of verbs: The -*ed* form signals the experiencer, and the -*ing* form marks the causer. The study was limited to those verbs that could take either form as predicate adjectives. This means that only sentences such as:

[2]   He is interested/interesting.

were the focus of instruction, but not

[3]   The wine list was promising (no corresponding past form, i.e., *promised*).

The second form chosen, the passive, was more complex. This form was rarely found in our learners' oral or written production. In addition, the instructional materials for their class contained little positive evidence or explicit instruction that would call their attention to this form. Thus this form is in keeping with Harley's suggestion (item 2) regarding forms that are not salient owing to their infrequency in the input. Furthermore, in contrast to the situation with participial adjectives, the formation and use of passive are neither transparent nor straightforward (although see Zhou, 1992). On the contrary, the passive is relatively complex, especially in combination with tenses other than the simple present, and the decision about whether to use it is also a difficult one. Instruction centered on passive sentences in which the agents were unimportant or unknown, because this type of passivization is more common in English.

Choice of instructional treatment

A variety of instructional treatments have been used in FonF studies, each an attempt to draw the learners' attention to the form in focus, and each offering its own advantages. For instance, the more implicit option of a flood of positive evidence may be less disruptive to meaning-based activities but may not be sufficient to get learners to notice forms in the input or, perhaps more important, to notice the gap (Schmidt & Frota, 1986) between those forms and their own IL forms. More direct instruction that provides negative evidence may be more appropriate in some cases. It is not clear what factors might be important in making such decisions, especially regarding the level of explicitness of instruction (see Doughty & Williams, Chapter 10, this volume).

In this study, two levels of explicitness were used. Three classes participated in the study: One acted as a control group (Group C), and the other two as experimental groups. The first experimental group (Group F) received a flood of positive evidence in their input, in the form of artificially increased incidence of the form in focus. A detailed discussion of materials and procedures is given in the section Instructional and Testing Materials later in this chapter. No explicit rules or instructions were provided, and no corrective feedback was given, but the teacher

TABLE I. ORDER OF INSTRUCTION

Class	Participial adjectives	Passives
1	I	F
2	F	C
3	C	I

deliberately used participial adjectives during class discussions. Thus this treatment entails a somewhat greater focus on form than a flood alone. The intention was that this kind of treatment would be effective in getting learners to notice these forms if they had not done so before. No prediction was made that the flood would lead them to notice the gap between their own production and the target materials. The control group worked with basically the same materials, but without the artificial increase in the number of forms in focus. The second experimental group (Group I) received explicit instruction and feedback. They received the same flooded input as Group F, but in addition, their attention was drawn to form, meaning, and use, and they were given a brief presentation of rules. These subjects participated in activities in which they both read and used the forms, and they received corrective feedback, not just for the instructional period but for the rest of the semester, though less intensively after than during instruction. This last step was taken because earlier studies had suggested that if focus on form is "parachuted in" and then dropped, its effects may not last (Spada & Lightbown, 1993).

For Group I, the intention was that those learners who had already noticed the form might be led to notice the gap – that they were in some sense ready to make changes in their ILs. At present, we have no documented developmental stages for these forms, but other studies have shown the importance of learner readiness for instruction (Pienemann, 1989). Bardovi-Harlig (1995), for instance, suggests that instruction on the use of the pluperfect is futile unless the learner has demonstrated stable use of the simple past and has begun attempts to express reverse-order reports, that is, to establish a context that would require the use of the pluperfect.

To ensure that any experimental effect was not due to the influence of a single teacher, the conditions were rotated for the two forms. In other words, Class 1 received explicit instruction for the participial adjectives but a flood for passives, and so on. The rotation is seen in Table 1.

It is important to emphasize again that, for us, focus on form does not mean that we asked the teachers to take some time out between writing assignments to do a few transformation drills on the passive. Instructional materials were carefully integrated into the content and skills that were the real focus of the course. Activities that were part of the experiment were similar to those done in the class on a regular basis. Because of this, it is difficult to determine exactly how much time was spent on FonF activities for each unit. Each unit lasted approximately 2 weeks. In addition, we should note that because these were ESL classes, it was impossible to control any input containing these forms outside of the classroom, though we assume that the groups were relatively equal in this respect.

Subjects

The subjects were all enrolled in intermediate ESL writing classes at the University of Illinois at Chicago that met for 2 hours twice a week for 15 weeks. Their placement in this class was based on a combination of their score on a multiple-choice placement test, given to all incoming students, and a holistic score on a timed essay. Students came from a variety of L1 backgrounds, including Arabic, Cantonese, Gujarati, Hindi, Khmer, Korean, Mandarin, Polish, Russian, Spanish, Tagalog, Thai, Urdu, and Vietnamese. The ESL composition program emphasizes the communication and organization of ideas over formal accuracy. Although sentence-level grammar instruction is one component of the course, it tends to occur on an ad hoc basis. Class size differed somewhat, but taking absences into account, eleven students in each class were present for the pretests and posttests and for the two instructional treatments.

Hypotheses

We have already noted that these two forms were used somewhat differently by the learners and, further, that the forms themselves are very different. Our overall expectation was, therefore, that FonF treatment would not produce the same results for the two forms or for the two conditions. In particular, since participial adjectives were already used, though often inaccurately, by the students, it was hypothesized that most of the students were ready for instruction on this form and that the instruction would have significant impact. An additional factor that we believed would favor our hypothesis is that the relationship between adjectival forms and meaning is relatively transparent. We hypothesized that, in general, a flood would be useful in getting learners to notice new forms in the input. However, since many of the subjects already seemed aware of participial adjectives and, to some extent, their use, it was hypothesized that the flood would have a less marked effect than more explicit instruction would. Taken together, these predictions are stated in Hypothesis 1.

H1a   Group F would show greater increases than Group C in accurate use of participial adjectives.

H1b   Group I would show greater increases than either Group F or Group C in accurate use of participial adjectives.

In contrast, the passive was infrequent in the ILs of most of the participants in the study. Its formation and use are also relatively difficult to master. It was therefore hypothesized that these learners would perhaps not be ready for focus on form on passives, particularly for explicit instruction; indeed, they had perhaps not yet started to notice the form and its use in the input. Although a flood of input might get them to start noticing and attempting the form, greater gains in accurate use were not expected from the instructed group. Taken together, these predictions are stated in Hypothesis 2.

H2a   Groups I and F would show greater increases than Group C in the (not necessarily accurate) use of the passive.

H2b   Groups I and F would show no significant differences in their accurate use of the passive.

Instructional and testing materials

Our goal in creating materials was to integrate focus on form into the course. All instructional material was piloted in an earlier study, and some material was substantially revised. Participles were introduced in the context of a unit on education and how it can be helpful in overcoming obstacles. The experimental portion of the unit was built around readings from *My Left Foot* by Christie Brown (1991), as well as the film of the same name (Pearson & Sheridan, 1989). All three classes read several chapters from the book and watched the film. All classes held discussions about the book and the film and also wrote multidraft papers on the topic of "overcoming the odds," as part of a unit in their textbook (Bates, 1993). In addition, the two experimental classes received written input that had been modified to include three times the number of participial adjectives contained in the original material. This was embodied in papers from former students on the same topic. Students were asked to do a peer review, discussing what points the student-authors were making and how well they supported their arguments. Groups worked with different papers, but each paper contained approximately fifteen instances of participial adjectives. In addition, the instructors in both experimental classes drew students' attention to parts of the material containing participles and questioned them on the points being addressed, for example:

[4] The author says Christie Brown's strength came from his disability and without it, his life would have been a lot less *interesting*. Do you feel that the author supports his point well?

Thus, the instructor drew the learners' attention to the form without focusing on it explicitly.

Group I received the same treatment as Group F, but in addition, received contextualized instruction and consistent corrective feedback. The instruction component began during the discussion of the reading. The teacher asked the students to think of words to describe Christie Brown. These adjectives were listed on the board. When some students offered the past participial adjective or the bare form, the instructor of Group I explained the causer-experiencer distinction and gave several examples, some of them humorous, for example, "I am so boring." The instructor checked the students' understanding with a series of oral fill-in-the-blank questions pertaining to the reading, for example:

[5] The story about Christie Brown was _____.

One week later, after viewing the film, the class had another discussion, this time ending with the participants' generating adjectives about how they felt about Christie Brown and the movie. The distinction was again reviewed by the Group I instructor, and comparative examples given, for example:

[6] I was touched.
The story was touching.

This time, the humorous examples elicited knowing nods and chuckles. The emphasis on the distinction between the two forms was carried over into the peer review activity described earlier.

The instructional treatment for the passive was integrated into a unit on cultural values. The experimental portion of the unit consisted of a survey from a textbook, *Reader's Choice* (Baudoin, Bober, Clarke, Dobson, & Silberstein, 1988), about obedience to authority. Learners were asked what they would do in various situations, for example, if they knew that a superior in the office was taking credit for work that was not his. They were then asked to gather responses to such questions from several members of their own speech community and then from the United States–born peers. They brought their results to class and used them as the basis of group discussions. They then wrote a short paper summarizing their findings. All three classes participated in this activity. The two experimental classes, however, received an altered version of the survey in which many of the questions had been modified to include the passive, for example:

[7]   You are working in a country that has a repressive government. You are asked to give information to the police about several of your colleagues.

The instruction for the assignment also contained numerous examples of the passive, for example:

[8]   Discuss how your information was collected and analyzed.

This material constituted the input flood. Group I also received brief explanations in the context of this activity about how to form the passive and why the author chose to use it, for example:

[9]   Write about how your information was collected and analyzed rather than how you collected the data, since the data, and not you, are important for your report.

The assignment also contained suggestions as to how Group I should complete the assignment, though learners were not explicitly told to use the passive, for example:

[10]   Start with the most important information, for example: "Five Koreans were interviewed."

And, as in the case of the participial adjectives, Group I received consistent feedback on the passive for the rest of the semester.

Several kinds of information were gathered to give a complete picture of the students' knowledge and use of these forms, including quantitative pretest and posttest scores on two tasks for each form. For the participial adjectives, this information consisted of two types of material.

Task 1 was a twenty-one-item grammaticality judgment (GJ) task that contained roughly equal numbers of correct and incorrect past and present participial forms as well as distracters, for example:

[11]   When I saw the magic trick, I was really amazing.

Task 2 was a ten-item sentence completion (SC) test, in which participants had to choose from a limited list of lexical items that included the past and present participle and the bare form of the verb, for example:

[12]   The lock on Michael's car door was frozen last week. He tried and tried to open it, but he couldn't. He was so _____. In the end, he had to take the El[1] to school.

The forms *frustrated, frustrating,* and *frustrate* appeared as items on a list accompanying the sentences.

For the passive, participants completed two types of tasks:

Task 1 was a more open-ended, picture-based, fifteen-item sentence

---

1 The El is the elevated train. All students in Chicago would be familiar with this term.

completion (SC) test in which they chose their own words and forms, for example:

[13]   Spring semester ends on May 7th. All grades _____ to students in the mail 2 weeks after the semester ends.

The accompanying picture showed stamped envelopes.

Task 2 consisted of two narratives (Narr) based on five or six pictures, for a total of eleven contexts for passive. For the narrative, participants were supplied with the patient as the initial word in an effort to elicit the passive, for example:

[14]   First, the grapes . . .

The narratives used nonhuman patients, with no agent shown, in processes, for example, manufacturing, that naturally admit the passive rather than the active form. Learners were expected to produce one sentence per picture; thus the essays were expected to be five or six sentences each, depending on the number of pictures in the stimulus. Pretests and posttests followed the same format, with different sentences and/or pictures. All test questions had been pilot-tested in an earlier study. Items that turned out to be ambiguous were discarded and replaced. Based on the results of the pilot study, learners were given between 7 and 12 minutes to complete each test. This allowed most of the students enough time to finish, but at a fairly rapid rate, without much time to look over their responses or revise them.

The pretests were administered 2 weeks prior to the beginning of each instructional treatment. Instruction on participles came first and was followed about 3 or 4 weeks later by the passive treatment. Two weeks later, the participle posttests were given, and finally, 2 weeks after that, the passive posttests. Thus, the posttests were given 4 to 6 weeks after treatment. Unfortunately, because of the time limits of the academic semester, no further posttests could be given.

Of course, these tests, which in some cases force the use of the forms in focus, tap only part of the learners' knowledge and use of this form. A more complete picture of the learners' use of these forms emerges in the more spontaneously produced data. In addition to the quantitative data, the assignments that were written as part of the instructional units were collected. This information was relevant primarily for the passive, however, since it was possible to give a writing assignment that encouraged the use of the passive but not possible to do this for participial adjectives. The learners were also recorded completing dictoglosses (see Swain, this volume) on the two forms, in an effort to gain some insight into their developing hypotheses as well as to check on their spontaneous productive abilities.

Results

Quantitative

All data were normally distributed; therefore, parametric tests were used. A one-way ANOVA revealed that the differences among the groups at Time 1 were insignificant (for participial adjectives: GJ: $F = .29$, $p = .750$; SC: $F = 2.27$, $p = .120$; for passive: Narr: $F = 2.15$, $p = .133$; SC: $F = 2.22$, $p = .127$), indicating that the classes were equivalent in terms of their ability to use these two structures at the outset. This means that differences across groups should be reflected in the posttest scores. However, as a cross-check, the gains in scores are also examined in the next section.

Participial adjectives

Hypothesis 1b was supported, but Hypothesis 1a was not (see Tables 2 and 3). A one-way ANOVA on the posttest scores revealed that the performances of the three groups were significantly different on both tasks (GJ: $F = 13.22$, $p = .0001$; SC: $F = 5.33$, $p = .01$). A Tukey's post hoc pairwise comparison showed a significant difference between Group I and Group C, as well as between Group I and Group F, but not between Group F and Group C. Thus, although the flood group made some progress, the gain was not significantly different from that of Group C. The same tests were applied to the gains in the scores between the pretest and posttest, with similar results (GJ: $F = 9.58$, $p = .0006$; SC: $F = 3.65$, $p = .038$).

Passives

The hypotheses regarding passive were partially supported (see Tables 4 and 5). An ANOVA applied to the posttest scores revealed that the groups performed differently on both tasks (Narr: $F = 4.95$, $p = .014$; SC: $F = 11.01$, $p = .0003$). However, for the narrative task, a Tukey's post hoc pairwise comparison showed that only the instructed and control groups' posttest scores showed a small significant difference, giving only partial support for Hypothesis 2a. When the same statistical tests were applied to the gains themselves, even this difference disappeared (Narr: $F = 2.2$, $p = .128$). In the sentence completion task, however, both Group I and

TABLE 2. TASK I – GRAMMATICALITY JUDGMENT (MAXIMUM SCORE = 21)

	Condition 1: Instruction		Condition 2: Flood		Condition 3: Control	
	$\bar{X}$	sd	$\bar{X}$	sd	$\bar{X}$	sd
Pretest	8.27	2.57	7.45	2.73	8.00	2.37
Posttest	12.82	1.72	9.18	2.14	8.73	2.24
Mean increase	4.55		1.73		0.73	

TABLE 3. TASK 2 – SENTENCE COMPLETION (MAXIMUM SCORE = 10)

	Condition 1: Instruction		Condition 2: Flood		Condition 3: Control	
	$\bar{X}$	sd	$\bar{X}$	sd	$\bar{X}$	sd
Pretest	5.55	2.50	4.09	1.64	5.82	1.89
Posttest	8.00	2.10	5.64	1.86	5.91	1.58
Mean increase	2.45		1.55		0.09	

TABLE 4. TASK I – NARRATIVE (MAXIMUM SCORE = 11)

	Condition 1: Instruction		Condition 2: Flood		Condition 3: Control	
	$\bar{X}$	sd	$\bar{X}$	sd	$\bar{X}$	sd
Pretest	5.64	2.98	4.64	3.44	2.82	3.25
Posttest	7.73	3.61	6.64	3.75	3.09	3.48
Mean increase	2.09		2.00		0.27	

TABLE 5. TASK 2 – SENTENCE COMPLETION (MAXIMUM SCORE = 15)

	Condition 1: Instruction		Condition 2: Flood		Condition 3: Control	
	$\bar{X}$	sd	$\bar{X}$	sd	$\bar{X}$	sd
Pretest	4.45	2.73	5.91	2.43	3.55	2.81
Posttest	6.82	3.03	7.73	1.49	3.18	2.44
Mean increase	2.36		1.82		-0.36	

Group F showed significantly greater increases than Group C but were not significantly different from each other, thus supporting Hypothesis 2b. This difference was sustained in the ANOVA on the gains (SC: $F = 8.51$, $p = .0012$).

Qualitative

At the time of the posttest, all groups also participated in a dictogloss activity (see Swain, this volume) to ascertain their productive abilities in a less restricted task. Students were read a short passage containing the form that had been the focus of instruction. They were allowed to take notes. The passage was read only once. Then, in pairs, they were to reconstruct the passage as best they could. The discussions of three pairs of students in each class were recorded, and all papers were collected. The reconstructed passages show the learners' knowledge of these forms in a somewhat more spontaneous task. In general, these results were consistent with those from the more structured posttests. The groups differed in the number of forms produced on the participle dictogloss, but differed not at all on the passive dictogloss. The latter is true because virtually no passives were used by any of the subjects (see Table 6). Some chose to write almost nothing, whereas others changed the passive verbs to active voice. The tapes also reveal the difficulty the learners had with the passive in the dictogloss, as well as their ignorance of its grammatical focus. In contrast, in the tapes of the participle dictoglosses, the participants in the experimental groups seemed to know quite clearly that they were being tested on participles (the subject even came up in one discussion in Group C). The choice of one participial adjective or the other was a topic of frequent discussion, whereas the use of the passive never came up in the tapes.

The latter result is also corroborated by the write-ups of the surveys that all the groups did in the passive unit. The passive was virtually absent from the writing of all the learners. The only exception was that, in Group I, a number of students began with the passive phrase that was given as a sample first sentence for the reports. After that, the explicit instructions given at the beginning of the assignment to focus on the patient were ignored by all Group I learners. In the write-ups of the two other groups, the passive was not used at all, suggesting very limited productive ability. Unfortunately, there is no analogous free writing sample for the participial adjectives because, as noted earlier, although it is possible, at least in principle, to build a piece of writing around the use of the passive, this cannot be done for participles without making it a purely structural exercise. Such a task would have been antithetical to our goal of contextualizing instructional tasks.

TABLE 6. MEAN SCORES ON DICTOGLOSSES

Forms	Condition 1: Instruction	Condition 2: Flood	Condition 3: Control
Participial adjectives (maximum score = 9)	6.45	5.27	3.45
Passives (maximum score = 7)	1.27	1.27	1.09

Discussion

The effect of focus on form seems apparent in both cases, though some-what different. Without any kind of focus on form, learners demons-trated very little progress in the use of the form in focus. This is borne out by most of the individual results as well as the pooled data, although there were two learners in Group C who seemed to make progress despite the lack of instructional focus on form. It should be emphasized that Group C was not, strictly speaking, a control group with no exposure; rather, the learners in this group received more limited input than did those in the experimental groups. Conversely, there were individuals in both of the experimental groups (one in Group I and two in Group F, all with low pretest scores) who seemed unaffected by either the flood or the instruc-tion. Several trends are suggested by these results. First, it seems that a good case can be made for individual readiness for instruction containing a focus on form (e.g., Bardovi-Harlig, 1995; Lightbown, this volume; Pienemann, 1989; Swain, this volume). This sample is too small to pro-vide convincing quantitative evidence, but it appears that the individuals who made the greatest gains with either type of focus on form, but especially with the instruction, were those who already had partial mas-tery of the form, that is, those who had at least moderate scores on the pretest. A number of individuals went from middle or high scores to almost perfect ones, and others went from low or middle scores to high ones. Those who had extremely low scores to begin with generally made little progress during the course of the semester. This pattern held true even for the few who made progress in Group C, suggesting that those who are ready may find the relevant data wherever they can, with or without instruction. This trend is most evident in the results on participial adjectives, where the gains in the experimental classes were the greatest.

The second implication of these findings is that not all forms are equal in terms of the effectiveness of FonF activities. And further, the interac-tion of instructional treatment, form type, and learner profile appears to be an important factor in effectiveness. As Sharwood Smith states, focus on form "admits of many degrees of both quantity and quality" (1991, p. 131). This may explain the ostensibly conflicting results found in many studies that attempt to demonstrate the superiority of inductive methods over deductive, deductive over inductive, explicit treatment over implicit, and so forth (Fotos, 1993; Herron & Tomasello, 1992; Zhou, 1992, inter alia). The results of this study suggest that the situation may not be nearly so clear-cut and that a blanket edict to focus on form is misguided and overly general. For instance, it has been reported that explicit feedback may be more effective in getting learners to drop their nontargetlike forms and begin using target forms (Carroll & Swain, 1993; Tomasello & Herron, 1989). Herron (1991) argues that it is the immediacy of feedback, as the learners are formulating relevant hypotheses, that engages them cognitively and makes such treatment effective and long-lasting. However, this was found to be consistently the case for only one of the forms in this study. Subjects responded less favorably to explicit and negative feedback on the passive than on participial adjectives. Zhou (1992), in contrast, found a strong effect for instruction, particularly for explicit instruction, on the use of the passive. However, initial scores are not reported; therefore, it is difficult to make a determination regarding learner readiness. It is possible that Zhou's learners were at a more advanced level and that our results are not, in fact, in conflict with Zhou's.

There may be several reasons for the differential effect of explicit instruction on the two forms discussed here. First, there are differences in the forms themselves. As we have mentioned, passives are considerably more complex (see DeKeyser, 1995, this volume; Doughty & Williams, this volume; Robinson, 1996b), in terms of both form and use, than participial adjectives. It may be that explicit treatment is more suited to more transparent forms such as the participial adjectives. Thus we might say that, although the forms of participial adjectives are easily confused, they are, perhaps almost as easily sorted out. In contrast, the form and use of the passive cannot be grasped by virtue of one straightforward explanation. A preliminary guideline, then, might be: Forms that are easily misinterpreted or misanalyzed by learners, but also easily explained, are excellent candidates for instruction containing more explicit focus on form, including the use of negative evidence, with learners who are ready. Another possible explanation of the results is that for both the instructional treatment and, to some degree, the tests, the participle material had greater task-essentialness (see Loschky, 1994) than did the passive material; that is, completion of the tasks required that the subjects attend to form as well as meaning.

Finally, we return to the issue of readiness. It may be that, in order for the more explicit treatment that Group I received to be effective, the learners had to be ready for it. In the case of these learners, many appeared to be not yet ready for an explicit treatment of the passive. Rather, they may have been just beginning to notice the form and its use, and for this reason, the flood treatment was almost as effective as the explicit instruction. Even at the end of instruction, development of the passive was tentative, with accurate productive ability still a long way off. It is possible that the same treatment provided later in these learners' development would yield different results. Further evidence for this interpretation can be seen in the individual results. Individual gains within groups are more consistent across the two tasks for the participial adjectives than for the passive. And in fact, the two passive tasks were more different from each other than were the two participle tasks. Both the participle tasks called on a rather limited ability to use the form, judging grammaticality and making choices from among a restricted list of items. Both the passive tasks were more demanding than this. The sentence completion task required subjects to supply their own choice of words. The narrative task was more demanding still, actually requiring them to create their own connected prose. Because of this level of difficulty, it is perhaps not surprising that the two experimental classes performed similarly on the narrative task. Although it may have been the most authentic test task of any in this study, it was also one that may have required the learners to draw on implicit knowledge that they did not yet possess. Thus, the participle tasks may not have required learners to apply their knowledge to new tasks and contexts to the same degree as the passive tasks did.

Additional evidence for the differential development of the two forms comes from the dictoglosses. The task of re-creating a text from aural memory proved to be difficult for all learners on both forms, but far easier, again for all of the learners, when the form focus of the passage was participial adjectives than when it was the passive. They struggled mightily with the latter, but in many cases managed only a few words, whereas the same students produced reasonable facsimiles of the text with participial adjectives. Since all students were in a different instructional condition for the two forms, ease of completion of the dictogloss appears to have had more to do with the form than the treatment. Therefore, it is likely that even with a more demanding task, such as the narrative used in the passive tests, performance on participial adjectives would remain strong.

These results suggest an important interaction between choice of forms and instructional treatment. Our initial hypothesis was that a flood would increase the chances that learners would notice the form. We further hypothesized that the instruction would do this and more; that is, it would increase the chances that the learners would notice the gap between their own use and the target input, resulting in increased accuracy in their production. If noticing a form is indeed a prerequisite to its acquisition, as Schmidt claims (1993a), then this may help to explain the lack of clear difference between the two experimental groups with the passive. In providing explicit instruction to a group of learners, most of whom had yet to notice the form in the input, we were perhaps trying in vain to circumvent this crucial step in the acquisition process; and in the end, the two treatments had the same effect: Learners noticed the form in the input and only then began attempting its use. For this form, for these learners, a more effective instructional strategy might have been the input-processing activities suggested by VanPatten (VanPatten & Cadierno, 1993a; Van-Patten & Sanz, 1995), which help learners to interpret input with the goal of incorporating this knowledge into their IL but does not require production. For the participial adjectives, the flood was enough to get some of the learners, who were ready, to notice how the input differed from their own production, but the more explicit treatment proved to be more effective for this job, leading to greater gains in Group I than in Group F.

Although it seems that the passive instruction was less effective than the participial adjective instruction, as reflected in the posttest scores, it is still possible to see changes in passive use. For instance, in the two experimental groups' results, there were attempts at the passive in the narrative task. To be counted as a full passive, the combined presence of either a *be* or a *get* auxiliary, and some past form of the main verb, was required (although regularized irregular past participles were accepted), and finally, the patient had to be in the subject position. There were many responses that contained some but not all of these elements, often along with the optional *by* phrase. Again, the N size is too small to permit clear conclusions, but there were a number of such attempts at the passive, among the responses of Group I in particular, such as:

[15]   The fish have chopped by the factory.
        The grapes are pick by the people.

This indicates that there is a growing awareness of the form and its use, even if the learners were unable to produce the full forms. This suggests several points: First, our test tasks may not have been sensitive enough for forms that are in early stages of development. A second, related issue is that we should perhaps not dismiss the effect of the passive instruction too soon. Indeed, it does appear that it was not optimal, nor was it entirely disregarded, as one might have concluded from the posttest and dictogloss results. Rather, it may be that it did have an effect in moving learners into a stage of development similar to that of the participial adjectives prior to instruction: In terms of receptive use, they began to notice the passive in the input, and in terms of productive use, they began to use it in a nontargetlike manner.

Conclusion

This study is a preliminary step in defining what is meant by *focus on form*. A more fine-grained analysis of what is meant by *formal* and *functional complexity* (see DeKeyser, this volume) is needed to differentiate among forms. In what way are passives more complex than participial adjectives? How can teachers and researchers gauge learner readiness in the absence of documented developmental stages for each individual form? Nontargetlike IL emergence is a rather primitive metric, but it seems to point in the right direction. Is there a more precise way of predicting the effectiveness of focus on form regarding learner development?

The pedagogical implications of the findings offer both promise and problems. Most generally, they point to the fact that focus on form is indeed useful and should be integrated into communicative curricula. However, they also suggest that each individual student has a point of readiness for focus on form and that every form may be ideally suited to different degrees and kinds of focus on form. This suggests the need for a greater awareness on the part of the teacher regarding emergence of forms in their students' ILs and for the development of alternative instructional strategies, particularly insofar as the level of explicitness of focus on form is concerned (see Doughty & Williams, Chapter 10, this volume).

Finally, it is important to view the results of Group C in a somewhat broader perspective. Group C consisted of the students in Class 2 for passives and the students in Class 3 for participial adjectives. In fact, then, this group represents two thirds of the participants in this study, and thus their behavior may be considered typical of this population when no FonF instruction is provided. Their lack of progress came in spite of the fact that they live in a world filled with spoken and written English and received plentiful input in comments, conferences, and conversation with dedicated teachers. This was their last ESL class, and it is unlikely that during the rest of their college career, they will ever again receive consistent corrective feedback or explicit instruction on their use of English. From now on, only authentic positive evidence will be available to them. Efficiency thus becomes an important issue. Learners who are ready seem eventually to be able to get the focus that they need without special treatment. However, based on these findings, providing such a focus as part of instruction does seem to get them there faster.

8 The role of focus-on-form tasks in promoting child L2 acquisition

Birgit Harley

Introduction

This chapter presents evidence from a classroom experiment showing that an instructional focus on form can have a lasting impact on the second language (L2) proficiency of learners as young as 7 or 8 years of age. In this study, the instructional focus is on grammatical gender in French, a quintessentially formal aspect of the target language that is generally lacking in semantic motivation. The learners are grade 2 students in early total French immersion, an optional school program that is now offered in a substantial number of Canadian schools.[1]

A major motivation for this study was to determine whether an early instructional focus on form could have an influence on proficiency in an area of French that has been found to be a persistent problem for immersion students. Students in the experiment were exposed to classroom activities designed to draw their attention to formal clues to the gender of French nouns: in particular, the information provided by the determiners *le/un* (masculine) and *la/une* (feminine) and the morphophonological clues provided by certain noun endings. The study was designed to test two hypotheses: first, that grade 2 immersion students receiving such focus-on-form (FonF) instruction would learn to assign gender more accurately to nouns in French than would their peers who did not receive this instruction; and second, that students who received the instruction would be able to generalize the knowledge they acquired about noun endings to new nouns that were unfamiliar to them.

After a summary of the study, its rationale, design, and test results, is presented, the learning tasks used in this experiment, and the extent to

The research described in this chapter was funded by the Social Sciences and Humanities Research Council of Canada (Grant No. 410-92-1614). I am grateful to Joan Howard, Yvette Michaud-Saranchuk, Louise Morrison, Doug Hart, and Fleur-Ange Lamothe for their role in materials development, data collection and analysis, and test scoring. I would also like to thank Catherine Doughty, Patsy Lightbown, and Jessica Williams for helpful comments on a previous draft of this chapter.

1 For a description of immersion programs and overviews of the research, see, for example, Genesee (1987); Lapkin and Swain (1990); and Swain and Lapkin (1982).

which they meet apparent requirements for instructional effectiveness, are discussed.

Rationale

Instructional conditions

To propose classroom treatment aimed at promoting attention to form among children in grade 2 may seem surprising, given that some educators would question the merits of consciousness-raising even among adult L2 learners (e.g., Krashen, 1985; Schwartz, 1993). It is, indeed, generally assumed that the acquisition of language by young children occurs incidentally as a by-product of communication without deliberate intention to learn the language for the purpose of mastering it (Schmidt, 1990, 1994b). This does not mean, however, that children's language learning occurs without any kind of conscious awareness. According to Schmidt, attention controls access to the conscious experience of *noticing*, that is, "registration of the occurrence of a stimulus event in conscious awareness and subsequent storage in long term memory" (1994b, p. 179). It is now conventional wisdom, he points out, "that target language forms will not be acquired unless they are noticed and that one important way that instruction works is by increasing the salience of target language forms in input so that they are more likely to be noticed by learners" (1994b, p. 195). This instructional principle would appear to apply equally well to the L2 learning of children as to adults. In French immersion, for example, it has been argued that simply exposing learners to language in a context that they understand, although necessary, is not sufficient to promote formal accuracy in some areas of the French language system. In achieving global comprehension of language in context, learners may often be able to rely on contextual cues and world knowledge, without paying attention to linguistic details (Swain, 1985). Communicatively expendable formal features of the second language may be overlooked as learners focus on making meaning in the new language in terms of the knowledge they already possess (Harley, 1992, 1993).

A number of instructional experiments in French immersion and intensive English programs in Canada have led to the conclusion that some kind of "input enhancement" (Sharwood Smith, 1991, 1993; White, Spada, Lightbown, & Ranta, 1991) can have a positive effect on the L2 proficiency of older children in grades 4 to 8 (Day & Shapson, 1991; Harley, 1989; Lyster, 1994a; Spada & Lightbown, 1993; White et al., 1991; Wright, 1996). These studies have been similar not only in attempting to focus the learners' attention on specific language features but also in their emphasis on focused productive, as well as receptive, use of the

L2 in communicative activities designed to be motivating for the age groups concerned. Language production, or output, according to Swain (1995), may have several learning functions: not only providing practice opportunities that encourage automatization of linguistic knowledge but also prompting learners to notice the gap between what they can say and what they want to say, enabling them to test hypotheses, and promoting reflection that permits them to "control and internalize linguistic knowledge" (p. 126). Affective considerations also have an important role to play in the design of FonF activities: Even children as young as 5 years of age are able to identify interest as a prime condition for attending to a task (Miller, 1985). To promote attention, learning activities need to be sufficiently stimulating yet not overly challenging for the age group concerned. Young children of 7 or 8 years of age cannot be subjected to the kind of metalinguistically oriented focus on form that relies heavily on the transmission of abstract rules. Instead, a more reasonable approach advocated, for example, by Loschky and Bley-Vroman (1993) is to introduce FonF activities that take the shape of tasks when the task demands themselves require the learners to attend to the relevant second language features.

In short, input salience, opportunities for focused output, and intrinsically interesting, age-appropriate tasks that cannot be performed without attention to the relevant forms are the principles underlying the instruction that in this study is aimed at facilitating the acquisition of communicatively nonessential formal features of the L2.

Choice of linguistic domain

Native French-speaking children reportedly acquire the essential characteristics of French grammatical gender by the age of 3 (e.g., Clark, 1985; Grégoire, 1947; Karmiloff-Smith, 1979). According to Clark (1985), for example, "By age 3, children appear to make few errors in their choices of articles," though they may still have problems with adjective agreement (p. 706). And, as Karmiloff-Smith (1979) has shown, native speakers as early as age 3 are able to predict the gender of unfamiliar nouns from reliable noun-ending clues, thus demonstrating system learning. In contrast to the research involving native French-speaking children, a number of studies carried out in French immersion programs have shown that grammatical gender is an area of French that is quite problematic for immersion students (Harley, 1979; Spilka, 1976; Stevens, 1984; Taylor-Browne, 1984). Their problems lie not only with adjective agreement but with articles too. After several years of early immersion, 11- to 12-year-olds have been found to be frequently overgeneralizing *un/le,* or sometimes *une/la,* thus rarely discriminating feminine from masculine nouns

(Harley, 1979; Stevens, 1984). It appears that they are overlooking gender distinctions. Taylor-Browne (1984) reports findings for a few grade 8 and 9 immersion students as well as younger ones. She found that the older students were able to predict the gender of unfamiliar nouns from some, but not all, of the reliable noun endings that were tested, and that errors were still being made in the gender of common nouns such as *tableau* – "blackboard," *pomme* – "apple," and *table* – "table." Further oral interview data from grade 10 immersion students collected in the context of studies at the Ontario Institute for Studies in Education (OISE) also show that article errors with common nouns such as **un voiture* – "a (M) car," **un ferme* – "a (M) farm," and **le raison* – "the (M) reason" are still in evidence at the high school level. In short, studies indicate that basic distinctions in French gender are a continuing problem for students in immersion programs, as indeed is typical for English-speaking learners in general. Grammatical gender is not something they appear to learn incidentally simply from exposure to the language from kindergarten on, even though immersion teachers, by using French day in and day out, are bound to expose students to numerous French nouns marked for gender. Frequency in teacher talk is clearly not enough in this instance. In short, gender in French appears to lack salience for these students.

There may be several reasons for this lack of salience. In the first place, their English-speaking background does not lead immersion students to look for grammatical gender in French.[2] They may in any case fail to notice the distinction between the articles *le* and *la* and between *un* and *une,* the most reliable indicators of noun gender in French, because in English the quality of the vowel used in an article, which is typically unstressed, can vary quite considerably without any grammatical consequences. With the focus of their early language learning on communication, there is little apparent motivation to pay attention to distinctions that are of minimal import for the expression of meaning. Furthermore, over time students will be exposed to much misleading input from their peers, which makes it difficult for them to establish the gender of individual items and to make appropriate generalizations. Teachers, too, as they

---

2 A study comparing performance in French gender attribution by university-level students, some with English L1 and others with German L1, produced evidence to suggest that the English native speakers were disadvantaged by the absence of grammatical gender in their L1, in contrast to the German native speakers, who appeared to benefit from their familiarity with the concept of grammatical gender in German (Marinova-Todd, 1994). Garavito-Bruhn (1986) also observed that French L1 learners of Spanish L2 at the secondary school level had a lower rate of error for gender than that found in previous research with anglophone learners. In this case, there may have been additional facilitation based on shared gender of cognates in French and Spanish, two Romance languages.

focus on subject matter content, may not notice that gender distinctions are not being made and that some students in their oral production become adept at using a conveniently ambiguous [lʌ] instead of *le* or *la,* which in context may be heard as correct.

Perhaps gender errors should not be a cause of concern. In one study of native speaker reactions to immersion speech (Lepicq, 1980), for example, gender errors were rated by adult French-speaking Canadians as the least serious type of error made by 11-year-old immersion students. Magnan (1983), in a study in France of reactions to various types of errors produced by an American learner, found similarly that adult native speakers rated gender errors among the least serious. However, adolescent native speakers in the same study rated the gender errors much more severely. So far there have been no studies of native speaker reactions to the errors of older immersion students, but there is anecdotal evidence to suggest that native French-speaking Canadians are disturbed by the gender errors of older immersion students when the errors are made in common nouns, perhaps because of high expectations for accuracy among older immersion students. Furthermore, it is evident that a lack of competence with French grammatical gender can result in errors in a high proportion of utterances (Surridge & Lessard, 1984, p. 48). In short, it appears well worthwhile from an educational perspective to attempt to improve immersion students' ability to make gender distinctions in French.

In this study, the focus was on formal rather than semantic clues to grammatical gender. One reason for this is that grammatical gender in French is largely determined by formal rather than semantic criteria. According to Corbett (1991), for example, although there is a core of nouns whose gender is determined by semantic considerations, "in French the major generalizations can be stated in terms of phonology" (p. 58). There is some debate as to whether phonology or morphology is the most important criterion for determining noun gender in French (see, e.g., Carroll, 1989), and it appears that there is often an overlap between the two types of criteria. Reliable indicators can be interpreted as nominal suffixes in morphological terms (e.g., /ɛt/, -ette as in *la bicyclette* – "bicycle") or alternatively as rhymes in phonological terms (/ɛt/ as in *la tête* – "head"). In any event, French native speaker performance data provide evidence that such formal "noun-ending" clues are important for deciding on the grammatical gender of unfamiliar or pseudonouns (Karmiloff-Smith, 1979; Tucker, Lambert, & Rigault, 1977; see also Hulstijn & Zekhnini, 1994, with respect to native speaker performance on Dutch pseudonouns). Karmiloff-Smith (1978, 1979), who studied the use of the determiner system in French-speaking children of different ages, also found that when phonological and semantic clues to noun gender were placed in conflict, the youngest children were the most likely to pay attention to the phonological clues to noun gender. Researchers studying first language acquisition in other languages have similarly concluded that early acquisition of grammatical gender is based on formal rather than semantic criteria (cf. Levy, 1983, on the acquisition of Hebrew; Pérez-Pereira, 1991, on Spanish).

The situation appears to be rather different for adult learners of English-speaking background. Whereas Hardison (1992) demonstrated that adult English-speaking learners of French were able to make use of noun endings as a guide to grammatical gender, Carroll (1993) found that semantic male or female gender clues were the most likely to be noticed. Likewise, Delisle (1985), who examined the strategies of English-speaking learners for assigning gender to borrowed nouns in German, found that, unlike native speakers, they based their decisions primarily on semantic considerations (whether the referent had male or female connotations). In French immersion, it seems that semantic criteria for determining the gender of nouns begin to appear around the middle elementary years (Harley, 1979), although little or no progress may have been made in using formal morphological or phonological clues (see also Stevens, 1984). The fact that formal clues to grammatical gender are primary for young native speakers of French and that English speakers in general seem to have trouble with formal clues suggests that they should be the primary focus of any instructional intervention.

Choice of grade level

As already indicated, Schmidt (1990) has argued that noticing is a prime requirement for language learning to occur at any age. There is considerable evidence to show that younger children have a phonological advantage in second language learning over older ones (for review, see e.g., Long, 1990). To the extent, therefore, that grammatical gender in French is phonologically determined, it makes sense to start drawing immersion students' attention to grammatical gender clues as early as possible, particularly in light of findings indicating that formal aspects of gender are learned early by French-speaking children (Karmiloff-Smith, 1979). Grade 2 was chosen for this instructional experiment in preference to grade 1 on the assumption that grade 1 students might not yet have a sufficiently large vocabulary for generalizations to be made. By grade 2, it is argued, students would be more likely to be using articles and would have larger vocabularies from which to generalize their learning. An early start to such instruction was also indicated as a preventive measure – as a defense against potential long-term exposure to misleading input from classmates and fossilization of *un/le* or ambiguous forms.

The experiment

Design

The FonF instruction in this experiment took place in six French immersion classes in the metropolitan Toronto area early in the grade 2 school year. Class sizes ranged from 19 to 26. The children in this study were mostly of English-speaking home background, and they were receiving all their schooling in the second language (French). They had been in French immersion since kindergarten. The activities in the instructional package were designed for 20 minutes of daily use over a 5-week period. Teachers were introduced to the material in a workshop prior to the experimental treatment, and in the course of the treatment they were asked to fill out evaluation forms each week. Each class was visited by a researcher on at least two occasions, to observe activities in use.

The students were pretested prior to the instructional treatment, posttested at the end of 5 weeks, and posttested again 6 months later, at the end of the school year. Scores on these delayed posttests were compared with end-of-year scores on the same tests for six classes of grade 2 students from the previous school year who had not received the experimental treatment. The comparison classes ranged in size from 16 to 24. The comparison students had been taught by the same teachers who took part in the instructional experiment. This design feature had the advantage of making it possible to control the teacher variable, generally recognized as an important factor in any classroom experiment. It did mean, however, that it was not possible to pretest in the comparison classes, since the schools were unable to determine so far in advance which of their teachers would be teaching at the grade 2 level during the following (experimental) year. The teachers who participated in the experiment were all women and were experienced immersion teachers. Three were native speakers of French, two were native speakers of English, and one was a native speaker of another Romance language.

Classroom materials

In designing the classroom material for the study, major emphasis was placed on creating activities in which the task demands would require close attention to gender distinctions. Many of the activities were based on children's games that involve the naming of individual concrete objects, thus requiring a choice of masculine or feminine article, *un* or *une*, *le* or *la*. Games such as "I Spy," "Simon Says," "Bingo," "Concentration," and "My Aunt's Suitcase" were adapted so that the contrast between masculine and feminine nouns would become an integral part of the game. In a variation on "Simon Says," for example, the game required students to perform contrasting actions depending on the gender of the noun that they hear in a brief sentence (e.g., touch their toes for masculine, hands on head for feminine). "Concentration" was adapted so that the purpose was to match pictures with a masculine or feminine noun ending. To win at "Bingo," it was necessary to name the objects in the row or column the student filled in and get their gender correct. In "My Aunt's Suitcase," the object was for each student in turn to add an item to a memorized list of items packed in the aunt's *valise*. These items could be all masculine, all feminine, all with a certain noun ending, and so forth. Picture cards that could be recycled in various games had the relevant word and the appropriate articles printed on the back (see Figure 1), so that once a game was played in a teacher-led, whole-class format, it could be played in pairs or small groups with access to the pertinent "feedback." Songs and rhymes provided further opportunities to practice producing the nouns with appropriate articles.

Daily activities were organized week by week for the 5 weeks of the treatment period (for a summary, see the appendix at the end of this chapter). For the first 2 weeks, the emphasis was on choice of determiner (*le* or *la, un* or *une*), and the main objective was to get students to "notice" (Schmidt, 1990) the fact that gender is an integral part of every noun in French. In subsequent weeks, emphasis was placed on the formal clues to noun gender provided within the noun itself (e.g., masculine nouns ending in /o/, /õ/, /ã/, and /ɛ̃/ and feminine nouns ending in /ɛt/, /ɛl/, /ɛz/, /as/, and /øz/).

Test instruments

Four tests were developed to assess the effects of the instructional treatment. Two of the tests were group-administered tasks presented on audiotape. Test 1 was an aural discrimination task designed to determine whether, when primed to do so, students were able to notice the difference between the masculine and feminine forms of articles in French: *le* versus *la* and *un* versus *une*. Each of the ten taped items on this test consisted of four nouns, accompanied by an appropriate masculine or feminine article. Three of the nouns had the same gender; one was different. Each set of four nouns was presented slowly twice, and on their answer sheet, which consisted of pictures of each noun, the students circled the one that was not like the others. The students were primed to focus on the article by means of an initial example. Test 2 was another group test presented on audiotape, along with pictorial answer sheets. This time, each of twelve items consisted of three nouns with the same ending, which were characteristically masculine (e.g., *-eau*, as in *bateau* – "boat") or feminine (e.g., *-ette* as in *casquette* – "cap"). The nouns were

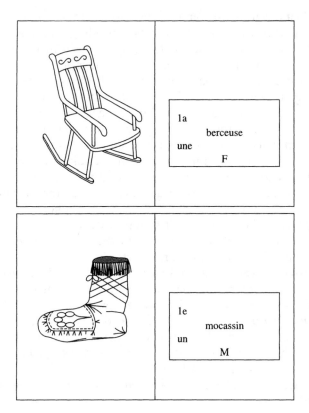

Figure 1   Sample cards used in games.

presented *without* articles, and the students' task was to circle *le* or *la* as appropriate for each item. At least some of the vocabulary on this test was assumed to be familiar to students in grade 2.

Test 3 was an individual production task that was administered to a random subsample of eight students in each class. The test was based on an experimental task used by Karmiloff-Smith (1979) in her study of native French-speaking children's use of the determiner system. Although Karmiloff-Smith was interested in how children would cope with conflicting semantic and morphophonological clues to the gender of invented nouns, in this study the focus of the task was exclusively on the morphophonological clues provided by noun endings. Test items were designed to elicit definite and indefinite articles in association with unfamiliar real nouns that represented inanimate objects, and whose endings provided gender clues (e.g., *tondeuse, sabot, brouette* – "lawn mower, wooden shoe, wheelbarrow"). The same testing procedure was used for each of twelve test items. The tester displayed a black-and-white picture of two objects (e.g., two wheelbarrows) and said: "*Voici l'image de deux brouettes. Qu'est-ce que ce sont?*" – "Here is a picture of two wheelbarrows. What are they?" When the student answered, with prompts if necessary, *deux brouettes* – "two wheelbarrows," the tester hid one object and, pointing to the other, asked: "*Et qu'est-ce que c'est?* – "And what is this?" This provides a context for the use of indefinite *une brouette* – "a (F) wheelbarrow." Replacing the original picture with a colored one (representing, e.g., one green and one red wheelbarrow), the tester then asked: "*Sur quelle image ai-je mis mon doigt?*" – "Which picture did I put my finger on?" The student was expected to answer with a definite article: "*Sur la brouette verte*" – "On the (F) green wheelbarrow." The entire test was recorded for later scoring.

Test 4 was also an individual production task. It was administered to the same subsample of students immediately following Test 3. In this case, the student was shown a colored picture depicting a variety of people, animals, and objects in a rural setting. The task was to name as many illustrated items as possible, many of which could be assumed to be familiar to grade 2 immersion students. There were twenty-four items that characteristically had masculine or feminine noun endings. This test was designed to elicit mainly indefinite articles (*un* and *une*). Again, the test was recorded for later scoring.

Results

Test reliabilities calculated on the pretest results of Tests 1 and 2 in the experimental group indicated a moderately good level of reliability for Test 1 (Cronbach's alpha = .70) and a somewhat lower level of reliability on Test 2 (Cronbach's alpha = .49), where a simple binary choice of *le* or *la* may have been affected by some guessing. Interrater reliabilities assessed on the production tasks of Tests 3 and 4 were based on a 10% random sample of taped responses from different testing sessions, including responses from both the comparison and the experimental groups. Scoring was blind with respect to group and testing session. An acceptable level of agreement between raters was found for both tests: They agreed on 84% of the item scores for Test 3 and 92% of those for Test 4.

In scoring Tests 3 and 4, it was noted that students were frequently obtaining very high scores on masculine items and much lower scores on feminine items, indicating that substantial overgeneralization of articles interpretable as *le/un* was taking place. Therefore, to avoid inflating gender accuracy scores for students who in effect were not making gender distinctions in their oral production, the analysis of results on Tests 3 and 4 was restricted to performance on feminine items.

TABLE I. MEAN SCORES OF EXPERIMENTAL GROUP ON PRETESTS, IMMEDIATE
POSTTESTS, AND DELAYED POSTTESTS FOR TESTS 1 TO 4

	Number of students	Pretest	Immediate posttest	Delayed posttest
Test 1				
(max = 10)	111	7.61	8.67	9.19[a]
Test 2				
(max = 12)	111	7.14	8.41	8.65[a]
Test 3[b]				
Indef. fem. (max = 6)	44	0.23	0.55	0.75
Def. fem. (max = 6)	43	0.70	0.58	0.60
Test 4[b]				
No. of fem. nouns	42	11.3	13.3	13.3[a]
% correct fem.	42	19%	42%	39%[a]

[a]Statistically significant linear contrast ($p < .001$) and quadratic contrast ($p < .05$).
[b]Ns for the student subsample on Tests 3 and 4 are less than forty-eight (eight students per class) owing mainly to the absence of individual students at one or more testing sessions. On Test 3, one student failed to produce definite articles, and on Test 4, two students were excluded who used feminine articles for 80% or more of all nouns on the pretest and/or immediate posttest.

Repeated measures analyses of variance were used to assess whether learning occurred between pretests and posttests in the experimental group. As Table 1 shows, mean scores increased from pretest to immediate posttest on three of the four tests (Tests 1, 2, and 4), and these scores were substantially maintained, or even slightly increased, at delayed posttesting 6 months later. The significant linear contrasts on these three tests confirm that statistically significant progress was made across time, and the significant quadratic contrasts capture the fact that the rate of progress that occurred between pretest and immediate posttest during the experimental treatment continued less rapidly (Tests 1 and 2) or simply stabilized (Test 4) in the ensuing months leading up to the delayed, end-of-year posttests. On Test 3, however, which required students in their oral production to use knowledge of noun-ending clues to predict the gender of unfamiliar nouns, no significant progress was made over time between pretest and posttests.

T-tests were used to compare the performance of the experimental and comparison groups on the four gender tests at the end of the school year. Again, on Tests 3 and 4, the analysis focused exclusively on feminine items in order to avoid inflating the scores of those students who might have appeared on the surface to be using masculine articles correctly but who were not actually making gender distinctions. Table 2 reveals that

TABLE 2. MEAN SCORES OF EXPERIMENTAL AND COMPARISON GROUPS ON END-OF-YEAR POSTTESTS

	Experimental		Comparison		Significance (1-tailed t-test)
	Number of students	$\bar{X}$	Number of students	$\bar{X}$	
Test 1					
(max = 10)	90[a]	9.12	96[a]	7.77	.000
Test 2					
(max = 12)	111	8.65	108	7.90	.008
Test 3					
Indef. fem. (max = 6)	44	0.75	47	1.34	.060
Def. fem. (max = 6)	43	0.60	38	0.39	.239
Test 4[b]					
Total nouns	45	25.8	47	26.8	.141
No. of fem. nouns	44	13.3	43	13.8	.187
% correct fem.	44	41%	43	27%	.015

[a]One school was eliminated owing to a nonstandard testing procedure used in the comparison class.
[b]Ns for the student subsample on Tests 3 and 4 are less than forty-eight (eight students per class) owing mainly to the absence of individual students at posttesting. On Test 3, some students failed to produce definite articles, and on Test 4, some students were excluded who used feminine articles for 80% or more of all nouns on the end-of-year posttest.

the mean scores of the experimental students were significantly higher than those of the comparison students on three of the four tests (Tests 1, 2, and 4). A comparison of the total nouns produced by the two groups in describing a farm scene in Test 4 indicates that the experimental students (mean = 25.8) and comparison students (mean = 26.8) were nonetheless comparable in their end-of-year knowledge of French noun vocabulary, thus adding confidence in the test results obtained by providing some evidence for equivalence of the two groups.

Discussion

The results of the testing in this study are in general accord with the first hypothesis, that grade 2 students receiving gender instruction in French would outperform students who received no systematic instruction in this grammatical domain. However, the results on Test 3 do not support the second hypothesis, that the instruction would enable students to generalize knowledge about noun endings to unfamiliar nouns. These findings appear to indicate that the experiment was more successful in inducing "item learning" than "system learning." Students in the experimental classes were successfully led to notice more often the gender of nouns they encountered in class and to distinguish more accurately between masculine and feminine articles in producing these familiar nouns, but they stopped short of generalizing from the input they received to the production of unfamiliar nouns containing the same reliable formal clues to their gender.

In association with Test 3, however, children were asked at the time of posttesting to comment on why they had responded as they did to certain items. Their responses revealed that some children were consciously aware of the relevance of noun endings for gender attribution even if they had not spontaneously produced the correct articles during the testing. Examples 1 and 2 come from the delayed posttesting session that took place toward the end of the school year. The student in Example 1 responded largely correctly on the test. The one in Example 2, however, did not, suggesting that some relevant explicit knowledge had been gained but that it had not, in general, been incorporated into the student's interlanguage system.

[1]   Interviewer: *Tout à l'heure tu as dit "le biberon jaune." Est-ce que tu peux me dire pourquoi tu as dit "LE biberon"?* (Just now you said "le biberon jaune" [the yellow baby's bottle]. Can you tell me why you said "*LE* biberon" [THE (M) baby's bottle?])

    Student: *Um. Parce que c'est "on" et c'est toujours masculin quand c'est "on."* (Um. Because it's "/ɔ̃/" and it's always masculine when it's "/ɔ̃/.")

    Interviewer: *OK. Bien.* (OK. Good.)

    Student: *Uh, pas "la maison."* ("Uh, not "*la maison*" [the (F) house.])

    Interviewer: *Pas "la maison," OK.* (Not "*la maison*," OK.)

[2]   [During the test, the student responded with *une tondeuse* – "a (F) lawnmower" – and *le tondeuse* – "the (M) lawnmower."]

    Interviewer: *Est-ce que le mot "tondeuse" est masculin ou féminin?* (Is the word "*tondeuse*" masculine or feminine?)

    Student: *Féminin?* (Feminine?)

    Interviewer: *Pourquoi tu dis féminin?* (Why do you say feminine?)

    Student: *Le "-euse" à la fin.* (The "*-euse*" at the end.)

    Interviewer: *Alors on dit "le tondeuse" ou "la tondeuse"?* (So, one says "the [M] lawnmower" or "the [F] lawnmower"?)

    Student: *"La."* ("The [F].")

Adequacy of the L2 input enhancement

One implication of the findings of this study is that the use of L2 tasks requiring close attention to formal features as part of the task demands is both feasible and helpful, even with young children. The tasks appear to have provided the kind of of salient L2 input, along with opportunities for output and associated feedback, that was needed to direct students' attention to grammatical gender. The fact that students made significant, long-lasting improvement in accuracy of gender attribution is convincing evidence that the activities had a positive effect.

It is worth noting some problems that arose, however, and that help to account for the fact that students did not go so far as to generalize their learning to the production of new nouns. From the observations and teacher reports, it appears that the first 2 weeks of activities, which focused on the gender information provided by the articles were the most successful. During these 2 weeks, much of the vocabulary that was used was probably already known to the students (the focus was on objects in the classroom in week 1, and on the theme of Hallowe'en in week 2). From the third to the fifth week, the focus was on the gender information provided by noun endings, and it is clear from consistent teacher reports that too much new vocabulary was involved. Teachers found that it took them too much time to teach the meaning of the vocabulary (the daily activities took 30–40 minutes rather than the suggested 20 minutes), and this led to curtailment of some activities, and elimination of others, particularly in weeks 4 and 5. Hence, one interpretation of the results of this study is that the input on noun endings was simply not available in sufficient quantity and intensity for the majority of students to establish the predictive relevance of the noun endings in question. Familiarity with a larger number of relevant noun exemplars may have been required. According to Hulstijn and Zekhnini (1994), for example, who found in their experiment involving Dutch pseudowords that intermediate and advanced adult L2 learners were less sensitive to formal patterns of gender attribution than native speakers, this was presumably because "nonnative speakers have taken in smaller amounts of input and have acquired smaller vocabularies and are therefore less susceptible to statistical tendencies (caused by rules or cues) than native speakers" (Hulstijn & Zekhnini, 1994, p. 5). The fact that so much of the vocabulary was new to the grade 2 students in this study may also have meant that the learners themselves were preoccupied with remembering the new words for objects featured in the activities and were thus not able to devote full attention to the formal aspects that were the intended focus of the activities.

Compatibility with the learning process

A key learning principle on which the activities in this study were based is that learning at any age depends on the ability to notice the relevant language features (Schmidt, 1990, 1994a, 1994b). Noticing requires attention, and for primary school children, it seems clear that attention is dependent on the intrinsic interest of the learning activities involved (Ceci & Howe, 1982). Hence, in this study, the emphasis was not only on making the forms salient but on using activities and material designed to be interesting and visually attractive to the age level concerned. From teachers' reports it appears that some of the more popular activities could have been recycled more often to good effect. Particularly with children, the introduction of new activities inevitably involves a certain amount of procedural familiarization, and the sheer variety of tasks introduced in this experiment probably added unnecessarily to the learning required.

There are indications that, among children at least, establishing a meaning for specific L2 vocabulary items precedes generalization of formal patterning (e.g., Harley, 1992; Viberg, 1993). Hence, one hypothesis for further investigation would be that instruction on the relevance of French noun endings should more deliberately focus on old, previously learned vocabulary, rather than incorporating so much new vocabulary in a short amount of time, as was the case in this study. More prior consolidation of item-by-item learning may be needed before the kind of susceptibility to cues or rules referred to by Hulstijn and Zekhnini (1994) can be induced. Students could have benefited from greater familiarity and a higher frequency of use of multiple nouns in each noun-ending category. Another possibility to be considered, however, is that learners base their formal generalizations on prototypical items rather than on a plurality of items, as was the assumption in this study. For example, it might have been more effective to work with one or two well-known words with the characteristically feminine ending of *-ette* as in *la bicyclette* – "bicycle," rather than introducing a number of new *-ette* words such as *la crevette* – "shrimp," *la salopette* – "overalls," *la casquette* – "cap," *la marionnette* – "puppet," and so on, as was done in the experimental treatment. According to Hardison (1992), for example, adult learners of French whom she studied appeared to develop gender attribution rules "based on the gender of the most salient member of each phonetic ending category in their input" (p. 296). Whether the same tendency would apply to young children, whose learning is assumed to be primarily incidental, rather than intentional, in nature, is an interesting question deserving of further investigation. It is clear, in any event, from Karmiloff-Smith's (1979) experiments with native French-speaking children that there is no intrinsic maturational barrier to system learning of grammatical gender in French by primary immersion students.

Congruity with the overall curriculum

There is another way in which the first 2 weeks of this experiment were more successful than weeks 3 to 5. In weeks 1 and 2, the activities were more clearly related to themes that teachers were emphasizing in their regular curriculum, whereas later weeks lacked any thematic thread that provided a context for the new vocabulary that was introduced. The words used in the various games that focused on noun endings were formally but not semantically linked, and this was found to be problematic in an elementary immersion curriculum that, like the regular English curriculum, is thematically based, and in which time must be economically used to permit coverage of a range of curriculum goals that go beyond language per se. The lack of congruity with the regular curriculum appears to have led at least one of the teachers to abandon the week 5 activities altogether.

Conclusion

This study lends support to the view that once a second language feature has been identified as problematic, there is merit in preplanning a segment of the curriculum to deal with it. Instruction for children requiring attention to form as an integral part of the task demands appears to be a promising approach that has its place in the context of a more broadly experiential type of second language program. The instructional activities developed for this study were compressed for research purposes into a 5-week period, but this is not necessarily an important feature of their use. In fact, the consciousness-raising the study produced among teachers led several of them to indicate that they would continue to pay more attention to the use of grammatical gender by their students. This study involved only an introduction to grammatical gender in French, and it is clear that further attention to this subsystem of French would need to be given in later grades.

It was suggested in this chapter that students may not have had the opportunity to focus intensively enough on the noun-ending clues that were introduced. It does not seem, however, that any absolute statement can be made as to how intensive this particular focus on form should have been. In principle, the intensity of focus on form is liable to vary, depending on the difficulty of the feature to be learned, how feasible it is to develop tasks that are compatible with the learning capacities of the age group concerned, and how easily the tasks can be made to fit into the general curriculum that is being followed. An important conclusion of this study is that a focus on form in a primary immersion context is most successful when it is well integrated with overall curriculum themes, and is, thus, not perceived as taking time away from other teaching objectives. It is possible that some of the activities used in this study would have been more effective among older children in grade 3 or 4, as indeed some of the teachers suggested. On the other hand, as noted at the beginning of this chapter, there are good reasons, in an immersion classroom context, for starting to make grammatical gender in French salient as early as possible. Clearly, this study of the role of focus on form among young classroom L2 learners leaves us with a number of issues that would benefit from further investigation.

Appendix   Outline of activities provided to experimental teachers*

Week 1
Monday: Students attach labels provided to objects in class-
                room; each label includes a masculine (M) or feminine
                (F) article as appropriate. Class sings song about M
                and F objects in the classroom (provided on cassette).
Tuesday: Each student highlights M and F nouns and articles in
                different columns on his or her song sheet. The song is
                sung again. Students do a word search for the same
                words (with articles).
Wednesday: The class plays "I Spy." The student giving the clue
                has to say whether the word is M or F.
Thursday: The teacher introduces the board game "The Race."
                When a student lands on a square, he or she has to
                pick a picture card and name the object with a correct
                article or identify the word as M or F. (The game is
                available for later play in pairs or small groups.)
Friday: Formative evaluation. The students label and cut out
                pictures of classroom objects and paste them in two
                columns – M or F.

Week 2
Monday: The teacher reads a Hallowe'en story. On the second
                reading, students listen for and name M and F words.
Tuesday: The students play a game of "Simon Says," with
                different actions for M and F words that the teacher
                produces in the context of short sentences. The class
                sings a Hallowe'en song that includes M and F nouns.

---

*It should be noted that there may have been a variation in the way that these activities were implemented in each experimental class, and that not all activities were completed in every class.

Wednesday: Each student begins a pair of personalized picture dictionaries – one for F, and the other for M words. Picture labels have to include *le/un* or *la/une*. Singly or in pairs, students do a Hallowe'en crossword puzzle of M and F words.

Thursday: The class plays a game of "Bingo" using Hallowe'en vocabulary. To win, a student must name the objects (with correct articles) in the winning row or column.

Friday: Formative evaluation. The students do a worksheet of Hallowe'en riddles. Each answer requires an M or F noun with article. The students create an oral Hallowe'en story prompted by picture cards. Each student adds a new sentence to the story.

Week 3   (M nouns ending in /o/ and /ð/ and F nouns ending in /ɛt/ and /ɛl/).

Monday: The students play a team game of "Concentration" using picture cards; the task is to match nouns with the same-sounding "ending," either M /o/ or /ð/ or F /ɛl/ or /ɛt/. The game is available for later play in pairs or small groups.

Tuesday: The students play a game of "Simon Says," with different actions for nouns with the characteristic M and F endings. "Concentration" is played again, with the class in two teams.

Wednesday: The students play a game of "My Aunt's Suitcase" using nouns that all have the same endings. Then they play a ballgame with an accompanying rhyme about *le ballon*.

Thursday: The students add to their M and F picture dictionaries using nouns with this week's endings. They make up rhymes about their pictures using rhyming adjectives with the same M and F endings.

Friday: Formative evaluation. The students color the items in a picture that shows a noun with the characteristic F ending /ɛt/. The students do a worksheet matching rhyming words and inserting correct M or F articles.

Week 4

Monday:	The class plays "Concentration" in two teams with a new set of picture cards representing nouns with typically M endings /ã/ and /ɛ̃/ and F endings /ɛz/, /as/, /iz/, and /øz/. A game of "Simon Says" focuses on contrasting nouns with the same M and F endings. The class listens to a recorded song, "La chèvre" ("The goat"), which features nouns ending in /ɛ̃/.
Tuesday:	The students play a team game of "Tic-tac-toe." Instead of using Xs and Os, the teams have to produce F and M items.
Wednesday:	The students add to their picture dictionaries using words from this week's vocabulary. They read aloud a rhyme that features nouns with characteristic M and F endings.
Thursday:	The students participate in a selection of small-group activities: for example, playing "The Race" board game or "Tic-tac-toe" with this week's vocabulary, using a commercial picture dictionary to find new nouns with characteristic M and F endings.
Friday:	Formative evaluation. The students match rhyming words on a worksheet and insert articles.

Week 5

Monday:	The students play a game of "Concentration" with new M and F vocabulary, including noun endings from weeks 3 and 4.
Tuesday:	"Simon Says" is played with M and F vocabulary from any week. The students do a word search involving nouns with characteristic M and F endings.
Wednesday:	The students add to their picture dictionaries, selecting nouns with characteristic M and F endings.
Thursday:	The students play a game of "The Race" using this week's vocabulary.
Friday:	Formative evaluation. The students do a new worksheet involving the matching of rhyming words and insertion of M and F articles.

PART III:
PEDAGOGICAL IMPLICATIONS OF
FOCUS ON FORM

9 The importance of timing in focus on form

Patsy M. Lightbown

Introduction

When does focus on form work most effectively to promote second language acquisition (SLA)? This question about timing in focus on form entails both psycholinguistic and pedagogical questions. Two broad aspects of timing will be discussed in this chapter:

1. Is focus-on-form (FonF) intervention more effective when it is timed to match learners' developmental stage in SLA, or is it more efficient when it targets features that characterize "advanced" stages, in which case learners are expected to have passed through the earlier stages without focused instructional intervention?
2. Should FonF activities be integrated into communicative activities, or is it better to have separate activities for formS focus and meaning focus?

Respecting developmental sequences

There is considerable evidence that specific sequences or stages of development characterize second language learners' progress. As this evidence began to grow, some researchers suggested that teaching might be most effective if learners were exposed to those features that were develop-

I thank Catherine Doughty for organizing the Focus on Form Symposium at the 1994 Second Language Research Forum in Montreal, where an early version of this paper was presented. I thank the participants in that symposium, both panelists and audience, for their provocative questions. I also thank Manfred Pienemann, Howard Nicholas, Laura Collins, Roy Lyster, and Nina Spader, for their comments on earlier versions, and Catherine Doughty and Jessica Williams for particularly valuable comments on later versions. I wish that I could have used their collective wisdom to overcome all the gaps and shortcomings, but I must take responsibility for the final product.

My own research, referred to in this chapter, is funded by the Social Science and Humanities Research Council of Canada and the Quebec Ministry of Education's Fonds pour la formation de chercheurs et l'aide à la recherche.

mentally "next" (e.g., Valdman, 1975). In fact, some research did show that learners benefited from instruction focused on linguistic features characteristic of their next developmental stage, whereas instructional intervention that targeted too high or too low a developmental level was either confusing or irrelevant (Pienemann, 1989).

Matching instruction to stage of development

The best-known and most extensive pedagogical recommendations following from the research on developmental sequences are Krashen's (1985) and Pienemann's (Pienemann, 1985, 1989). Although both researchers based their conclusions, in part, on the discovery that learners proceed through predictable stages as they acquire a second language, their resulting pedagogical proposals are quite different.

Krashen recommends that teachers "cast a wide net," that is, that they not attempt to "time" instruction to match learners' development at all. Rather, he suggests that teachers can count on the availability of the linguistic features at the appropriate next developmental level (which he called $i + 1$) in any rich enough source of comprehensible input. Krashen's proposal includes a virtual prohibition against targeting any specific linguistic form for focused attention and emphasizes the value of language teaching methods based exclusively or primarily on the provision of comprehensible input. Krashen argues that neither formS-focused nor FonF instruction will aid or alter language acquisition. It may appear to have such an effect, Krashen says, but this is because learners getting focused instruction "learn" certain metalinguistic information and then use it to "monitor" the output that is generated by the interlanguage they have "acquired" through "comprehensible input" (see Krashen, 1982, 1992, 1993; see also 1985, for his definition of these terms, 1992 for his reaction to research on attention to form).

Pienemann's pedagogical recommendation, based on his "teachability hypothesis," was first proposed in detail in 1985. Pienemann differed from Krashen in that he did consider it appropriate to identify the developmental stage at which learners are functioning and to target the next stage in creating or selecting instructional materials. Unlike Krashen, Pienemann did not take a position on *how* to teach (teaching "methods"), restricting his pedagogical recommendations to considerations of *what* to teach (the linguistic features that are likely to be affected by instruction) and *when* (in developmental terms) such features are best taught. A series of experimental studies provided some support for his recommendations (Pienemann, 1989). In these studies, learners of German as a second language benefited differentially from instructional intervention according to the stage of readiness they had reached when the intervention took place. This research was carried out with both young learners of German as a second language in Germany and adult learners of German as a foreign language in Australia. In both studies, there was evidence that only those learners who were at a stage immediately prior to the stage represented by the intervention materials benefited from the instruction. Those learners who were at lower stages either gained nothing from the intervention or showed signs of being somehow confused or disadvantaged by the intervention, which was not timed to their interlanguage developmental stage. Not only did learners fail to progress to the next developmental stage following instruction that was too advanced, some learners performed less well than they had previously done. The negative effects were seen even in features characterized as *variational,* that is, features whose acquisition does not appear to progress in a fixed sequence (Meisel, Clahsen, & Pienemann, 1981). It was as if too much effort and attention were being expended in trying to learn features that were developmentally too difficult, leaving learners with little "processing space" for the variational features. These findings were interpreted as suggesting that teaching that targets a developmental level which is too high can lead to problems rather than progress.

Although they disagree on pedagogical recommendations, Krashen and Pienemann appear to agree on the assumption that learners themselves will process and use for acquisition only that which is developmentally appropriate. In previous works, I have had occasion to discuss both proposals. Like many SLA researchers, I have questioned Krashen's complete confidence in comprehensible input and his dismissal of focused instruction, especially for learners whose development takes place principally or only within a classroom context (Lightbown, 1991). Some recent classroom-based research has yielded evidence that learners not only benefit from, but may sometimes require, focus on form to overcome incorrect or incomplete knowledge of specific target language features (e.g., Lightbown & Pienemann, 1993; Lyster, 1994a; Swain, 1991b; L. White, Spada, Lightbown, and Ranta, 1991).

I expressed concern about some limitations to the implementation of teaching procedures based on Pienemann's proposal in a discussion chapter (Lightbown, 1985a) reacting to the original presentation of his pedagogical recommendation (Pienemann, 1985). First, I pointed out some practical concerns. For example, even now, more than 10 years later, the developmental stages we have identified cover only a tiny fraction of the structural features of English and German, and still less of other languages. We are currently in no position to create a syllabus that would adequately cover what learners need to learn. In addition, the heterogeneity of classes is a well-known reality, one that would make developmentally targeted teaching very difficult to organize.

At a more theoretical level, I argued that it was precisely because learners in such a wide variety of learning environments seemed to pass through similar developmental stages that we should question the efficacy of step-by-step teaching of specific features of the second language. SLA research showed that learners acquired features in a predictable sequence whether or not they got specific instruction on one feature or another. Indeed, much of the research prior to 1985 was based on subjects whose exposure to their second language took place exclusively, or to a large extent, outside classrooms. One could thus assume that they were exposed to a wide variety of linguistic features, in no particular order, from the beginning. This tended to confirm that the sequences were a result of mechanisms or processes internal to the learners rather than to any consistency in the input to which they had been exposed.

Furthermore, some research (including my own) showed that the only learners whose development seemed to differ from the emerging "universal" sequences were those learners in instructional settings that rigorously controlled their access to linguistic forms that had not already been taught. I argued that learners who were not exposed to a full range of natural language could be said in a sense to be learning a different target language, with resulting effects on patterns of development (Lightbown, 1985b). I reasoned on the basis that the acquisition sequence might actually depend on learners being exposed to a variety of features, rather than having features presented one at a time, in an order determined either by hypothetical "linguistic simplicity" or by observed "developmental sequences."[1]

Planting the seeds for later-stage development

In the early 1980s, when I wrote the discussion chapter responding to Pienemann's proposal, I think that I was closer to Krashen's view that formal instruction was neither necessary nor desirable (Lightbown, 1985a). My studies of the effects of the massively distorted input characteristic of Audiolingual teaching led me to fear that choosing features for focused instruction might bring about the disruption of learners' interlanguage development (Lightbown, 1983; Lightbown & Spada, 1978). However, a number of years of research in classrooms in which focused instruction was virtually absent and comprehensible input was the principal basis for language acquisition led me to share the view of a number of researchers – that focused attention to language features is often beneficial and sometimes necessary (Lightbown, 1991; see also Long, 1991; Long & Robinson, this volume; L. White, 1987, 1991).

---

1 Pienemann did not argue that learners should be prevented from hearing a wider range of structures than those which were targeted. However, he concluded that his research showed that focusing on what was developmentally too advanced could sometimes interfere with learners' progress.

LEARNER OUTPUT AS AUTO-INPUT

Whereas the value of certain types of instructional intervention now seems to be well established,[2] the question of the *timing* of the attention to form has been explored by far less research. Some of the work by the Concordia/McGill research group led me to think again about Pienemann's recommendation that focused instruction should target the next developmental stage. For example, in a study of the acquisition of English by young francophone learners, an instructional treatment was introduced that involved some explanation, considerable comprehensible input, and opportunities to practice question forms. The forms presented by the instructional materials were representative of the most advanced stage in the acquisition of questions (see further details later in this chapter). We found that students who got instruction and corrective feedback improved in accuracy more than an uninstructed comparison group did. That is, they advanced in their ability to recognize and produce correct question forms (L. White et al., 1991). More important in this context, they also advanced in their developmental stage in forming questions in communicative interaction (Lightbown & Spada, 1997; Spada & Lightbown, 1993). This development was described in terms of the framework of developmental sequences that Pienemann, Johnston, and Brindley (1988) elaborated for ESL (see Figure 1).

The instructional input that was provided to students in this study focused mainly on question forms that would be placed at Stage 4 or Stage 5 in the Pienemann, Johnston, and Brindley framework.[3] Learners who were at Stage 1 or Stage 2 on the pretest neither stayed put at Stage 1 or Stage 2 nor jumped ahead to Stage 4 or Stage 5 utterances. Instead, they tended to advance along the stage continuum, adding Stage 3 questions where there had been only Stage 1 or Stage 2 forms before. Sometimes their progress was apparent more in terms of what they left out; that is, they produced fewer Stage 2 questions and more Stage 3 questions after instruction.

Another finding from this recent research merits closer attention, however. Following the instruction, many students whose overall preference was clearly for Stage 2 utterances did produce a small number of Stage 4 and/or Stage 5 questions (Lightbown & Spada, 1993). For example, learners might use the Stage 4 questions "Where is the dog? Where is the

2 The reference list to support this statement, too long to place here, would include Long (1983a), Lightbown (1983), Lightbown and Spada (1990), Doughty (1991), Lyster (1994a), Kowal and Swain (1994), VanPatten and Cadierno (1993a), and many of the chapters in this volume.
3 In the speech of native speakers of English, questions in Stages 1, 2, and 3 are often pragmatically appropriate. However, except for some rote-learned chunks in Stage 1 or do-fronted questions in Stage 3 (e.g., "Do you have a dog?"), they are not fully formed grammatical questions in English.

Stage 1

Single words or fragments
A spot on the dog?
A ball or a shoe?

Stage 2

Subject-verb-object with rising intonation
A boy throw the ball?
Two children ride a bicycle?

Stage 3

Fronting
  Do-fronting
  Do the boy is beside the bus?
  Do you have three astronaut?

  Wh-fronting
  What the boy is throwing?
  Where the children are standing?

Stage 4

Wh- with copula BE
Where is the ball?
Where is the space ship?

Yes/no questions with AUX inversion
Is the boy beside the garbage can?
Is there a dog on the bus?

Stage 5

Wh- with AUX second
What is the boy throwing?
How do you say "lancer"?

Figure 1   Developmental stages in English questions (adapted from Pienemann, Johnston, and Brindley, 1988).

shoe? Where is the spaceship?" or the Stage 5 questions "How do you say *tâches* in English? How do you say *lancer*? How do you say *extra-terrestre*?" – with essentially slot-substitution variations. These questions appear to be quite sophisticated in the speech of a learner with an over-whelming tendency to use Stage 2 questions. However, I would not con-clude, contrary to the strictest interpretation of Pienemann's model, that students producing these questions could be said to have reached Stage 4 or Stage 5 because these structures had "emerged" in their speech. It seemed much more likely that these questions were made up at least partly of unanalyzed chunks in which a variety of noun phrases could be inserted. As such, they did not necessarily provide evidence that learners were actually using subject-auxiliary inversion or "AUX-second" rules for forming questions.[4]

On the other hand, even if the Stage 4 and Stage 5 questions were essentially chunks, the learners usually appeared to know what they meant. They knew when it was appropriate to use these questions and what information they could expect to gain by asking them. One might say that, in asking these questions, they were providing themselves with meaningful, comprehensible input. A longitudinal follow-up showed that the learners continued to advance in their ability to use question forms after the specific teaching materials on questions had been withdrawn (Spada & Lightbown, 1993). It may be that these chunk or semichunk utterances were serving as available input to the learners' own developing systems. That is, although these utterances had not been integrated into the learners' interlanguage systems at the time when the learners first began to use them, the utterances were nevertheless there, "available" as input for later integration.

I believe that this explanation is consistent with a proposal that Sharwood Smith (1981) made in describing a possible role for instruction in a model of language acquisition that was largely compatible with Krashen's view. In this model, metalinguistic knowledge or memorized utterances do not directly alter the structure of the learner's interlanguage, but they can play an important role by permitting the learner to produce useful input to his or her own system.

Acquisition from one's own "monitored" or memorized utterances is only one plausible explanation for the usefulness of practicing language forms that are beyond the current developmental stage. Another hypothesis, compatible with cognitive approaches to SLA, is that through exposure to instruction, learners have acquired "knowledge" of these features but have not yet acquired "control" of them (see, e.g., Bialystok, 1994a; McLaughlin, 1987). It is hypothesized that opportunities to use the utterances in discourse-appropriate contexts help learners get this control (see DeKeyser, this volume, for a detailed discussion of cognitive approaches).

---

4 Technically, of course, unanalyzed chunks should be eliminated from the analysis or classified as Stage 1 utterances. However, when there are several different sentences ("How many boys do you have?" How many spaceships do you have?" "How many fish do you have?"), it is more difficult to say with confidence that these are truly "unanalyzed" and therefore not relevant to stage determination. If the criterion for eliminating them is a flexible rule such as "Eliminate utterances that are too far removed from those that are more typical of the learner's behavior," one ends up with a purely circular definition of *stage assignment*.

PRIMING SUBSEQUENT NOTICING

An alternative hypothesis is that the benefit of the instruction did not derive from learners' own production of advanced forms. It might instead have been due to the fact that instruction led learners to notice those forms when they occurred in communicative input (Schmidt, 1990). Clearly, "self-input" was not the only source of correctly formed questions in the input. In normal classroom events, the learners continued to hear many questions.[5] The focused instruction equipped the learners to notice language forms that they did not notice when they focused on meaning. Thus it might be that the benefit they derived was not due to their production of the forms but rather to the attention they gave the forms when they heard them. This role for focused instruction would be in keeping with VanPatten's input processing model for SLA (VanPatten & Cadierno, 1993a).

Of course, these hypotheses about how instruction may have affected the learners' behavior are not mutually exclusive. The evidence does seem to suggest, however, that making "advanced" question types the focus of instruction permitted learners to make progress in their acquisition of this aspect of English, even if the advanced question types were presented in the instruction to learners at Stage 1 or Stage 2. Thus, although immediate effects might be expected if the instruction targets (accidentally or intentionally) a learner's next developmental stage, learners may be able to assimilate advanced-stage input gradually over time, especially if opportunities to use the features continue to occur in meaningful contexts.

Facilitating acquisition by teaching advanced features

Other SLA studies provide evidence that focused instruction can be effective in furthering SLA when it does not specifically target the learner's next stage, or even correspond to it. Several researchers have explored the acquisition of relative clauses in terms of the Keenan and Comrie (1977) Noun Phrase Accessibility Hierarchy (NPAH). This research has shown that, as with all languages of the world, learners' interlanguages relativize syntactic units in a predictable order (Doughty, 1988; Pavesi, 1986). Specifically, languages (and interlanguages) that permit relativization on noun phrases in a given syntactic function also permit relativization on all those "to the left" of it (see Figure 2). For example, the existence of indirect object (IO) relativization in a language (including an interlanguage) implies the presence of subject (SU) and direct object (DO) relativization.

5 Students in the classes in which the research was carried out always had rich communicative language interaction throughout the day. The instruction took up only a fraction of their daily exposure to the language over a period of 2 weeks.

SU > DO > IO > OPREP > GEN > COMP

SU (subject): The man who came to dinner . . .
DO (direct object): The ball that he kicked . . .
IO (indirect object): The child I gave the book to . . .
OPREP (object of preposition): The girl I'm having dinner with . . .
GEN (genitive): The family whose house is next door . . .
COMP (object of comparison): The only colleague I'm older than . . .

Figure 2   Noun phrase accessibility hierarchy (NPAH) for relative clauses (adapted from Keenan and Comrie and applied to SLA research by Gass, 1982; Eckman, Bell, and Nelson, 1988; Doughty, 1991; Hamilton, 1994; and others).

Researchers have found that learners who are taught relative clause types that are well beyond the level at which they are currently operating may progress through several of the levels following instruction (Doughty, 1991; Eckman, Bell, & Nelson, 1988; Gass, 1982; but see footnote 1 in Long & Robinson, this volume). There is some difference among the findings as to whether learners acquire all the relativization positions that are implicated by the one that is taught, that is, to the left of it in Figure 2. In some cases, learners appear to learn the relativization position that is taught as well as all those that are implicated by it. This has led to the "maximality" hypothesis: that all implicated positions will be acquired when a more advanced one is. Further, it was observed in some studies that learners learned *only* the relativization positions to the left of the one that was focused on in instruction. This led to the "unidirectionality" hypothesis: that generalization will take place only to the left of the position taught.

Hamilton (1994) questioned both the maximality and the unidirectionality hypotheses. He suggested that the evidence, in both his study and some of those that preceded his, yielded somewhat ambiguous results regarding these hypotheses.[6] On the one hand, there was evidence that not all learners learned up to and including the level at which they were taught (i.e., the learning was not "maximal"). On the other hand, some learners learned not only up to and including the level at which they had been taught but seemed to have acquired knowledge of the more advanced (nonimplicated) position levels as well (i.e., learning was not "unidirectional"). A study by Ammar (1996) provides further evidence

6 Hamilton's study involved the use of both the NPAH and another implicational framework that he called the *SO hierarchy*. Details of the two hierarchies are beyond the scope of this chapter, but the findings that Hamilton reports are consistent for both with regard to the issues raised here.

for the learners' ability to generalize *beyond* the level at which they were taught.

What was consistent in all the studies, however, was what Hamilton referred to as the *cumulative constraint*. Hamilton's results and those of the other studies confirmed the existence of an implicational relationship, that is, whether or not what they learned went beyond what they were taught, learners followed the same sequence of implicational relationships. Hamilton observed that learners made progress along the relative clause hierarchy, adding positions to the right of those they knew before the instruction, but not necessarily learning the position that was taught or everything to the left of it. Instead, they might simply move a step or two beyond their current level, but always in the predicted sequence, and without skipping steps.

Other research that seems to point to the efficacy of exposing learners to the most advanced features or structures in an implicational relationship is that of Zobl (1985) and of J. White (this volume) on the acquisition of possessive determiners in English by francophone learners. Both Zobl's and J. White's studies show that the most advanced stage has been reached when learners can reliably choose the correct possessive determiner (*his* or *her*) in cases in which the possessed "object" is a human being whose natural gender is different from that of the possessor (e.g., *his mother, her father*) and when body parts (*his arm, her head*) are also matched with the correct possessive determiner.[7] Learners who can do this will also tend to choose the correct forms for inanimate objects possessed, but the reverse is not true (see Figure 3).

Both J. White and Zobl increased students' exposure to correct uses of possessive determiners in contexts in which the meaning was clear. In both studies, students' exposure to these linguistic features was embodied in enhanced input (increased frequency and/or salience of possessive determiners for a limited period of time) rather than more traditional instruction providing rules and explanations. In both studies, learners' developmental stage advanced. Not only the most advanced students but also learners who started at low levels benefited from the focused exposure. In Zobl's study, learners who were exposed only to examples of possessive determiners with human entities (nouns reflecting natural gender) tended to progress more than those exposed only to examples of

---

7 Note that the cross-linguistic problem for body parts is not the same as the one for entities with natural gender. In French, there is a preference for using definite articles rather than possessive determiners with body parts (*Il prend la main de sa mère* = He takes *the* hand of his [feminine agreement] mother). The difficulty with natural gender is the tendency to use the French rule, making the possessive determiner agree with the gender of the possessed rather than that of the possessor. Grammatical gender does not seem to create so lasting a problem. That is, there seems to be a greater tendency to "transfer" natural rather than grammatical gender.

Stage 1: Preemergence – avoidance of *his* and *her* and/or use of definite article instead of *his* or *her.*

The boy gave the boat to the mother.

Stage 2: Preemergence – use of *your* for all persons, genders, and numbers; some very rare uses of *his* or *her.*

The boy gave your boat to your mother.

Stage 3: Emergence* of either or both *his* and *her;* use is occasional but not to criterion.

The boy gave his boat to the mother.

Stage 4: Preference for *his* or *her.*

The boy gave his boat to his mother.

The girl gave his (girl's) boat to his (girl's) mother.

Stage 5: Differentiated use of both *his* and *her,* to criterion with inanimate nouns but not reliably with body parts or "kin-different" nouns (when the gender of the possessor is different from that of the possessed).

The boy gave the boat to her [boy's] mother.

He has Band-Aids on the arm.

Stage 6: Differentiated use of both *his* and *her,* to criterion for inanimate nouns and, in some kin-different contexts, correct for *his* or *her.*

Stage 7: Differentiated use of *his* and *her,* to criterion for inanimate nouns and kin-different human nouns but with errors still made on body parts.

His (boy's) father put Band-Aids on the arm.

Stage 8: Error-free use of *his* and *her* in all contexts, including kin-different natural gender and body parts.

*Stages refined and adapted by J. White (1996), based on research by Zobl (1985). J. White used a minimum number of examples in learners' spontaneous oral production as the criterion for stage assignment.

Figure 3   Stages in the acquisition of possessive determiners.

possessive determiners with nonhuman entities. In J. White's study, very few learners reached what she characterized as *Stage 8* (error-free application in all contexts), but even fewer remained at the lowest stages.

It may be that questions, relative clauses, and possessive determiners are different in terms of the kind of acquisition sequences they represent.

Doughty (1991) has suggested, for example, that, with regard to relative clauses, the developmental progress is from "no relativization" to "some relativization" and that there is no real sequence of development among the individual relative clauses. Furthermore, in the relative clause sequence, performance at any stage can be grammatically correct, whereas performance at earlier stages in the acquisition of questions or possessive determiners entails the production of ungrammatical sentences. Nevertheless, in the research on relative clauses, observations tend to confirm that the presence of certain features in a learner's language implies the previous or concurrent presence of other related features. The features that imply the presence of others, previously or concurrently, are being treated in this context as *more advanced developmentally*. It would be less controversial to say simply that they are *implicationally related*.

Clearly, there are many questions raised by these findings that suggest the need for further research. From a pedagogical perspective, it is important to know whether focus on form that is not timed to match learners' developmental stage is necessarily inefficient or even counterproductive – as suggested in different ways by both Krashen and Pienemann. To this end, it is important to have a clearer understanding of the types of input learners are able to use in pushing their interlanguage development forward.

The notion that only instruction that is "timely" in terms of developmental level is fascinating, and teachers are enthusiastic about finding sequences that will guide their teaching. However, the pedagogical implications of such a recommendation are cause for considerable concern. Some of the problems associated with the implementation of developmentally timed instruction were mentioned earlier in this chapter (Lightbown, 1985a). Another potential problem with such a proposal is that teachers and syllabus writers could come to treat developmental sequences as a new basis for syllabus or materials design, returning to the teaching of language features in isolation, something that no research in SLA or language teaching currently supports (Long, 1985; Long & Robinson, this volume).

In summary, the current state of research on the possible advantages of matching instructional intervention to developmental readiness suggests that we should avoid pushing the idea too far in pedagogical contexts. The evidence, although suggestive, is far from overwhelming that learners benefit only from developmentally matched instruction. Further research may continue to support the hypothesis that, although FonF instruction cannot induce learners to skip stages, providing focus on form – even if it is beyond the next developmental stage that learners are expected to attain – can move learners along the sequence more quickly than they could move without it and lead them further toward mastery (see Long, 1991, 1996). If this is so, then the daunting pedagogical task of selecting teaching points in terms of their developmental appropriateness is somewhat ameliorated. That is, teachers need not fear that they will cause harm by focusing learners' attention on something which is "too advanced." Rather, they can use their knowledge of developmental sequences to shape their own expectations of what learners will be able to do following instruction, not expecting that learners will immediately begin to use the most advanced forms they have been taught, but that they will make developmental progress toward those forms (see Lightbown, 1985b). It is certainly valuable for teachers to know that developmental progress is not always manifested as an immediately higher percentage of accuracy in spontaneous production, and that it takes time for learners to traverse the stages of acquisition of particular linguistic features.

This long-term view of acquisition does not answer the other question posed in this chapter: whether focused instruction should be incorporated into communicative classroom activities or presented separately. Should teachers prepare students for communicative activities by providing information about the linguistic features that are likely to be needed in the communicative task? Or should they intervene only after learners attempt to say something for which they do not yet have adequate linguistic resources? Should focus on form be offered in separate lessons or integrated into communicative interaction? These questions about timing are discussed in the next section.

Integration of attention to form

Some teachers believe that integrating attention to form into communicative activities increases the likelihood that learners will attend to, notice, and then be able to use the information. They expect learners, in these contexts, to make a link between their own intended meaning and the formal feature of language that is focused on. On the other hand, teachers who favor separation of communicative activities and focus on form often do so on the basis of concerns for learners' motivation. They fear that there may be negative affective reactions if learners' attention is drawn to form in any way when they are concerned about expressing a particular meaning.

Exclusive attention to meaning

In the 1960s, when I was first trained as a teacher, and in the 1970s, when I began to do classroom research, almost everything students said during their second or foreign language class was shaped by the teacher's model. Teachers practiced what might be called *preventive pedagogy:* Students were prevented from saying anything unless they had just heard the model they were to echo or had practiced it thoroughly and could say it without making mistakes. Based on an interpretation of psychological learning theory and the descriptive linguistics of the period (see, e.g., Brooks, 1964; Lado, 1964), the principle underlying this approach was the importance of practicing correct forms, which led to the formation of habits and subsequent learning by analogy.

As a result of both changes in linguistic theory and frustration with some of the outcomes of language instruction, this approach was subsequently discredited and replaced by approaches that put more emphasis on getting learners to use language with a focus on meaning. New approaches, often referred to as *communicative language teaching,* were based on recommendations from applied linguists (e.g., Breen & Candlin, 1980; Brumfit & Johnson, 1979). SLA researchers and theorists (e.g., Dulay & Burt, 1975; Krashen, 1982) also encouraged teachers to allow learners to use language freely, to provide substantial amounts of comprehensible input, and not to worry about the production of perfect utterances. Errors were seen as a natural part of language acquisition, and they were expected to work themselves out eventually, if learners remained motivated and if they continued to have access to sufficient comprehensible input and/or opportunities for communicative interaction.

Many teachers resisted this approach for a while, and some have never really accepted this version of communicative language teaching – indeed, some have never accepted any version of communicative or task-based language teaching. Eventually, however, many experienced teachers have come to acknowledge that the old methods were often ineffective, or at least that the new ones were more fun for everyone. And new teachers, trained in university programs by applied linguists who were supporters of the new approach, were convinced from the outset that language teaching that put the emphasis on meaning, not forms, was the "right" way to teach. This now includes a whole range of classroom approaches, from some fairly radical language classes in which there is no practice or speaking at all – only listening and/or reading (see Lightbown, 1992) – through task-based instruction (see Crookes & Gass, 1993a, 1993b; Long & Crookes, 1992), to immersion and other content-based instruction in which language is to be learned incidentally as learners focus on learning history or math (see Doughty & Varela, this volume; Genesee, 1987; Swain & Lapkin, 1982).

The impact of the new approaches to language teaching is often brought home to me when classroom teachers give me minilectures on the value of unfettered communication in the classroom, the power of comprehensible input, and perhaps, above all, the danger of raising the affective filter by correcting learners' errors when they are in the midst of a communicative act (Krashen, 1982)! If language is to be the focus of the learners' attention at any time, they argue, it should be in their home study materials or in a separate lesson. Sometimes these separate lessons may be motivated by consistent errors that the teacher is aware of, but errors should not be pointed out in the midst of a task or other communicative activity. Such a view is explicit, of course, in the "natural approach" of Krashen and Terrell (1983), but I am fascinated by how this has – at least among many teachers – become the new orthodoxy, embraced by many teachers who would not be able to trace its origins.[8]

Continuous integration

The logic of this position is powerful, and it permeates communicative language teaching. I am increasingly convinced, however, that, like the earlier belief in the value of practice (read *rote drill* and *preventive pedagogy*), it is based more on intuition than on what is actually known about SLA. A number of things make me doubt that focus on formS should be restricted to separate language lessons or home study. It is not that I am convinced that these are without value. Indeed, I will mention at least one important role for them. However, it seems increasingly likely to me that this separation was at least part of the reason for the apparent ineffectiveness of the now-rejected traditional approaches to forms-based instruction for promoting spontaneous language development. That is, learners learned to treat *language instruction* as separate from *language use*. This would contribute to a self-fulfilling prophecy along the lines of Krashen's monitor model: that learners would simply store metalinguistic information about the language in one metaphorical place, and interlanguage rules, developed in interactive contexts, in another.

Lyster (1994b) and Swain and Carroll (1987) have observed that it is not the case, as is often believed, that French immersion students are never taught grammar. Indeed, they often have quite significant amounts of formal metalinguistic instruction in language arts periods of their school day. Lessons and exercises on verb conjugations, the intricacies of agreement in the noun phrase, and the correct spelling of homophonous forms (e.g., *c'est, ces, ses*) are typical. However, as a matter of pedagogical principle, when meaning is paramount, for example, in a history or mathematics lesson, many immersion teachers consider error correction and attention to form to be inappropriate.

Furthermore, research on classroom-based second language learning

---

8 Colleagues and students often remind me that this version of communicative language teaching is more prevalent in North America than in most other parts of the world and that it is more typical of second language than of foreign language instruction.

has shown positive results for learners who have experienced an integration of forms and meaning in their instructional environment. Research in intensive ESL classes with young francophone learners has shown that teachers who focus learners' attention on specific language features during the interactive, communicative activities of the class are more effective than those who never focus on form or who do so only in isolated "grammar lessons" (Lightbown, 1991; Lightbown & Spada, 1990; Spada & Lightbown, 1993). These effective teachers tend to provide focus on form on the fly, without causing the interaction to be interrupted or learners to be discouraged. Similarly, Lyster (1994a) described a French immersion teacher he observed who seemed particularly adept at getting learners to correct their own errors. The teacher did this mainly by asking students pertinent questions about how they thought the language worked, always in the context of communicative interaction. Lyster called this *negotiation of form,* something different from the *negotiation of meaning* that is typical of communicative language teaching.

VanPatten's research finding (1990) that learners have difficulty focusing on forms and meaning at the same time might appear to be an argument against the feasibility of integrating attention to form into meaningful interactions. It does not seem so to me. In fact, VanPatten's experimental research on input processing suggests that learners benefit from this joint focus when the form in question is crucial to the meaning being conveyed. It is when the targeted forms (e.g., verb endings) do not contribute crucially to the principal meaning in focus (e.g., inflation in Latin America) that learners experience acute problems in attending to both. When the *form in focus* (e.g., the subject and the object of the verb in a sentence with unfamiliar word order or missing pronouns) is an important carrier of the *meaning in focus* (who did what to whom), learners do benefit from the dual focus on forms and meaning.

There will, of course, be situations when the form that is being targeted is not crucial for the meaning that is in focus. In these cases it may be necessary to stop the communicative activity for a few seconds and to make the focus on form quite explicit – albeit brief. For those few seconds of focus on form, students should know that their attention is being drawn to forms, not meaning. This can help to avoid the situation, so frequent in communicative language teaching, when teachers offer a gentle implicit correction, and learners hear the correction as a continuation of the conversation:

Student: I don't speak very well English.
Teacher: You don't speak English very well?
Student: No.

The student's response is conversationally appropriate but shows no evidence that the corrective feedback has been noticed (Schachter, 1981).

As Lyster and Ranta (1997) found in French immersion classes, when teachers' feedback is provided via recasting, with no explicit indication that form is in focus, students give evidence of uptake only 30% of the time. To be sure, this is not, in itself, proof that the learner did not notice it (see Mackey & Philp, 1998). The challenge of determining what learners actually notice remains a difficult one. However, explicit correction *can* be given without stopping the flow of interaction. It may be sufficient to intervene for less than a minute before resuming the task or conversation at hand. But the explicit focus on form will have been provided at precisely the moment when the learner is able to see the relationship between what was meant and how it should be said. The goal is to ensure that the learner notices a difference between his or her own utterance and the target form. The fact that the learner does not make an immediate behavioral change cannot be taken as evidence that there is no effect of the focus on form. Nor can a corrected response from the learner be taken as evidence that the more correct or advanced form has been integrated into the learner's interlanguage. Nevertheless, a reformulated utterance from the learner gives some reason to believe that the mismatch between learner utterance and target utterance has been noticed, a step at least toward acquisition.

Some further evidence in support of FonF instruction that is made available in the midst of students' attempts to use the language appropriately comes from research by Tomasello and Herron (1988, 1989). They have found evidence for the greater effectiveness of explanation and focus on form during, rather than preceding, learners' attempts to use certain structures of the new language. Their research was carried out in university foreign language classrooms where there was always more emphasis on metalinguistic information and formS-based teaching than is the case in communicative classrooms. Nevertheless, their findings do suggest that learners are better able to attend to and use information that is presented to them at a moment when they are the initiators of the utterance than when the attention to form is presented only "preventively." (See Long, 1996, for extensive discussion of the differences between the Tomasello and Herron research context and procedures and the research carried out in mainly communicative or task-based language teaching.)

Finally, there is a basis for the integration of attention to form within communicative activity in psychological research on learning and memory. This research shows that we remember best when we are back in the context in which the learning took place. Thus, rules and forms learned in isolated grammar lessons may be remembered in similar contexts, but they may be harder to retrieve in the context of communicative interaction (Segalowitz & Gatbonton, 1994). Language features noticed in communicative interaction may be more easily retrieved in such contexts.

Arguments for occasional separation

Notwithstanding the importance of continuous integration of focus on form, I believe there is a role for "grammar instruction" that is separate from communicative activities and yet is integral to the lesson as a whole. For one thing, if there are to be brief and nondisruptive moments of focus on form within communicative events, there needs to be a shorthand that will permit the teacher to communicate concerns about formal aspects of the language in ways that are clear and informative. In separate lessons, learners can be provided with some specific metalinguistic information and explanations of problematic linguistic features. They can also be taught a set of nonverbal signals that the teacher can use to draw their attention to the formal features of what they have just said, as well as – or instead of – to its meaning in a communicative activity. For example, a teacher's raised eyebrows may sometimes be sufficient to elicit self-corrections in learners' utterances (Lightbown & Spada, 1990). Schachter (1981) described a hand signal system that might be effectively used to let learners know that they need to attend to the linguistic form of their utterance. But raised eyebrows and hand signals will not work unless the students have some source of knowledge to call on in order to reflect on what they have just said. That is, there is no point in knowing that they have made an error unless they have some way of knowing what they should have said. If fear of dampening learners' motivation is a concern in error correction, it is certainly the case that to tell a learner that he or she has made an error without providing the means of correcting it would be the most serious threat to motivation.

The brief focus on form in context is not the right moment for explanations or presentations of grammatical points. When explicit grammar teaching is done, however, VanPatten's "input-processing instruction" is a good model of the type of grammar teaching that these separate lessons or minilessons might take (VanPatten & Cadierno, 1993a, 1993b). In these contexts, where the emphasis is on understanding the linguistic features rather than on producing them, students can get clear examples, simple explanations, and some experience in paying attention to one thing at a time. The emphasis in VanPatten's model of instruction is not on rote practice or accuracy in the output but, rather, on developing recognition and understanding of the grammatical features in question. Work on improving output is better done in the context of more interactive activities, in which the main focus is on communication, but in which the accuracy or sophistication of the communication can be improved via focus on form via feedback and learners' self-corrections. Lyster and Ranta (1997) have identified several techniques that French immersion teachers effectively used to elicit self-corrections from students. Another successful model is the intensive, focused recast suggested by Doughty and Varela (this volume).

Related to the issue of integration versus separate lessons is another continuing debate in communicative language teaching: How should teachers decide what linguistic features they will target with focus on form? Should teachers plan tasks or other communicative activities with particular linguistic features in mind? For example, should a teacher plan a unit on biographies of famous people because it will give students an opportunity to hear and use the past tense? Some researchers have proposed the creation of tasks that, by their nature, require the accurate use of a particular feature (Fotos & Ellis, 1991; Loschky & Bley-Vroman, 1993). Some theorists and practitioners object to classroom activities that are planned with specific linguistic features in mind (Long & Robinson, this volume). However, one potential advantage of planning of this kind is the fact that some linguistic features are simply very rare in the "natural" interaction that emerges in activities which are not planned in terms of the linguistic features they may elicit. Thus, strictly meaning- or content-based instruction may leave learners in the position of failing to learn certain language features simply because they are not available in the language that occurs in the classroom environment. This includes such relatively ordinary linguistic features as past tense forms (Harley & Swain, 1984), adverbs (L. White, 1991), and forms of polite address (Lyster, 1994a).

Classroom activities that tend to elicit specific linguistic features need not be awkward and unnatural. They can incorporate the principles of communicative language teaching and task-based instruction while, at the same time, maximizing the likelihood that learners will have adequate opportunity to be exposed to, use, and receive feedback on a wider range of linguistic features. Teachers are not "traitors" to the cause of communicative language teaching if they plan activities in which they know that learners will almost inevitably need to use specific linguistic features. An assessment of learners' needs for language outside the classroom is a useful starting point for creating activities that lead to the use of those features. Alternatively, teachers can analyze existing classroom activities and identify language features that may benefit from some focused attention (Doughty & Varela, this volume).

Conclusion

It is neither necessary nor desirable to attempt to teach students all aspects of the second or foreign language they are learning. That is fortunate, for it is also clear that it would be impossible to do so. There is no doubt that a great deal of language acquisition will take place without focused instruction and feedback, when learners are exposed to comprehensible input and opportunities for meaningful interaction. However, some features of a language are very difficult – or perhaps impossible – to acquire in this way. Future research should focus not only on identifying such features but also on seeking to understand what makes them difficult or impossible to acquire without guidance. Valuable research is currently under way to identify the features for which learners seem most likely to benefit from some kind of focus on form (for some examples of this work, see Doughty & Williams, Chapter 10, this volume; Harley, 1993; Long, 1996; L. White, 1991).

Knowing which features are likely to benefit from or require focus on form is one step toward providing second language instruction that takes account of the psycholinguistic facts of second language acquisition. Knowing *when* to offer such focus on form is another step. There is a need for considerably more research that starts from this question.

10 Pedagogical choices in focus on form

Catherine Doughty
Jessica Williams

Introduction

In this final chapter we attempt to place the research findings presented in this volume, as well as the body of research that has motivated our studies, firmly into the context of the language teaching professional. From our perspective, the fundamental goal in the classroom is to teach language for communication. Accordingly, the larger context of interpreting focus-on-form (FonF) research must be the act of communication and the development of communicative competence. Ultimately, the aim of FonF studies is to determine how learner approximation to the target can be improved through instruction that draws attention to form but is not isolated from communication. Thus, precisely whether, when, and how to facilitate the deployment of language forms to accomplish a communicative purpose in a language classroom is the context of the discussion in which we engage in this chapter.

To frame the discussion, we briefly examine a range of classroom learning contexts and conditions that necessarily have an impact upon FonF considerations. We then address six pedagogical decisions in detail. We first tackle the question that may be in the mind of the skeptical reader and certainly has been a subject of discussion in the SLA research literature: Should there be any attention to language form at all? After some discussion of arguments outright against, and, after noting the very few language forms that may not be amenable to instructional intervention, plus the somewhat greater number of easily learned forms for which focus on form may be unnecessary, we take the decision that some focus on form is applicable to the majority of linguistic code features that learners must master. This is mainly because second language learning is not identical to first language learning, and so we do not consider leaving learners to their own devices to be the best plan. Does this mean that practitioners should take up the opposite position – that focus on form is appropriate for all forms for all learners all the time? We think not and believe that, between the two poles, there are many ensuing pedagogical decisions to be made. At the outset, it must be said that it is not the case that adult SLA cannot take place in the absence of instructional focus on form; for many learners, clearly much of it can. However, our interest is not limited to what is merely possible, but extends to a determination of what would comprise the most effective and efficient instructional plan given the normal constraints of acquiring a second language in the classroom.

We will break down this complex determination and look at each part of it in turn. An obvious pedagogical choice to be made is whether to take a proactive or reactive stance to focus on form. That is to say, a proactive approach would entail selecting *in advance* an aspect of the target to focus on, whereas a reactive stance would require that the teacher notice and be prepared to handle various learning difficulties as they arise. In our opinion, the jury is still out regarding which of these two stances is more appropriate. Furthermore, since both are reasonable, in the end it may turn out to be the case that both are effective, depending upon the classroom context. Thus, in this chapter we discuss the merits and disadvantages of each approach.

In the case of the proactive stance, for which the teacher must make a determination as to which form – among the language forms that are potentially good candidates for focus – to select for attention at any particular time, we base our suggestions on interwoven considerations of individual learner differences, developmental language learning sequences, input quality, formal and functional complexity, and L1 influence on SLA processes. Thus, although preselection of forms may, at first blush, resemble traditional structural approaches, in fact, it stands in sharp contrast to curricula and texts that present isolated forms in sequences based on intuition.

We next turn our attention to the pedagogical decisions that must be made in planning the implementation of focus on form once the choice to do so has been made, and, with the exception of purely reactive focus on form, the target of instruction has been identified. Throughout this discussion of implementing focus on form, we attempt to keep in mind the language learning goals that teachers and learners set at various stages of language acquisition, as a guide to determining whether and when to focus on form along the way to fluent and accurate L2 use. In other words, some learners may require more attention to form than others, given their relative and differing aims for ultimate attainment, as well as the wide range of classroom contexts and pedagogical choices. Furthermore, since we believe that these decisions are necessarily based on the teacher's understanding of the language learning process, the implementation decisions are discussed in the context of our views on the nature of SLA.

Once it has been decided which forms to address, perhaps the most vexing decision concerns the degree of explicitness of FonF activities. As can be seen across the contributions to this volume, the extent to which attention to form should be explicit is still largely a matter of debate (see especially the chapters by DeKeyser, Harley, and Swain in this volume). In other words, should tasks and/or techniques aim to draw learner attention to form unobtrusively or, instead, to direct learner attention to the problem area more explicitly? Will focus on form involve mere enhancement of the materials themselves so that the learners will notice target forms, or will it include an attempt to teach them in the more traditional sense? Will the goal be to engage particular language learning processes and, if so, which ones? It is apparent that in earlier approaches to second language teaching and learning, the attention to forms was too heavy and isolated, but it is not clear how much directed attention is needed to be effective. Therefore, we discuss practical issues, such as separation versus integration of attention to form into a communicative lesson. Then, in addition to detailing how various researchers have operationalized and, thereby, implemented focus on form, we discuss the contexts in which each type of task may or may not be effective. The more unobtrusive the nature of the focus on form, the more important the pedagogical consideration of task demands on the linguistic production of learners becomes. In the L2 curriculum section, we discuss overall curricular integration, as well as the factors of intensity and duration of the focus on form. Finally, we provide a taxonomy of tasks, ranging from those that require implicit attention to form to those that require explicit attention.

By way of summarizing what we have just outlined, the six pedagogical decisions that we consider in light of both the contributions to this volume and the wider body of FonF empirical research are listed here:

Decision 1   Whether or not to focus on form
Decision 2   Reactive versus proactive focus on form
Decision 3   The choice of linguistic form
Decision 4   Explicitness of focus on form
Decision 5   Sequential versus integrated focus on form
Decision 6   The role of focus on form in the curriculum

We turn now to a consideration of the classroom context in which teachers must make these decisions.

The classroom context for focus on form

In attempting to maximize any pedagogical strategy, it is important not to accept blanket edicts, but instead to take into account the differing circumstances under which classroom SLA takes place. In this volume alone, several different learner populations and learning contexts are represented, and these differences may have important consequences for decisions regarding focus on form. In the French immersion classrooms of Ontario, Canada, such as those described by Swain or Harley (both this volume), for instance, many students are highly proficient (for their age levels). Although they hear and use little French outside of school, in the classroom they have had years of meaning-focused input, as well as many output opportunities. Viewed in terms of Skehan's (1996) three goals for language instruction, their language is *fluent* and *complex,* and yet their level of *accuracy,* even in basic areas, such as gender assignment and auxiliary choice, remains low. This situation differs markedly from that of the students in J. White's study (this volume). These learners are in an intensive ESL program in Quebec and do not receive instruction in the second language in content classes, except for a half year of study at grade 5 or 6. The rest of their second language study is limited to 2 hours per week, and they are considerably less proficient than the learners in the Swain study. They report using only French outside of school, reminiscent of an EFL situation.

Compare this to ESL contexts in the United States described in this volume (Doughty & Varela; Williams & Evans). First, and perhaps most important, they are second language contexts in which often the second language is both the object and the medium of instruction. In addition, the target language is generally available outside of the classroom. Like the learners in Swain's study, some of these learners are fluent but inaccurate producers; others lack fluency as well. These characteristics would have important consequences for decisions regarding focus on form. For instance, a teacher in this context could feel comfortable with an unobtrusive FonF activity designed to get learners to notice a form in their input, knowing that there is plenty of input available to the learners. This contrasts with the input of foreign language learners, for instance, learners of English as a foreign language in traditional classroom settings, such as those found in Japan or Korea, or learners of a variety of foreign languages in the United States, who present a very different profile (DeKeyser, this volume). Most have had years of overtly metalinguistic instruction and yet have had limited meaning-focused input and few opportunities for output. In addition, there may be institutional and cultural limitations on pedagogical practices, such as large class size or a tradition of teacher- or exam-centered language instruction. It is unlikely that they will benefit from the kind of output activities advocated by Swain for metalinguistic reflection. On the other hand, some of the other FonF activities might well facilitate the additional functions of output described by Swain: noticing and hypothesis testing. Any of these learning context variables can influence whether and what kinds of focus on form are implementable, a consideration that will be important to bear in mind as we examine the six pedagogical decisions that arise when focusing on form.

Decision 1: Whether or not to focus on form

It is possible in the case of some or, by a few accounts, all aspects of language that instruction is not necessary, or at least is not an efficient use of time and resources, which are already woefully inadequate in many language programs. There may be a number of reasons to think so. First, there is the somewhat fuzzy notion of "easy rules," which perhaps need not be taught. However difficult such a concept is to state theoretically, most teachers have an intuitive sense that there are certain aspects of the target grammar, perhaps for example, basic word order (Rutherford, 1983) or even aspects of the phonological system (Eckman, 1977), that come to learners fairly easily. These will be treated at greater length later (see the section Decision 3). In contrast, there are some forms, such as the English article system, that seem strangely impermeable to instruction and so, for that reason alone, perhaps should not take up valuable class time (Celce-Murcia & Larsen-Freeman, 1983; although see Master, 1994, 1995; Mellow, Reeder, & Forster, 1996; Muranoi, 1996).

More recently, some theory-driven research has suggested other reasons for why instruction may not be needed. It has been claimed that forms need not be taught if they are a part of Universal Grammar (UG). (See also DeKeyser, this volume.) If the assumption is made that UG in some form remains accessible to adult second language learners, then, in order for these forms to emerge in the learners' interlanguage (IL), all that is needed is triggering evidence in the target language (TL) input. In this sense, forms need not be taught because they do not have to be learned; they simply emerge as appropriate data interact with UG, in a process similar to the one of grammar development in children learning their first language.

There is some debate on the nature of that triggering evidence. The issue is whether positive evidence, that is, information about what is possible in the target language, is the driving force (Carroll, 1996; Schwartz, 1993), or whether negative evidence, that is, information about what is not possible in the language, may also be necessary or at least helpful (Lyster & Ranta, 1997; Oliver, 1995; Trahey & L. White, 1993; L. White, 1987, 1991). Schwartz has argued that instruction that includes negative evidence has little impact on forms within UG anyway, since it will change (temporarily) only language behavior and not IL grammars. In this view, changes in IL grammar occur solely in response to positive linguistic evidence. If this is the case, it would mean that all explicit instruction and corrective feedback could be immediately abandoned for these forms. The question of the utility of negative evidence becomes particularly important if the L2 structure stands in a subset relation with a related L1 form, since this situation would require that learners withdraw from a UG-based hypothesis, one presumably based on their L1. It has been suggested that negative evidence is at least helpful (Lin & Hedgcock, 1996; Mackey & Philp, 1997; Oliver, 1995), and perhaps necessary, in these cases (Long, 1996; L. White, 1991).

If a UG-based explanation were to prevail, regardless of whether a role for explicit and negative evidence in SLA is rejected or accepted, then teachers would simply have to wait for the results of linguistic research to determine precisely what resides in UG and do their best to provide the appropriate triggering data in their classes. This route has been suggested by Cook, who states: "As the Universal Grammar in the student's mind is so powerful, there is comparatively little for the teacher to do" (1991, p. 119). Although this point of view is theoretically plausible, it is not likely that the suggestion that teachers contribute little to classroom language learning will have much resonance for classroom teachers. Furthermore, we could make the observation that any useful change in linguistic behavior, irrespective of changes in competence, would be perfectly acceptable to many language educators. Indeed, many researchers are convinced that adult SLA is not at all the same process as child first language acquisition, and thus that Cook's proclamation is not helpful. That is to say, even if the UG in the child's mind is powerful, adults may rely on entirely different, perhaps general cognitive (i.e., nonlanguage-specific) and/or problem-solving processes, during SLA.

So far then, it has been suggested that focus on form might be ineffective on two counts: first, because it is unnecessary, and second, perhaps less plausibly, because it cannot result in real change. The second position also finds some support in the notion of a critical period, especially as it applies to specific aspects of IL development. It has been suggested, for instance, that older learners will never fully master the target system (Long, 1990, 1993), either its phonological aspects (Scovel, 1988) or even some aspects of syntax (Coppieters, 1987; Johnson & Newport, 1989). Although putative counterexamples to both these claims have been presented (Birdsong, 1992; Flege, 1987), in general, it has frequently been demonstrated that ultimate levels of L2 attainment are widely variable and, indeed, usually fall short of nativelike. Pedagogical questions, however, are quite different from those regarding ultimate attainment that bedevil researchers. It has not been claimed, for instance, that adult learners are completely impermeable to instruction in these aspects of IL development, that is, that instruction has *no* effect. Rather, the claim is a more limited one: It may be impossible for even the best adult second language learner to reach a level of competence such that he or she is indistinguishable from a native speaker (though see L. White & Genesee, 1996). However, since attainment of native speaker ability is not necessarily the goal of second language learners or teachers, these research results can only temper instructional strategies; they cannot guide them. Even if a learner's eventual attainment falls short of native speaker status, there is still much work to be done along the way to largely fluent and accurate target language use.

Perhaps the greatest impediments to the introduction of focus on form in L2 classrooms have been the influential claims of the "noninterface position" proposed by Krashen. These claims emanate from the learning/

acquisition hypothesis of his Monitor Theory of SLA, in which it is proposed that knowledge of consciously learned language is distinct from unconsciously acquired language knowledge (dual representation), that only the latter can be deployed in fluent (unmonitored) language use, and, furthermore, that there can be no interaction between the two knowledge systems (Krashen, 1982, 1985). In particular, "learned" knowledge can never become "acquired" knowledge.[1] The impact of these claims is exacerbated by the consistent and pervasive observation of classroom language learner performance that reveals two kinds of language use: fluent use of language, which seemingly involves intuitive knowledge, and more deliberate language use, which appears to depend upon expressible linguistic knowledge. Whereas there is little disagreement that both kinds of performance exist, what kind of knowledge underlies each and whether there is any connection between the two during SLA and use are issues that are far from resolved.

It is well known that proponents of this position, which Long and Robinson (this volume) refer to as the *noninterventionist position,* see no role for focus on form in language teaching (Krashen, 1992).[2] However, it should be pointed out that noninterventionists have not, as yet, provided any other *expedient* solution to the lack of adult classroom L2 learner accuracy. The dual-representation plus noninterface claims have been particularly problematic, since they have perpetuated the notion that the only effective kind of learning is learning that occurs without conscious awareness and without tangible understanding. Furthermore, placing the emphasis on acquiring intuitive, implicit knowledge has made the teaching-for-accuracy problem unresolvable because the way in which implicit knowledge is gained cannot be explained in any but the most abstract terms (e.g., "only by comprehensible input"; see also the chapters by DeKeyser and Lightbown, this volume). In other words, the lack of an explanation for how to remedy any specific language learning problems has led directly to the laissez-faire attitude toward the development of learner accuracy that we have noted.

Dissatisfaction with the constructs of Monitor Theory has led researchers to examine more deeply the dimensions of learning and performance in linguistic and other domains and has given rise to many alternative views of the mental representation of second language knowledge.[3] Two plausible positions – one retaining the dual (or even multiple) repre-

1 Unless otherwise defined, as done here, the terms *learning* and *acquisition* are used synonymously throughout this chapter.
2 For a more extensive discussion, the reader is referred to an interesting *TESOL Quarterly* exchange (Vols. 26/2 and 27/4) between Krashen (1992, 1993) and Lightbown and Pienemann (1993).
3 By *mental representation*, we mean how language is stored in the brain (i.e., in memory).

sentation of language knowledge but positing a synergy among levels (Carr & Curran, 1994), and the other severely limiting the role of implicit knowledge (Bialystok, 1994a) – will be discussed briefly here with the aim of dismantling the learning/acquisition distinction and, consequently, removing this barrier to teachers' and learners' attending to form in the L2 classroom. At issue for both alternative theories is the teasing apart of learning (processes) and mental representation (memory) in terms of their implicit versus explicit qualities and the causal relations among processes and knowledge.

The multiple representation model suggests that both implicitly and explicitly processed instances of a linguistic feature can be stored as implicit knowledge (e.g., remembering a set of examples) and then, through the additional processes of cognitive comparison and abstraction, can become represented as rule-based knowledge (i.e., in such a way that the knowledge contained in the examples can be deployed in previously unencountered linguistic situations; Carr & Curran, 1994). According to this model, it is not the degree of implicitness that leads to successful SLA; rather, success depends instead on what kind of cognitive processing engages the implicitly *or* explicitly stored language knowledge (see the section on Decision 4 for discussion of how this happens).

An alternative possibility, explored in the second alternative model, is that the only truly implicit knowledge is limited to innate linguistic knowledge.[4] The innate knowledge serves to structure all incoming input, and more important, language acquisition processes are geared toward the entire system becoming more explicitly represented in terms of the target language(s) (Bialystok, 1994a). The advantage here is that this model leaves aside the difficult problem of determining how learners can acquire implicit knowledge by claiming that all implicit knowledge is innate language knowledge and that all language knowledge, whether innate or subsequently acquired, becomes more and more detailed and language-specific in its representation through the two psycholinguistic processes of *analysis* (e.g., figuring out the rules of the linguistic system) and *restructuring* (e.g., organizing those rules for efficient and fluent use). As is the case with the multilevel representation of knowledge, no one kind of learning is claimed to lead to a particular (or even desirable) kind of knowledge representation. Instead, all internalized linguistic knowledge is always moving in the direction of more analyzed, detailed, and targetlike representation. Furthermore, in contrast to the noninterface position, these models propose a strong interface that allows for the interaction between implicit and explicit knowledge during language acquisition. Thus these researchers suggest that teachers are not faced with the impossible task of bringing learners to high levels of accuracy solely

---

4 Bialystok remains neutral as to the nature of innate knowledge, leaving open the possibilities of UG principles and parameters or cognitive or semantic primitives.

via indefinable, implicit language acquisition but, rather, can depend upon the learners' cognitive processing capabilities to integrate explicitly learned and represented knowledge into the developing IL system, thus permitting a role for focus on form in instruction.

Summary

In this section, we have considered the overarching decision of whether or not, in principle, to focus on form in the L2 classroom. Although we disagree with the complete prohibition of its use by the "noninterventionist" and the "no negative evidence" positions, we recognize that some forms do not need or may not benefit from instructional focus. Far more of language, however, is likely to be more efficiently acquired in the L2 classroom with the kind of instruction that engages the cognitive processing ability of the learners. The job of the teacher then becomes one of providing assistance to the learner, who needs to attend to particular aspects of language in order to analyze them, to compare them to the developing IL, and to restructure the developing IL for more efficient use. For this, teachers need to stay informed about empirical research on the psycholinguistic processing that occurs during SLA. We will take up these considerations as we discuss the remaining pedagogical decisions to be made, once the decision to focus on form has been taken.

Decision 2: Reactive versus proactive focus on form

A major curricular choice involves whether to be proactive or reactive in focusing on form. That is to say, teachers can plan in advance to ensure that a focus on form will occur, or they can wait for a pressing learner need to arise and develop an "on-the-spot" FonF lesson in response. The reactive stance is the approach that Long (1991) appeared to have in mind in the conceptualization of focus on form:

> [W]hereas the content of lessons with a focus on *forms* is the *forms* themselves, a syllabus with a focus on *form* teaches something else – biology, mathematics, workshop practice, automobile repair, the geography of a country where the foreign language is spoken, the cultures of its speakers, and so on – *and overtly draws students' attention to linguistic elements as they arise incidentally in lessons whose overriding focus is on meaning or communication.* (Long, 1991, pp. 45–46; latter emphasis ours)

Long continues to define *focus on form* as a responsive teaching intervention that involves occasional shifts in reaction to salient errors using devices to increase perceptual salience (Long & Robinson, this volume). The reactive stance would seem to be most congruent with the general aims of communicative language teaching. In other words, when in the course of communicating a message, a second language learner is frequently inaccurate, the teacher – or another learner (Williams, 1997) – could draw attention to the problem. There are several additional advantages to adopting the reactive stance. For instance, the burden of choosing which form to focus on is eased somewhat (see the section on Decision 3). The choice is restricted to classroom learner errors that are "pervasive," "systematic," and known to be "remediable" for learners at this stage of development (Long, 1991, 1996; Long & Robinson, this volume). In addition, it appears that recasts of learner utterances are more effective than teacher models (cf. Long, Inagaki, & Ortega, 1998; Ortega & Long, 1997). Thus the main concern of the teacher who takes a reactive stance is to resist attending to errors that, for reasons we outlined earlier, may not be amenable to focus on form. Furthermore, according to Long, the teacher also needs to be aware of the constraints of developmental readiness (see also Pienemann, 1987, 1989; the section Decision 3). In other words, teachers should not aim any instructional intervention too far beyond the developmental stage of the learners. Lightbown (this volume), however, warns against pushing this idea too far in the classroom and proposes several convincing arguments against teaching *only* to the next phase of any developmental sequence:

1. In most classrooms, this is impractical, given the wide range of learner abilities.
2. Learners do internalize advanced language, and this can eventually become auto-input for future restructuring.
3. Learners acquire knowledge first and then gain control over that knowledge (and, to our way of thinking, perhaps control over knowledge is what is constrained by development).
4. Focus on form causes later noticing in the input that facilitates the internalization of the input.

Even if the constraints of developmental readiness are loosened, reactive focus on form may still be difficult in practice, particularly when there are learners of different L1s, of differing abilities, or of such high ability that errors go unnoticed by the teacher or other learners, since the message is successfully delivered. The reactive stance may be most appropriate when the learners are of the same L1 background, and the teacher is experienced enough to have some idea of what to expect. Furthermore, it has to be said that reactive focus on form, by its very "on-demand" nature, places considerable requirements on the teacher's "on-line" capacity to notice and assess the need for the intervention, and instantly to devise consistent FonF interventions for learner errors, even as he or she must attend to other pedagogical problems.

Perhaps a testament to the difficulty of an entirely reactive focus on form is that there are few classroom studies that have investigated the effectiveness of such a completely unplanned instructional intervention.

Indirect evidence may be gleaned, however, from the teaching practice of a "wayward" control group teacher who focused on form even though it was believed that she, like previously observed teachers, was purely communicative in her approach to language teaching (Spada & Lightbown, 1993). Her technique was to correct learner errors and to remind students of a metalinguistic lesson that she had apparently provided at an earlier class session. Further indirect evidence may be marshaled from controlled experimental studies that have investigated classroomlike behaviors. Carroll and Swain (1993) compared various types of responses to learner errors in English double object dative alternation, all of which were more effective than no response:

[1]   Responses to learner error

Treatment A: Explicit hypothesis rejection

Expect an explanation   Response = "Wrong" plus metalinguistic
statement

Treatment B: Explicit utterance rejection

Expect an indication   Response = "Wrong"
of correctness

Treatment C: Implicit negative feedback

Expect a correction   Response = Recast

Treatment D: Implicit negative feedback

Expect a cue   Response = "Are you sure?"

Since the L2 subjects were told what kind of response to expect and that the information would be related to the quality of their utterances, and since the measure of success was simply telling the researchers which sentences in a list could alternate, these findings must be interpreted with great caution. In real classrooms, learners are often faced with the problem of what is called in the first language literature *blame assignment,* which means that they must figure out what is at fault in their utterance when they receive a response from the teacher. Nonetheless, if a reactive approach to focus on form is to succeed, then it seems that the pedagogical emphasis must be placed on developing a repertoire of techniques that can be easily deployed as needed.

In a classroom study of the effectiveness of various feedback techniques, Lyster and Ranta (1997) found that recasts – although the most widespread response to learner error – were, in fact, the least effective in eliciting immediate revision by learners of their output, what they term *uptake* (although see Doughty & Varela, this volume). Instead, the provision of metalinguistic clues, clarification requests, repetition of learner error, and teacher elicitation of a repaired response were the most effective in stimulating learner-generated repairs. However, uptake may not be the most revealing indication of acquisition, a process that is not usually instantaneous. In fact, in an experimental study, Mackey and Philp (1998) found a delayed effect for intensive recasting of questions. Clearly, the effectiveness of the techniques described in Example 1 should be tested in a classroom-based study; if the findings are confirmed, this would suggest that such responses may be added to the teacher's repertoire of reactive FonF techniques.

In the majority of language class settings, however, a more proactive FonF approach is likely to be more feasible. In other words, the teacher may want to make an informed prediction or carry out some observations to determine the learning problem in focus. For instance, the language learner's often observed predilection for forming useful generalizations across similar contexts can be utilized by the teacher in predicting learning problems and developing tasks that lead students to greater accuracy. Tomasello and Herron (1988, 1989) have demonstrated that, when learners are in the process of generalizing and make an error of overgeneralization, a very effective technique is to point out this error at the moment the generalization is made, for example:

[2] Garden path technique

The path
C'est le tableau de Monet. C'est son tableau.
This is Monet's painting. It's his painting.

C'est la sculpture de Monet. C'est sa sculpture.
C'est l'art (art = M) de Monet. C'est son art.

The exception (use the masculine *son* for vowel-initial feminine nouns)
C'est l'image (image = F) *de Monet. C'est son image.*

(Tomasello & Herron, 1988, p. 241)

This so-called garden path technique was shown to be more effective than telling learners in advance about a linguistic regularity plus its exception (see Beck & Eubank, 1991; Long, 1996, however, for discussions of the methodological problems of this study). Strictly speaking, this is not yet a FonF technique, since the main aim of the lesson was to elicit sentences with the grammatical generalization and there were no subsequent communicative activities (see the sections on Decision 5 and Decision 6). Furthermore, the assessment of language ability was a set of rather discrete point tests, such as filling in the blank. Nonetheless, this technique would seem to be a promising one to try in more communicative lessons. An example of this is to have the students judge a fashion show (adapted from Stein, 1995), providing them in advance with carefully ordered adjectives that characterize the prizes to be awarded. The ordering would lead students to overgeneralize – in this case twice, as indicated by the asterisks in Example 3 – and the teacher would then point out the error. Tomasello and Herron stress the importance of indicating to students that they have made a *logical* error, one based on the natural process of generalizing to new contexts:

[3]   Garden path adjectives

Path
cute   the cutest
sexy   the sexiest
grand   the grandest

Exception
beautiful   the *beautifulest → Point out error here

Path
outrageous   the most outrageous
expensive   the most expensive

Exception
good   the *goodest or *the most good → Point out error here

Not all learning processes are as predictable as is the tendency toward overgeneralization. Consequently, one of the greatest problems of the proactive stance is to get the learning difficulty to occur in the classroom discourse in such a way that it can subsequently be brought into focus. In other words, once a learning problem has been identified, and the teacher has some basis upon which to believe that an instructional intervention would be effective, he or she must develop a task in which learners are guided to comprehend or produce messages involving the learning difficulty. Loschky and Bley-Vroman (1993) have identified three degrees of involvement of a linguistic form in a task: task naturalness, task utility, and task essentialness, defined as follows:

In task-naturalness, a grammatical construction may arise naturally during the performance of a particular task, but the task can often be performed perfectly well, even quite easily, without it. In the case of task-utility, it is possible to complete a task without the structure, but with the structure, the task becomes easier. The most extreme demand a task can place on a structure is essentialness: the task cannot be successfully performed unless the structure is used. (p. 132)

For the purposes of focus on form, task essentialness would be most useful, particularly when a proactive rather than a reactive approach to a known learning problem has been decided upon. However, as Loschky and Bley-Vroman admit, such tasks are difficult to conceive of. They suggest that task essentialness can more easily be incorporated into comprehension tasks, whereas production tasks may only rarely go beyond fostering task naturalness or task utility. An example of a task in which it is essential that the learner grasp a formal distinction is the input-processing, match-the-picture task in Example 4 (Cadierno, 1992). For this task, the student has to imagine that he or she is one of the characters in the picture (women or girls imagine that they are the female character, and men or boys that they are the male one). While viewing pictures that clearly show either a man looking for a woman or a woman looking for a man, students listen to sentences and select the picture in which the message of the sentence is true *for their situation,* as in Example 4:

[4]   Match the picture.

    A. *Te busca el señor.*   versus   B. *Tu buscas al señor.*
       The man is looking for you.   You are looking for the
                                                         man.

The key distinctions to be made are the subject and object markers (the pronouns *tu* and *te;* with or without the preposition *a* in *al* and *el*). Note that even if the more natural *Buscas al señor* is used as sentence B, the distinction is still almost as hard to hear, because the student is more likely to be attending to the end of the utterance, where the distinction between *el señor* and *al señor* is merely the slight difference between two vowels /ɛ/ and /a/.

Production involving task essentialness is much harder to achieve, in the sense that the communicative goals and the FonF goals may come most into conflict. Getting the learner to produce *anything meaningful* could be thwarted by any teacher control. Perhaps the dictogloss described by Swain (this volume; see also Wajnryb, 1990) offers a partial solution. In the dictogloss, texts are created that contain forms known to be difficult for students. Students hear the text and work together with a peer to reconstruct it exactly. The effect of the goal of exactness is that students negotiate the forms that are difficult for them to produce on their own. Even so, LaPierre (reported in Swain, this volume) has pointed out that students do not always negotiate the forms that were thought to be in focus in the texts.

Given that task essentialness is an elusive component, task naturalness and task utility may be more realistic to aim for in developing classroom activities. For instance, in describing the steps of an experiment conducted during a previous class, it is most *natural* to use past tense ("First we measured the distance"), though students may avoid the past by using a more instructional mode of discourse ("First you measure the distance") (Doughty & Varela, this volume). Example 3 shows the *utility* (bordering on essentialness) of adjectives in judging any kind of contest for the purpose of awarding prizes. Which of these levels of form involvement in tasks to aim for will depend primarily on the length of time the teacher has to bring learners to the desired level of accuracy. If class time is short, materials preparation ensuring task essentialness will be time well spent.

Summary

In this section, we have considered the decision of whether to take a proactive or a reactive approach to focus on form. At the present time, there is no definitive research upon which to base a choice of one over the other; rather, it seems likely that both approaches are effective, depending upon the classroom circumstances (but see Ortega & Long, 1997). The implications of the choice are, nevertheless, important, for they involve different emphases in curricular planning: Reactive focus on form involves developing the ability to notice pervasive errors and have at the ready techniques for drawing learners' attention to them. On the other hand, proactive focus on form emphasizes the design of tasks that ensure that opportunities to use problematic forms while communicating a message will indeed arise.

Decision 3: The choice of linguistic form

Particularly in the case of more proactive focus on form, in which the decision has been made in advance to attend to a specific learning problem, and tasks are to be designed in which a particular form is natural, useful, or essential, the next critical decision is that of *which* particular form to focus upon. (In the case of reactive focus on form, the consideration is more one of which problematic forms *not* to react to.) Since it is widely accepted that not all grammatical structures are acquired in the same way (Larsen-Freeman, 1995), a logical extension of this assumption would be that instruction, including focus on form, should not be applied to all forms in the same way (see Hulstijn, 1995, for a related discussion). In this section, therefore, we examine how forms may differ with respect to the effectiveness of focus on form, and how teachers can make informed choices among forms.

Several avenues may be followed in determining what feature of the L2 should be in focus during instruction. In our discussion of these possibilities, the terms *form* and *rule* are both used, since learners are engaged in acquiring both. That is to say, SLA is essentially a process of working out the entire system of the L2, a system that is composed of interrelated forms. Put simply, rules describe the realization, distribution, and use of forms. Thus, for us, both forms and rules are subsumed by the more comprehensive term *form*. Furthermore, it is important to note that every hierarchical level of language – from phonology to morphosyntax to the lexicon to discourse and pragmatics – is composed of both forms (e.g., phonemes, morphemes, lexical items, cohesive devices, and polite-ness markers) and rules (e.g., devoicing, allomorphy, agreement, colloca-tion, anaphora, and in-group vs. out-group relationships).

Thus, although SLA is most often thought of in terms of the develop-ment of the IL sound system and grammar, other levels of linguistic form cannot be ignored as potential candidates for focus on form. This view counters the common, perhaps justified, but nonetheless *mis*perception of focus on form seen here:

> We must note, however, that the notion of "focus on form" has typically been understood as focus primarily on the grammatical regularities of the "linguistic code features" . . . of the L2, whereas the direct approach we have in mind would also include a focus on higher level organizational principles or rules and normative patterns or conventions governing language use beyond the sentence level (e.g., discourse rules, pragmatic awareness, strategic competence) as well as lexical formulaic phrases. (Celce-Murcia, Dörnyei, & Thurrell, 1997, p. 147)

In fact, focus on form embraces this "direct approach." For example, even though it is commonly held that vocabulary is best acquired in purely meaning-focused instruction, and Krashen (1989) maintains that extensive reading is the best route in lexical acquisition (this position is labeled *context alone* by Coady, 1997, p. 275), it is likely that focus on form can enhance lexical acquisition. Indeed, several contributors to this volume assume that this is the case and have referred to lexical examples in their discussion of focus on form (e.g., Long & Robinson, this volume; Swain, this volume). And, there is mounting evidence that, in the acquisi-tion of lexical items, as with that of grammatical structures, some inter-vention is helpful (see Coady, 1997, for review). Paribakht and Wesche (1997) and Zimmerman (1997) provide the clearest evidence of the supe-riority of reading plus contextualized vocabulary instruction over reading alone. Furthermore, although there is, as yet, little evidence of the efficacy of attention to the form of language at the discourse and pragmatic levels, we believe that the principle will still apply. Thus, it is important to see the term *form* in the broadest possible context, that is, that of all the levels and components of the complex system that is language. With this in mind, we turn now to a detailed consideration of several important fac-tors that should inform the decision regarding which particular aspect of form to focus upon.

Perhaps the most obvious is the time-honored tradition of choosing forms that appear to be problematic for a particular group of learners; this, of course, is one choice implicit in reactive focus on form. Learner error or difficulty comprises the basis of most proactive remedial ap-proaches to instruction (R. Ellis, 1993) and has high face validity, in that teachers are closely connected to instructional decisions. Another advan-tage of this approach is that information about learner error is quickly and easily accessible for action research by teachers (see Nunan, 1992). We need not wait for the results of extensive experimental research to implement decisions regarding focus on form in instruction. However, teacher intuition and needs assessment evidence of learner difficulty alone may be insufficient or, at least, may not be the most efficient basis for making instructional choices. Unless more is known about why specific learners commit these particular errors at a given time in their language development, teachers' efforts to correct them may be futile.

For instance, it may be that learners demonstrate difficulty precisely because they are not ready to learn a particular form, or because they are thinking about something else, or because the linguistic regularity is too complex to be learned in the way that it is being presented. There may be many reasons for learner error, and simply focusing on the form again and again may not always be the solution. Therefore, although learner profiles are an appealing starting point for decisions regarding focus on form, those decisions informed by research on learning and learnability may be more efficient and more effective in the long run. As we will note later, however, this by no means suggests that the status of a given form in a learner's IL should be left out of consideration. Rather, it indicates that a simple error analysis may not be a sufficient basis for pedagogical choices.

Basing decisions on research results is not without its own problems, however. Many SLA researchers have been warning for years that we should be careful about extrapolating from experimental results and/or mining experimental results for classroom applications (Hatch, 1978; Lightbown, 1985b). One of the biggest obstacles is that such research often produces conflicting results. Lightbown (1985a) describes the by now familiar conundrum presented by research on acquisition orders. Pienemann (1987, 1989) maintains that, within developmental sequences, it is not possible for learners to acquire, and, therefore, it is not possible to teach, structures that are far beyond the learner's current stage of development. In other words, it is not possible to skip steps in an established sequence. Although Pienemann's original work was primarily on word order rules in German, he and others have sought to extend this notion of teachability to other languages and other aspects of morphosyntax (Pienemann & Johnston, 1986; Spada & Lightbown, 1993). Apparently contradictory results are found in "projection studies," in which learners were given instruction on structures that were more than one step ahead in the developmental sequence (Zobl, 1983). The learners were able to generalize this knowledge of the more distant and, presumably, harder-to-learn structures to ones that were adjacent in the learning sequence, in spite of the fact that they had received no instruction on the adjacent ones. In other words, these learners indeed skipped a step (but not a "stage," as discussed later). The most notable of these studies addresses the teaching of relative clauses (Doughty, 1991; Eckman, Bell & Nelson, 1988), although there have also been studies involving other instructional targets, such as determiners (Zobl, 1985) and articles (Muranoi, 1996).

However, Doughty (1991) and Pavesi (1986) have shown that, although at first blush seemingly contradictory, psycholinguistic readiness and typological projectability can be combined to the advantage of the learner. In Doughty's study, learners were first determined to be capable of the complex syntactic process of embedding, as evidenced by the emergence of subject relative clauses in their IL. The majority of learners, however, had not extended their knowledge of relativization to the other five contexts, which are typologically more marked. Upon encountering an input flood of very marked contexts, even the control group improved slightly in relativization. The instructed groups, each receiving a different kind of more or less explicit FonF instruction, made significantly even greater progress in extending their contexts for relativization. (See the section Decision 4 for a discussion of the range of types of focus on form.)

Thus we can sometimes explain or, when necessary, accept apparently conflicting research results as interim steps toward a better understanding of the second language learning process, and begin to formulate the questions we would like to ask of research. Insofar as choice of form is concerned, the central question is: What makes one form more learnable than another? Or put in other ways: Why do L2 learners learn one form before another? Why does one form appear easier to learn than another? And, once we establish the answers to these questions, which of these forms should be the focus of instruction? In short, what research-based claims can be made regarding differentiation among forms, from which we might draw implications for teaching?

The body of research that has most often been the basis for pedagogical recommendations is the studies that offer increasing evidence that many forms are learned in predictable stages. As noted earlier, some researchers have concluded that instruction is not likely to have any significant impact if the learner is at a developmental stage that is much earlier in the sequence than the focus of instruction. The first, albeit rather loose, acquisition orders to be documented in SLA research were the morpheme orders (e.g., Dulay & Burt, 1974), but little was provided at the time in the way of explanation as to why these particular orders should obtain. Early studies did indicate, however, that efforts to teach morphemes that appear late in the natural order (e.g., third person singular -s and possessive 's) to beginning learners were counterproductive (e.g., Lightbown, 1983).

In addition to those based on Universal Grammar (UG) analyses (e.g., Tomaselli & Schwartz, 1990; Zobl, 1995; Zobl & Liceras, 1994), several explanations have been advanced for why such orders obtain or why some forms appear to be easier to acquire than others. In this discussion we will distinguish between the staged acquisition of a system and the relative order of acquisition of several different forms or structures, for example, the morpheme orders.[5]

Evidence of staged acquisition of a linguistic system includes the early studies of negation and interrogation (e.g., Cancino, Rosansky & Schumann, 1978), studies of pronouns (Zobl, 1985), and J. White's investigation of possessive determiners (this volume). In early stages of acquisition, forms may or may not be targetlike. For example, in J. White's data, at an early stage of development (Stage 2) of possessive determiners, a learner's production might be targetlike if it is used to refer to second person determiners (*your*); however, this same form, *your* used for third person, would not be targetlike. The distinction being made here is that this is a stage of development along the way toward mastering the determiner system. In other words, we are not viewing this as the relative order of acquisition of the forms *your* and *his,* as separate items.

The staged acquisition of a linguistic system has often been explained in terms of increasing processing complexity and capacity, generally with movement in the direction of the target. Probably the most well-known work in the area of developmental stages is that of Pienemann and his colleagues (Pienemann, 1987, 1989; Pienemann & Johnston, 1986). Essentially, the claim is that constructions that involve little manipulation of elements or little demand on short-term memory tend to be acquired early. According to Pienemann, there is an independent cognitive basis for the speech-processing strategies that constrain learner production. These strategies are rooted in cognitive factors, such as perceptual salience and continuity of elements. Each stage is a prerequisite for the next, as learners shed these constraints one by one. Learners are initially tightly constrained against movement and separation of elements, and produce primarily formulas. Gradually, as they move from stage to stage, they begin to move elements around in their sentences and establish long-distance relationships. Within each stage, evidence of acquisition can be found in the extension of learned operations to a wider range of contexts. This process may be concurrent with the emergence of the next stage. For Pienemann, the teaching implications of the model are quite clear: It is not possible to learn, and therefore not possible to teach, a structure that lies within a stage far beyond the learner's present stage. Thus, for example, there would be little profit in introducing dative movement (deemed to be Stage $X + 4$) in the instruction of an L2 English learner who had yet

5 As Ingram (1989) notes, there are multiple definitions of the term *stage* (see also Atkinson, 1982). In the morphemes studies, the term was used to describe transitional phases, that is, stable use of the form. Others (e.g., Pienemann, 1987, 1989; J. White, this volume) use some variant of an emergence criterion; that is, a new stage is reached when is it used in a (small) specified number of times.

to acquire preposition stranding (deemed to be Stage $X + 2$). There is some counterevidence to this position, however. Weinert (1994) found that formal practice that required learners to produce complex target forms beyond their current stage of development of L2 German negation allowed them to skip the earliest stages, such as external negation (**nein spielen Katze* = no play cat), characteristic of naturalistic learners. Spada and Lightbown (1993) also observed instances of learners producing occasional later-stage question forms subsequent to instruction. As we have already noted, Lightbown currently suggests that a pedagogical focus on advanced forms can have some long-term, if not immediately noticeable, effects.

Processing explanations have also been advanced to explain other aspects of second language development. Hawkins (1989), for instance, argues that the order of relative clause acquisition in L2 French is based on the distance of the head noun from the extraction site. A more distant relationship (*dont*-genitive) is presumably harder to process and thus is acquired later than relative clauses in which the two are adjacent (*qui*-subject).

[5]   Distance of relative clauses

    La femme qui _____ *aimait Jean est morte.* (SS)
    The woman who loved John is dead.

    La femme que Jean aimait _____ *est morte.* (SO)
    The woman who(m) John loved is dead.

    La femme dont Jean avait admiré la peinture _____ *est morte.* (SG)
    The woman whose painting John admired is dead.

Tarallo and Myhill (1983) present similar conclusions for relative clause acquisition in English.Wolfe-Quintero (1992) also claims that the order of acquisition for complex WH-questions and relative clauses is based on processing constraints. She maintains that learners are sensitive to the degree of discontinuity created by the extraction, with those sentences causing the greatest discontinuity acquired last.

These accounts are appealing in that they provide an independent explanation of learner data, from which predictions of learner performance can be made, both in and out of the classroom (though see Larsen-Freeman & Long, 1991; Towell & Hawkins, 1994, for critiques). For the teacher, these results may mean rethinking some instructional sequences or at least rethinking expectations about learner progress. Here we may find an explanation for why learners continue to produce questions such as:

[6]   Late errors

    *Why you left so early?
    *I don't know what is she doing?

If learners show other signs of being in an earlier stage of IL development, in which such stagewise development is known, for instance, in negation, tense marking, and pronoun use, it may make sense not to focus on these kinds of errors and, instead, concentrate on structures within the next stage of development, such as inversion with questions containing the copula. Evidence of staged development may also indicate, for instance, based on Hawkins's work, that teachers of L2 French should introduce, and allow their students to practice, the subject relativizer *qui* well before introducing the object and genitive relativizers *que* and *dont*. Most textbooks introduce, and encourage practice of, *qui* and *que* simultaneously.

As encouraging as the results of these studies are, as Lightbown (this volume) points out, the inventory of documented developmental sequences remains small and insufficient for designing effective pedagogical strategies. Further, even when more is discovered about the language forms that develop sequentially, not all prerequisites for moving from one stage to another are based on processing constraints. There may be other important developmental signposts for teachers to watch for. For instance, in a study of the emergence of the pluperfect (e.g., *had given*), Bardovi-Harlig (1995) found that stable use (80% in obligatory contexts) of the simple past always preceded the emergence of the pluperfect. A second requirement seemed to be the context or, we might say, the communicative pressure, for the pluperfect, as in the use of what Bardovi-Harlig calls *reverse order reports*. These are contexts in which chronological order is not followed; rather, the later action precedes the earlier one in an utterance. It is only when the communicative need for a second, relational, past arose that learners began to produce the pluperfect. Bardovi-Harlig examined the effect of formal instruction on acquisition of the pluperfect and found that, for learners whose production did not show evidence of these two prerequisites, instruction did not have a significant effect. Most of the learners who had produced reverse order reports and showed stable use of the simple past, on the other hand, began to use the pluperfect after instruction. These results offer significant support for Pienemann's teachability hypothesis. However, Bardovi-Harlig can only speculate that this instruction may have increased the rate of acquisition, that is, may have prompted emergence earlier than would have occurred without instruction, because hers was an observational and not an experimental study.

Lexical meaning itself may affect ease and order of acquisition. It has been suggested that some "core" meanings may be acquired before more peripheral ones. Most studies in this area have addressed the acquisition of tense and aspect systems and have focused primarily on untutored learners (see e.g., Andersen, 1993, for summary; Meisel, 1987). Bardovi-Harlig, however, has examined this issue in acquisition by classroom learners (Bardovi-Harlig, 1995; Bardovi-Harlig & Reynolds, 1995). Instructed and uninstructed learners alike appear to follow a predictable order of acquisition of lexical verb classes based on the internal structure of events and situations. Learners begin by marking simple past on achievement verbs (those with an end point but no duration, e.g., *find something*), then on accomplishment verbs (those with an end point and duration, e.g., *eat dinner*), and finally, activity verbs (those with duration but no end point, e.g., *eat*). The learners whom Bardovi-Harlig and Reynolds studied had undergeneralized grammars, with activity verbs characteristically marked with progressive -*ing* but rarely for simple past. They found that after receiving a flood of positive evidence and performing focused activities, learners increased their marking of simple past on activity verbs and that these changes remained in a delayed pretest. Since there was no control group in this study, it is impossible to unequivocally attribute these gains to instruction. However, the results appear to be consistent with those of the study of the pluperfect: Formal instruction cannot change the route of development, but it may accelerate progress through an established acquisition order.

Developmental orders have also been attributed to typological differences among forms. This approach offers a description of the facts and may even point to predictions, but does not tell us why learners do what they do. Typological explanations are based on the idea that structures that are rare across languages are likely to be acquired late, if ever, and, conversely, those that are relatively common will be acquired early, without necessarily offering an account of why this should be the case. Probably the best-known examples of this are, once again, relative clauses, based on the Noun Phrase Accessibility Hierarchy (NPAH) of Keenan and Comrie (1977). Briefly, their account showed an implicational relationship among relative clause types, with subject extraction being the most common, and object of comparison the least. A number of studies have shown that SLA orders mirrored the typological findings, that is, that learners tend to acquire the common structures first and the rare ones last, if at all (e.g., Eckman, Bell, & Nelson, 1988; Gass, 1982). It may be that the findings of these studies are not so different from those described earlier, as seen in the work of Tarallo and Myhill (1983) and Hawkins (1989), who offer processing explanations for the descriptions offered by typological approaches.

Other examples of typological explanations are those posited for acquisition of interrogatives (Eckman, Moravscik, & Wirth, 1989) and acquisition of aspects of the phonological system, such as consonant clusters (Eckman, 1991; Eckman & Iverson, 1993). From a pedagogical viewpoint, the most interesting question that these studies raise concerns the nature of instructional intervention. The results of several studies of relative clauses demonstrate that when forms are implicationally related, it may be possible, and even more efficient, to teach the more difficult forms first. Eckman, Bell, and Nelson (1988) and Doughty (1988, 1991) both found that when learners were taught the more difficult forms in the implicational order, but not the less difficult ones, they improved not only on the difficult forms that they had been taught but also on the easier ones that they had not been taught. This strategy has even been suggested for teaching pronunciation (Eckman & Iverson, 1997). In this case, pronunciation of an L2 sound would be taught first in the most difficult, latest-acquired environment, the hope being that mastery of this environment would entail mastery without instruction of all other easier ones. So far, however, this has been successfully demonstrated only on (nonphonological) forms that are implicationally related, based on typological data, suggesting that a call to teach all late-acquired structures first would be overly general and probably ill-advised. That is to say, these results would not imply that we should ignore Pienemann's teachability hypothesis and, for example, start teaching late-acquired word order rules to beginning learners.

We now turn to an examination of our second issue: why some unrelated target forms seem to be acquired earlier than others or with greater ease. For ESL, why does *-ing* precede plural *-s?* There is as yet no evidence that the former is a prerequisite for the latter; *-ing* just emerges first. However, it is possible to propose some plausible bases for this phenomenon. In fact, a number of explanations have been offered for the relative ease and order of acquisition of different forms. Most of them fall within the following categories:

1. Salience in the input: If learners notice certain forms or constructions, for whatever reason, for example, frequency or unusualness, they are more likely to acquire them than they are to acquire forms they have not noticed in any way.
2. Communicative function or meaningfulness in the output: Even if learners notice a form, or if it is pointed out through instruction, without a communicative need, or if language forms fulfill no (unique) function, acquisition may be delayed.
3. Inherent difficulty of rules: Learners tend to acquire "easier" rules early and indeed may never acquire "hard" rules. The definition of *easy* has variously included functional and formal complexity, reliability, scope, and prototypicality (see DeKeyser, this volume).

Salience and communicative function

As we discuss at length later (see the section Decision 4), noticing forms in the input has been proposed as a prerequisite for acquisition (Robinson, 1995b; Schmidt, 1990, 1994a; Skehan, 1996). If this is the case, it stands to reason that forms that are noticed will be acquired before those that are not. This is an area of great interest to teachers, since, unlike the situation with status in UG or with allegedly immutable acquisition orders, it may be possible to change the level of salience in the input and encourage learners to notice what, under other circumstances, they might not. Such a promising possibility begs the question: What causes learners to notice or ignore forms in the input? As noted earlier, frequency has been proposed as one feature. Bardovi-Harlig (1987) explained the earlier acquisition of preposition stranding ("He's the one who I came with") as opposed to the later acquisition of the less typologically marked pied-piped construction ("He's the one with whom I came") in terms of the relative frequency of the two structures in the input, in addition to the novelty of pied-piping. Other studies (Day & Shapson, 1991; Trahey & L. White, 1993) also show the benefit of instruction that increased the frequency of troublesome forms. However, Williams and Evans (this volume) found that increasing the frequency of the form in focus resulted in improved performance on participial adjectives, yet not on the passive. It seems clear, then, that frequency cannot be the whole story. Otherwise, why would any learner have trouble with the acquisition of the ubiquitous article, either in L2 English and L2 French? (See Harley, this volume.) Forms such as articles, and often the gender or case assignments encoded in them, are frequent and yet appear to lack salience for second language learners. Harley argues that there is little semantic or communicative motivation for gender assignment; thus failure to assign gender accurately does not result in loss of meaning. Similar observations can be made about frequent, but semantically redundant, forms such as English third person singular -*s*.

For forms that are frequent in the input and yet still seem to lack salience for learners, it may be that other means are required to induce learners to notice. Some studies have used enhancement techniques that are not based on increased frequency. For instance, J. White (this volume) used typographical enhancement to encourage students to notice possessive determiners, generally a source of learner difficulty, in the input but did not find a significant difference between the accuracy of learners who received enhanced input and the accuracy of those who received unenhanced input. Jourdenais, Ota, Stauffer, Boyson, and Doughty (1995), Leeman, Arteagoitia, Fridman, and Doughty (1995), and Shook (1994), in studies of acquisition of L2 Spanish preterit and imperfect verb forms, also used typographical enhancement of input. In contrast to J. White, they found a significant difference in noticing of target forms and accuracy of subsequent output. The forms examined in the Spanish studies are both frequent and semantically important and perhaps more meaningful than J. White's possessive determiners. In the case of Spanish aspect, learners may indeed notice the forms but may require assistance in sorting out their distribution.

In some cases, it is difficult to distinguish what is, in fact, noticed from what may be noticed at some level, but ignored as unimportant relative to other items in the input. Hammarberg (1985) notes that learners of L2 Swedish invert the subject and verb in questions long before they do in declarative statements containing adverbials or other items preceding the subject. Inversion is required in both structures in Swedish. Why is there a lag in applying the exact same strategy to one of the contexts? Hammarberg argues that it is because learners perceive a pragmatic function – questioning – for the interrogatives but not for declaratives with preposed items, in which inversion is a purely formal requirement.

Inherent difficulty of rules

Relative difficulty of acquisition is not limited to implicational relationships, processing complexity, or perceptibility. Some language rules evidently are easier to learn and thus may be learned earlier than others (recall our discussion of rules, forms, and form at the beginning of this section). The distinction between "easy" and "hard" rules has a long history, although it is far from clear what is meant by these terms (see Robinson, 1996b). DeKeyser points out (this volume) that rules are generally classified by linguistic rather than processing complexity. For instance, English verb phrase morphology in the simple present is formally simple, since it is essentially a predictable alternation between -$\varnothing$ and -s. Compare this to the variety in Romance or Slavic verb phrase morphological forms. These would be examples of formal complexity. However, many ESL teachers have wondered whether it is really accurate to say that the English verbal morphology system is easy to learn, because third person singular -s continues to be a bête noire for many learners. Although the concept of agreement may be transparent, one difficult aspect of agreement that has been noted is that there is considerable distance between the noun and the verb with which it must agree (DeKeyser, this volume; R. Ellis, 1990). Thus, language form considerations extend across elements in an utterance, making a seemingly simple concept difficult to acquire and use.

Functional complexity is another aspect of rule difficulty and refers to the multiplicity of form-function relationships. The article system in German, for instance, is functionally complex, in that each article is associated with several meanings: case, number, gender, and definiteness. In addition, the same form may have several meanings (e.g., *die* marks both plural and feminine singular in nominative and accusative cases). We might hypothesize, then, that rules that are formally and functionally complex are learned late, but it is not entirely clear what role focus on form might play in their acquisition. Finally, in discussing difficulty, it is important to distinguish between acquisition and use. DeKeyser and Sokalski (1996) point out that some forms are easy to notice and comprehend but difficult to produce. Other forms may be difficult to notice but, once noticed and learned, are produced rather easily.

Ultimately, however, some rules for use are so complex that they cannot be stated clearly or exhaustively, even by linguists. Westney (1994) places two types of rules in this category. The first type includes those sets of forms, such as verbs that do or do not enter into dative alternation in English or gender assignment in French, that defy satisfactory rule formulation without recourse to extensive and, as yet, incomplete lists of exceptions. In a study of L2 acquisition of dative alternation, Fotos and R. Ellis (1991) found that the learners were unable to generalize their knowledge much beyond the words they were given as examples, displaying an absence of what has been called *system learning*. Instead, gains were limited to the example items themselves, what is generally known as *item learning*, essentially what occurs in lexical acquisition. Similar findings of item learning are reported in a study of another complex rule, the affixation of *-age* versus *-ment* in L2 French (Carroll, Swain, & Roberge, 1992). Hulstijn (1995) recommends lexical learning rather than focus on form as a possible way of approaching instruction, since these complex rules are, indeed, essentially lexical. For instance, instead of trying to learn the phonological and morphological rules for gender in French, students should simply learn gender assignment along with the word itself, in effect, memorize it. Some support for this view is presented by Harley (this volume), who found that her learners probably improved their performance through item learning rather than system learning. According to Hulstijn and De Graaff (1994), direct instruction will be less effective in the case of item learning, in which rule application as the basis of production is eschewed in favor of storage and retrieval of individual forms.

The second type, such as English articles, Westney calls *semantically complex* because, although formally simple, the rules for their use are tied to both semantic and discoursal concerns that are too numerous for the learner to grasp easily. Another example of the second type is the distinction between preterit and imperfect in Spanish. Hulstijn claims that such rules must be stated in what he calls vague *soft metaphors,* such as perspective. In these cases, Hulstijn (1995, p. 379) claims, there are certain to be learning difficulties, particularly if the relevant semantic distinctions do not exist in the L1, as would be the case in the acquisition of Spanish verb forms by L1 English learners (described in the previous section). These rules, he suggests, must be learned by "feel," and pedagogical intervention, in this case, is best limited to a few rules of thumb, coupled with repeated exposure to illustrative examples. This reasoning may explain the findings in the studies of Spanish verb tense cited earlier (Jourdenais et al., 1995; Leeman et al., 1995; Shook, 1994). Indirect support for this contention also comes from Green and Hecht (1992), whose study of L2 English reveals that vague rules, for example, aspectual distinctions, engendered the greatest divergence between the learners' abilities to state the rules and to provide a correction for an errorful utterance. The learners were far better at correcting these utterances than at giving a rule. On straightforward rules, in contrast, such as SVO order and the ± animacy distinction for *who* and *which*, their rule and correction scores were much closer.

Not all studies corroborate this view, however. In an experimental study of L2 English dative alternation, Carroll and Swain (1993) found that a variety of types of feedback were more effective than no treatment. Generalizing to the classroom, they suggest that "instruction" might be helpful even for rules that are not clear-cut. Muranoi (1996) and Master (1994, 1995) also claim success for FonF instruction on the notoriously complex and difficult rules for the English article system. This may, in part, be due to the fact that Master successfully reduces this complex system to a few reliable rules of thumb – that is, that all NPs can be categorized as ± classified and ± identified – that work most of the time, and this is precisely what Hulstijn suggests for these cases. We will extend this consideration of how to teach inherently difficult rules in the section Decision 4, which examines implicit and explicit focus on form.

Several of these examples illustrate one important sense in which complex rules cannot be stated clearly, that is, when they can be stated only probabilistically. For English past tense, for instance, this means that the odds are in favor of any given past form being regular. It also means that there are clues that indicate whether a form will take a regular or irregular past and, if the latter, which kind of irregular. However, these are only odds and clues; they are not entirely reliable. In this sense, complexity is related to what Hulstijn and De Graaff (1994) have called *reliability*. Reliability refers to how dependable a rule is. For example, a reliable rule might be that all English adjectives or adverbs with three or more syllables form the comparative with *more* + adjective or adverb. Although there are a few exceptions (e.g., *unhappier*), the rule is a highly reliable one. Compare this to the same rule applied to two-syllable words, which have all sorts of exceptions that cannot be stated simply or exhaustively. Reliable rules are easier to learn and presumably easier to teach.

In addition to consistency of application, the scope of application of rules should be considered. Reliable rules themselves may have large or small scope (Hulstijn & De Graaff, 1994), depending on how many forms the rule applies to. An example of a rule with large scope would be the affixation of plural -*s* in English. Although there are exceptions, the vast majority of nouns in English pluralize with -*s*. An example of a reliable rule with small scope is an aspect of the diminutive affixation rule in Dutch, in which the suffix -*je* is added to the end of nouns. One of the subrules for this form is that, for all nouns containing a single vowel followed by *r* or *l* and then ending in *m,* or for those ending in a diphthong or unstressed vowel followed by *r* or *l* and then ending in *m,* a -*p*- must be inserted prior to the addition of the diminutive suffix -*je* (e.g., *boompje,* "little tree"). This is a very reliable rule; yet it has a very narrow scope. We can hypothesize that those rules with high reliability and broad scope are acquired before those with low reliability and narrow scope, although this has not been shown conclusively. Certainly those with broad scope are the most useful, and based on this fact alone, we suggest selecting them prior to selecting rules with narrow scope in any syllabus. Hulstijn and De Graaff argue that the advantage of instruction is greatest with rules that have both wide scope and high reliability. Their definition of *advantage* is not entirely clear, however. It certainly seems more efficient to concentrate on rules with larger scope, as we have noted, but it is not clear that this necessarily means that acquisition is easier and quicker for those rules than for rules with narrower scope. Such an ease of acquisition advantage remains to be demonstrated by SLA research.

Reliability and scope, as described here, apply to what Hulstijn (1995) calls *lexical rules,* that is, morphophonological rules. We can talk in similar terms about nonlexical rules, such as word order rules. Here, the term more often found in the literature is *L2 consistency.* Numerous studies have pointed to the evidence that, when the L2 is inconsistent, it presents greater difficulties for the learner. This effect has been found to be particularly strong when L1 predispositions favor one variant of the structure. For instance, if the L2 word order is inconsistent, as say in the case of French and Spanish SVO clitic placement, violating the more expected, typologically canonical SVO order, acquisition may be delayed. In this case, the likely result from the imposition of the expected order yields sentences such as:

[7]   Processing errors

    Je vois les
    I see them

                                               (Zobl, 1980)

In other cases, L2 inconsistency may not result directly in learner error but may lead to learner misanalysis and subsequent extension of this misanalysis to new contexts. Yuan (1995) demonstrates that L1 English learners misanalyze L2 Chinese sentences, such as the following, to be evidence of subject-predicate word order:

[8]   Learner misanalysis

wode didi	*xihuan chi*	*pingguo*
my brother	like eat	apples

My brother likes to eat apples.

Instead, this represents what Yuan calls *base-generated topics* and contains a topic ("my brother"), followed by a comment structure in which the redundant personal pronoun (*ta* = "he") is omitted. Yuan's results indicate that acquisition of this class of target structures, base-generated topics, comes extremely late, with many fairly advanced learners never mastering it at all.

By now it is evident that the issue of determining what is an easy or hard rule is a complex one, and the pedagogical implications of such a determination of easy versus hard are not immediately apparent. On the one hand, Pica (1985) suggests that it is the acquisition of easy rules, especially those which apply to nonsalient forms, that benefits most from instruction. She defines *easy rules* as those with clear form-function relationships, such as plural -s. Robinson (1996b) also found a clear superiority for instruction on simple rules (as ranked by experienced teachers), in this case, the rule for SV inversion with fronted adverbials (Into the house ran John/John ran), arguably a more difficult "easy" rule than plural -s. Williams and Evans (this volume) find a similar benefit for instruction of participial adjectives (interesting/interested), which despite their confusing phonological similarity follow a clear form-function rule, but not for the use of the passive, a rule that falls squarely into Hulstijn's category of rules that require vague language and soft metaphors for their explanation (although cf. Zhou, 1992). Hulstijn and De Graaff (1994), on the other hand, suggest that easy rules are relatively straightforward for learners to discover on their own, and therefore, perhaps not the best use of instructional time. It is possible that this is indeed the case for rules that are both easy and apply to salient forms. In short, there seem to be many shades of *easy*.

Once criteria are established for what makes learning a form or rule hard or easy, we must then address the issue of what this means for the classroom. Put simply, given a finite amount of instructional time, should we teach the easy-early ones first, assuming that they form the foundation for the acquisition of the later ones, which will be acquired though exposure? Or should we focus on the harder-later ones, and assume that the easy ones will look after themselves? Both time and learning context are important determining factors. When class time is limited, but input is available, learners can be left to discover certain rules on their own, and teachers can concentrate on guiding learners to acquiring more difficult ones. This makes the most sense in a second language situation, where learners have the opportunity to make such discoveries. In foreign language classrooms, however, it may be more effective to assist learners even in figuring out rules they might discover on their own, given time and input. We must heed Westney (1994), however, in his admonition that some rules are just too complex to be taught directly.

First language influence

Finally, many of the features discussed thus far interact with one of the most important factors in the process of second language learning: the influence of the first language. There is an enormous literature on this topic, and an exhaustive review is beyond the scope of this chapter. For our purposes, it will be sufficient to note that a learner's previous linguistic knowledge influences the acquisition of a new language in a principled, if not straightforward, contrastive way. To show the importance of this influence on focus on form, we will offer just a few examples. Selinker and Lakshmanan (1992) have proposed the *multiple effects principle,* which they apply to stabilization, but which could be understood more broadly to mean that when more than one factor in SLA work in tandem, they will have greater impact than one factor alone. Selinker and Lakshmanan also hypothesize that L1 influence has a privileged status among these factors. In some cases, they argue, this combination of factors may even lead to IL features that are apparently impermeable to destabilization through instruction. In particular, they examine cases in which L1 influence may interact with principles of UG. This combination of factors has been investigated extensively, most notably by L. White (e.g., 1988, 1989), in whose view one of the most intractable difficulties that learners face is having to retreat from a UG-based grammar, that is, when the L1/IL form is part of a less conservative grammar than the L2 form. In this case, the learner must notice that the IL form is not present in the L2; positive evidence will not supply this information. In the case of adverb placement in L1 French/L2 English, the learner must notice the absence of utterances such as "*He gobbled hungrily the doughnut," which display word order that is grammatical only in the L1. In these instances, L. White (1991) argues, explicit and negative evidence may be required, or at least helpful.

Typological universals may also interact with the L1 and have implications for pedagogy. Greatest learner difficulty and L1 transfer are predicted when the L2 contains forms that are typologically marked and the corresponding L1 forms are unmarked (Eckman, 1977). On the other hand, when both the L1 and the L2 contain marked forms, although the unmarked version may make an early appearance in the IL, it may give way to the target marked form of its own accord and require little pedagogical intervention. Hyltenstam (1987) uses this notion to explain acquisition order and difficulty for postverbal and postauxiliary negation, which is marked in relation to preverbal negation, and for inversion in interrogatives, another marked form. Eckman's (1991) position on universals is even stronger, essentially relegating the influence of L1 to a much lower priority. Using his phonological example of terminal devoicing of obstruents, he claims that the unmarked feature, devoicing, requires no instruction, regardless of the L1. Although it is unclear what effect instruction might have on acquiring the more marked value, the terminal ($\pm$ voice) distinction does not come easily, again regardless of the L1 markedness of the feature in question.

In many cases, it is the L2 input that determines whether L1 influence will cause learner difficulty, perhaps requiring focus on form. The L2 may contain potentially misleading information, so that learners will assume that their L1 forms are directly transferable to the L2, as in Andersen's "transfer to somewhere" principle (1983). Several examples, such as those for L1 English learners trying to learn French or Chinese word order (Yuan, 1995; Zobl, 1980), are given in Examples 7 and 8. Lightbown (1991) provides other cases of how classroom input, in particular, may provide learners with a distorted sample of the target discourse, as in the disproportionately high frequency of *have* as an introducer, instead of *there is/there are*, in the speech of the teachers in the L1 French/L2 English classroom, strengthening the influence of the L1 form, *il y a* (from the verb *avoir*, "to have").

L1 influence has also been shown to interact with developmental sequences, for instance, Zobl's description of L1 Spanish learners of English whose negation development remained in the No V stage longer than learners whose L1 did not contain this type of negation (1980). Finally, L1 forms may have an effect on the salience of L2 forms. Harley (this volume) argues that L1 English predisposes learners not to notice grammatical gender in L2 French, and Ringbom (1990) makes a similar point regarding Finnish and Swedish learners of English. Swedish contains articles, whereas Finnish does not, and therefore, he claims, Swedish learners are more likely to notice this relatively nonsalient feature of English. Clearly, L1 influence is an important factor in second language learning, and this importance may increase when it acts in combination with other factors. This phenomenon may have significant pedagogical implications; yet it is not clear that these combined forces make the prospects of intervention dim, as Selinker and Lakshmanan conclude, or whether, instead, they present the very situation in which instruction is the most important, as Lightbown (this volume) has suggested.

Summary

Thus far we have examined the pedagogical decisions involving whether to focus on form; whether to plan the pedagogical intervention in advance or to maintain a reactive stance; and, once the decision to focus on form has been made, how to select from among the many occurring or potential learner errors or potentially difficult TL features which forms will be the focus of instruction. The remaining decisions will assume a mainly proactive approach, in which the target form has been identified by the teacher, who must now consider *how* to implement the focus on form in lessons and, ultimately, into the curriculum. We believe that these decisions should be based upon the research findings on learnability of forms just discussed, as well as on studies that have investigated the learning processes of the adult L2 acquirer, to which we will now turn.

Decision 4: Explicitness of focus on form

Even though, as is the case with any pedagogical decisions, many task and technique design choices will be determined to a certain extent by practical considerations, such as the context of instruction, the particular learning problems of students, and as we have just discussed at length, in some cases by the nature of the linguistic form itself, FonF design decisions also require the teacher to reflect on several aspects of SLA. More specifically, the type of task or technique employed will be directly related to the teacher's perspective on the following difficult questions:

1. How does the L2 learner mentally represent[6] knowledge of the TL?
2. How is language knowledge accessed during language use processes, such as production and comprehension?
3. What is the role of metalinguistic ability in language acquisition?

The larger SLA processes that will be of greatest interest in our discussion are:

1. Analysis, which, in considering whether to focus on form at all, we defined earlier as the "figuring out" of systematic rules.
2. Restructuring, which essentially involves the reorganization of those developing IL rules to be most effectively deployed during language use and, eventually, to become more targetlike. Language learning subprocesses which are engaged during analysis and are catalysts for restructuring are:
   - Hypothesis testing
   - Cognitive comparison
   - Noticing IL/TL differences (often called *gaps*)
   - Noticing IL deficiencies (or "holes"; see Swain, this volume)

There is considerable agreement that learner attention is required in order for any of these processes and subprocesses to be engaged. However,

6 That is, store in memory.

although it is incontrovertible that perceptual attention is required, there is some debate as to whether conscious, focal attention is necessary for acquisition to take place (Schmidt, 1995; Tomlin & Villa, 1994). This is an important distinction because the choice has an impact on the degree of overtness or obtrusiveness of the focus-on-form technique, as well as on the extent to which the techniques *direct* versus *attract* learner attention to the linguistic material needed to notice, test hypotheses, make cognitive comparisons, and so on. The final learning process that is vital to targetlike language ability is:

3. Gaining control over the knowledge in order to use it fluently and skillfully.

In considering the development of control, we have come full circle to the common observation that we noted is often used to justify the learning/acquisition distinction and the noninterventionist position: Language use tends to be of two types – highly skilled and effortless versus halting and deliberate. The processes by which deliberate language use can be automatized are far from well known. However, it is already clear that the starting point for discovering them is the distinction between *focus on form* and *focus on formS,* the latter entailing the well-known pitfall that too much attention to form results in deliberate rather than automatic language use. Long's operationalization of focus on form is an attempt to draw a line between traditional grammar teaching and FonF instruction, which is integrated into communication-oriented instruction.

In Table 1, we try to represent, in a concise format, the implicit/explicit dichotomies that are so pervasive in the SLA research literature and that generate complex debate, typically because each of the domains of language knowledge, use, and learning is envisioned as being potentially more or less "explicit," and the degree of explicitness is purported to be directly connected, either positively or negatively, with ultimate attainment in language learning.

The tendency has been to assume that all pedagogical choices must be made within one vertical column (see Table 1), based on whether it was assumed that language learning is overall and essentially *either* an implicit, experiential process *or* an explicitly "taught" process. We hope that our discussion of the initial decision regarding whether or not to focus on form thus far has suggested that such rigid constraints are not effective. Further, since we believe that the noninterface position does not hold, choices *across* the columns in Table 1 can be made, and their success will necessarily depend upon other considerations, such as degree of integration of attention to form and meaning and the duration of attention to form within primarily meaningful activities (as we will see in the sections on Decision 5 and Decision 6). For example, we believe that, even when the aim is *fluent and automatic access* (choices from the

230   *Catherine Doughty and Jessica Williams*

TABLE I. IMPLICIT AND EXPLICIT LANGUAGE LEARNING

Domain	*"Implicit"*	*"Explicit"*
IL knowledge (mental representation)	• Innate (universal) • Intuitive • Example-based	• Explicit (analyzed; language-specific) • Rule-based
Access to and/or use of IL knowledge	• Automatic (effortless) • Fluent, skilled	• Deliberate (effortful) • Halting

Learning
  Analysis
    Hypothesis testing
    Cognitive comparison
    Noticing gaps or holes
    Restructuring
	• Inductive
	• Incidental
	• Inherent
	• Unaware
	• Imperceptible
		• Deductive
		• Intentional
		• Aware
		• Noticed

Attention	• Attracted • Unconscious	• Directed • Conscious
Development of control	• Experiential • Automatized	• Practiced • Proceduralized
Teaching intervention	• Unobtrusive or none	• Overt • Obtrusive • Metalinguistic

"Implicit" column), the learning can involve *overt noticing* (choices from the "Explicit" column). The full details of these complex debates are beyond the scope of this chapter; however, the interested reader may consult several sources for a more thorough discussion (Carr & Curran, 1994; Schmidt, 1993a, 1995; Tomlin & Villa, 1994). We do suggest, however, that in choosing or designing FonF tasks, teachers must have some conception of how language knowledge is stored, accessed, and used by learners engaged in particular tasks.

At this point, it is useful to clarify what we mean by the terms *implicit* and *explicit* by recalling their ordinary senses:[7]

Implicit a. Implied or understood though not directly expressed.
b. Contained in the nature of something though not readily apparent.

Explicit a. Fully and clearly expressed, defined or formulated. b. Readily observable.

Applying these definitions to language teaching, it is clear that there is a two-part distinction between implicitness and explicitness (the a and b

7 Copyright © by Houghton Mifflin Company. Adapted and reproduced by permission from *The American Heritage Dictionary of the English Language, Third Edition.*

definitions). This dual distinction has been a continual source of confusion in terminology, because implicit-a versus explicit-b comparisons and vice versa are sometimes made. The first distinction is primarily a linguistic one concerning the degree of detail in the expression of the formal aspects of the linguistic element at hand. In recent communicative language teaching practice, the prohibition against teaching linguistic forms in isolation has been a reaction to one particular approach to the explicit expression of linguistic elements, that is, metalinguistic rule presentation. The prohibition has furthermore, but perhaps unjustifiably, been broadly interpreted as one against any form of explicit language teaching, leaving learners on their own to induce the rules of language.

As we have already pointed out, the most extreme followers of this prohibition take the noninterventionist approach to language teaching, which is based on the theoretical belief that implicit, *uninstructed* learning is the only successful kind of SLA. However, we emphasize the unproductive nature of these kinds of all-or-nothing choices between the implicit and the explicit, such as those shown in Table 1, which result in inflexible approaches to language teaching. That is to say, expecting that all language learning problems can be resolved in the same way strikes us as odd. Teachers may want instead to recognize the synergistic and dynamic possibilities offered by accepting the interventionist view that knowledge can be gained and represented *either* implicitly *or* explicitly. In other words, in contrast to the noninterventionist view – that implicit learning implies no instruction – we believe that instructional intervention designed by the teacher may be either implicit or explicit and that the choice for instructional technique or task depends ultimately upon many other considerations, such as the nature of the aspect of language being taught and learned, the language learning processes being engaged via the task or technique, the degree of integration of form and meaning in the teaching approach, the level of the learners, and so forth.

The pedagogical question of whether learning and instruction are most effective when implicit or explicit is not unique to language teaching. The issue is debated vigorously in cognitive psychology, where the emphasis is on general learning processes. Moving on to the b definitions of the terms *implicit* and *explicit,* we note that the "readily observable" versus "not readily apparent" distinction here is a cognitive rather than a linguistic one that pertains to factors such as perceptual salience, consciousness, and attention. It is interesting to note that there is very little empirical evidence in the cognitive psychology literature in favor of implicit learning. Thus, whereas in the field of applied linguistics the burden of proof currently seems to be on those researchers who claim that explicit learning is possible, cognitive psychologists are attempting to discover evidence of the superiority of implicit learning (DeKeyser, 1994). In any case, the cognitive studies have served as motivation for a number of recent experimental SLA studies that have examined implicit and explicit learning under various conditions.

N. Ellis (1994c, pp. 2–3) has defined *implicit learning* and *explicit learning* as follows:

(i) Implicit learning: a nonconscious and automatic abstraction of the structural nature of the material arrived at from experience of instances.

(ii) Explicit learning: conscious searching, building then testing of hypotheses; assimilating a rule following explicit instruction.

Since it appears to be unrealistic to expect SLA to be entirely effortless, inductive, and incidental, Ellis proposes that there are three ways to learn and that adult L2 learners are likely to engage in all of them. Depending upon the requirements of the learning situation, SLA may proceed (1) explicitly, via given rules (i.e., assimilation of rules *following* instruction), (2) explicitly through selective learning (i.e., searching for information and building, and then testing hypotheses), or (3) implicitly (i.e., unconscious-automatic abstraction of the structural nature of the material derived from experience of specific instances). Inherent in Ellis's discussion of ways to learn is the recommendation that there are also various ways to teach which range along the explicitness continuum. We offer at least the following two pedagogical approaches, emphasizing considerations of the degree to which the teacher guides the learners into the kinds of language processing known to facilitate SLA and the extent to which the focus on form intrudes into the processing of meaning:

1. Implicit focus on form: The aim is to *attract* learner attention and to avoid metalinguistic discussion, always *minimizing any interruption* to the communication of meaning.
2. Explicit teaching: The aim is to *direct* learner attention and to *exploit pedagogical grammar* in this regard.

Long and Robinson (this volume) discuss a number of the experimental studies that have compared the effectiveness of implicit and explicit teaching-learning conditions. We refer readers to that chapter for the details of the studies and, for convenience, only briefly summarize some examples of the findings of these experimental studies (see Table 2). We have tried to extract the learning task, the learning mode (implicit vs. explicit), the target of instruction, and the learning outcome of each experiment.

Taken together, these findings certainly suggest that explicit focus on form is better for simple rules[8] than implicit learning is. The findings are less clear-cut for complex rules, which generally appear to be difficult for

---

8 See the discussion of inherent rule difficulty in the section Decision 3.

learners in all conditions (DeKeyser, 1995; Robinson, 1996b). DeKeyser found that learners performed somewhat better in learning complex allomorphy (in an artificial language) when merely exposed to thousands of exemplars than when they were given rules to approximate the allomorphic formulation and distribution. On the other hand, N. Ellis found an advantage for explicit instruction over implicit learning on complex rules, but it should be noted that the explicit instruction was of a particular type, that is, rules blended with especially relevant examples. In fact, the combination of rules plus carefully considered examples of the rules – a condition evident in all three studies – appears to be the most effective learning condition for complex rules, at least insofar as has been revealed by effects of nonclassroom, experimental learning on knowledge, and, as measured by grammaticality judgments, picture-sentence matching and metalinguistic ability to state rules. Carroll and Swain (1993) also suggest that explicit instruction combined with explicit metalinguistic feedback may be helpful for rules that are not clear-cut. In their experimental study of L2 English dative alternation, which we discussed earlier (see Example 1), it was found that, although *all* forms of feedback were more effective than no treatment, those subjects who received explicit instruction combined with metalinguistic feedback performed better in extending their knowledge to novel exemplars than did those who received implicit feedback.

The studies discussed thus far have all been controlled, laboratory experiments, which have the advantage of examining FonF techniques in isolation in order to determine their effectiveness but may be lacking in external validity, given that such tightly controlled conditions rarely exist in language classrooms and that the assessment measures used do not resemble everyday language use. What is more typical in a language class, as well as in classroom SLA research, is a pedagogically motivated combination of two or more techniques, as needed according to classroom conditions. Thus, although it may not yet be appropriate to extrapolate from this research whether one, another, or a combination of techniques is needed to promote IL restructuring, it is nonetheless possible, based on the growing body of investigations of focus on form in classroom studies, to discuss promising examples across the whole range of implicit to explicit FonF techniques. In addition, more, though still not all, of the classroom studies have attempted to employ valid measures of language ability and have made efforts to assess the permanence (vs. short-term laboratory effects) of the observed learning outcomes. Accordingly, we will now review a number of these classroom-based studies, moving approximately from the more implicit to the more explicit FonF interventions and concluding with some examples of successful combinations of FonF techniques.

TABLE 2. EXPERIMENTAL FOCUS-ON-FORM STUDIES

Learning Task	Learning Mode	Target	Outcome
N. Ellis, 1993 Learn translation equivalents	*Implicit:* Viewed randomly ordered examples	Complex rule of Welsh	Did poorly on grammaticality judgments and could not state rule
	Explicit: Taught rules and then given examples		Could state rule but could not transfer to new grammaticality judgments
	Explicit: Taught a rules and related examples blend		Did well on grammaticality judgments and could state rule
DeKeyser, 1995 Study pairs of sentences and pictures	*Implicit:* Just viewed the pictures and induced rules	Categorical (simple) vs. probabilistic (complex) rules of a real-language-like artificial language	Did well on matching pictures to sentences with the categorical rule but only in previously viewed contexts; did well on the probabilistic rule
	Explicit: Some brief rule instruction at the start of a few (but not all) of the sessions given in order to promote deduction of the rules		Did well on the categorical rule but only in previously viewed contexts and could also generalize to about two of three new contexts; did not do well on the probabilistic rule

TABLE 2. CONTINUED

Learning Task	Learning Mode	Target	Outcome
Robinson, 1996		Complex vs. simple rule of English	Comparative results on simple rules as measured by grammaticality judgments. Complex rules were difficult under all conditions:
"Remember the sentences viewed"	*Implicit:* Viewed grammatical sentences, answered questions about whether word pairs occurred, and received feedback		1. Implicit = incidental for speed and accuracy
"Read the sentences for meaning"	*Incidental:* Read for meaning, answered comprehension questions, and received feedback		2. Instructed > rule search for accuracy and rule search may be > all others for speed
"Find the rule in the sentences"	*Implicit rule search:* Directed to induce an unknown rule without feedback		3. Explicit instruction is most effective for accuracy (but not speed) on both complex and simple rules
"Learn these rules, read sentences and answer questions"	*Explicit instruction:* Directed to deduce form-function connection; first were given rules to learn, then read sentences that exemplified the rules, and then answered questions about rules		4. None of the subjects could state rules well

We began this chapter by noting that classroom studies show that the most implicit approach to L2 teaching – for example, unfocused exposure to input, as in immersion classrooms – is not effective for many aspects of language, a result that corroborates the experimental findings just discussed. The limitation of exposure only notwithstanding, it is sometimes possible to aim more or less implicitly to attract the learner's attention to linguistic features and promote the processing of these features without providing any sort of explicit guidance in how or when to do so. Such techniques simply try to increase the possibility that the linguistic material needed to solve a learning problem will come into the learner's focal attention. Two highly implicit techniques that may be employed in this regard are the input flood and the use of tasks in which the learning target is essential for successful task completion. In the case of the input flood, the principle is simply that the more opportunities there are in the input for learners to notice a linguistic feature, the more likely they are to do so. Using a task in which a feature is essential goes one step further to ensure that the learner will at least need to attempt to produce or process the form. However, as suggested by J. White (this volume), input flooding alone may not be particularly effective, and, as we noted earlier in our discussion of proactive approaches to focus on form, task essentialness is an elusive component and certainly cannot be devised for linguistic features that are optional. Thus other, increasingly explicit, devices may be needed to attract learner attention.

Highlighting, color-coding, and font manipulation are examples of the kind of visual input enhancement that aims to attract learner attention. Intonational focus on learner errors is an auditory version of input enhancement. These techniques are still relatively implicit, for they simply make forms perceptually salient without offering any explicit expectation as to what kind of processing should ensue. For example, J. White (this volume) attempted to make English third person singular possessive determiners perceptually salient to francophone ESL learners. The techniques she employed, in addition to increasing the frequency of encounters with the form via a book flood, involved highlighting the graphical appearance of the forms via bolding, italics, underlining, and font size. In addition, the types of enhancements were varied from text to text to increase the likelihood that they would be noticed. Three specific conditions of learner engagement with input were compared: a natural input[9] condition, an input enhancement condition, and an enhancement plus book flood condition. The book flood began prior to the 2-week natural/enhanced exposure period and continued during and after the enhancement. The idea was to provide the book flood subjects with a greater

---

9 Since possessive determiners are frequent, most natural texts involving entities and their possessions can be expected to contain them.

number of opportunities to detect the forms in the enhanced texts during extensive high-interest pleasure reading (without enhancements).[10]

The findings of this study suggest that all three conditions were somewhat beneficial to the learners, since the performance of all three groups had improved by the first posttest. Furthermore, some advantage obtained for the enhancement plus book flood on the immediate posttest; however, the other two groups had caught up by the time of the delayed posttest 1 month later. J. White discusses a range of explanations for these findings, including the possibility that the pretest and posttest language assessment, which typically required learners to choose between the masculine and feminine possessive determiners, may have increased noticing for all groups. Furthermore, it is entirely possible that all three types of attention to form (natural exposure to interesting texts, textual enhancements, and book flood) were all equally, but minimally, effective because of their implicitness.[11] As J. White suggests, perhaps the learners needed more assistance in using the input to construct the determiner system.

Clearly, there are many possible ways to manipulate and enhance the input. However, as Sharwood Smith (1991, 1993) has cautioned, it is inappropriate to assume that external manipulation of the input is the only mechanism that will increase learners' attention. He stressed that artificially induced noticing might not result in the target forms being incorporated into the developing IL. In other words, forms may be noticed perceptually, but not linguistically: "Although learners may notice the signals, the input may nevertheless be nonsalient to their learning mechanisms" (1991, p. 121). Accordingly, the determination of effective means of getting learners to focus on form is an important research aim. A study by Jourdenais et al. (1995) is promising in this regard, since it was demonstrated that learners are more likely to notice visually enhanced linguistic material than the same material in unenhanced format. In their study, Spanish preterit and imperfect endings were encoded in larger fonts than the rest of the characters, and all exemplars of each category of morpheme were encoded in the same color and font, which contrasted with the color and font representation of other categories. The discrepancy in findings between these two studies may simply have been due to the fact that J. White's subjects were children who are still developing their L2 reading ability and thus may have encountered a cognitive overload. If it is the case that there are limits to attentional capacity, then such conditions are important to take into account. Furthermore, it should be

---

10 Since this was the aim, it could be argued that the effect of the flood would have operated only in the last 2 months rather than throughout the 5 months.
11 Unfortunately, the lack of a control group prohibits us from making a conclusive analysis here.

noted that the Jourdenais et al. investigation was not a study of acquisition, because the effects of this increased noticing on IL restructuring were not examined. Thus, further research is needed in this area, but it seems likely that input enhancement could be an effective implicit FonF technique, at least for adult learners.

Given the possibility that input flooding and input enhancement may sometimes be too implicit to be maximally effective, one of the central issues in FonF research is how to lead the learner's attention to a linguistic mismatch between IL and TL. Lightbown proposes that the aim is to draw learner attention to the fact that "what they [are] saying is not what they meant to say" (1993, p. 719). Accordingly, Swain has questioned whether input, though clearly essential, is sufficient to enable this kind of cognitive comparison. For Swain, the role of output in noticing and paying attention is crucial to SLA because the L2 learner is pushed to a new level of processing in which IL deficiencies may become more salient. More specifically, Swain (1995, p. 126; see also this volume) suggests that being pushed to produce output has three learning functions:

1. A noticing function: Learners may notice a gap between what they want to say and what they can say, leading them to notice what they do not know at all, or what they know only partially.
2. A hypothesis-testing function: Output may test a hypothesis that may attract feedback that can then lead learners to "reprocess."
3. A metalinguistic (conscious reflection) function: "[a]s learners reflect upon their own target language use, their output serves a metalinguistic function, enabling them to control and internalize linguistic knowledge."

Thus there are two ways to promote IL restructuring, according to Swain: production of output plus feedback, and production of output plus metatalk.

Negotiation tasks are well established as ways to engage learners in pushed output that attracts feedback from a peer interlocutor. In particular, learner output must be restructured in response to signals of comprehension difficulty (e.g., clarification requests). Pica (1992, 1994) claims that the segmentation, movement, and reformulation features of negotiated interaction are useful mechanisms for linguistic hypothesis testing. However, it has thus far been difficult to establish empirically the connection between negotiation and SLA (Doughty, 1996, in press; Gass & Varonis, 1994). Takashima (1994) has also argued for the value of what he calls *output enhancement,* which refers to clarification requests that target specific grammatical features, as opposed to confirmation checks, which seek to resolve communication breakdowns. Takashima compared the effects of output enhancement with mere participation in communication tasks in an EFL setting in Japan, and found that the output enhancement condition led to scores in speaking and writing that were higher than those of the comparison group (see also Noboyushi & R. Ellis, 1993).

The degree of explicitness of attention to form is increased further still when tasks direct learners to reflect upon, discuss, or process linguistic form in particular ways. Three examples of such techniques are metatalking during dictogloss tasks, consciousness-raising tasks, and input-processing instruction. We have already presented the dictogloss as an example of a kind of task in which production of the targeted form is highly likely to occur (i.e., nearly essential), since the dictogloss is constructed by the teacher to include well-known learning problems (see the section on Decision 2 and also Swain, this volume). The additional feature of directing the learners to discuss the language which they are reconstructing, Swain claims, pushes them beyond simple noticing to noticing the gap and noticing the holes in their IL. Furthermore, collaborative metatalking during the dictogloss engages them in syntactic rather than semantic processing, which may be necessary for IL restructuring to occur. Whether this generalizes to more natural production is yet to be shown. However, analysis of the transcripts of collaborative interaction during dictogloss reveals that learners do engage in the kind of syntactic processing that Swain claims is necessary in order to go beyond communicative effectiveness to a fully accurate L2.

Consciousness-raising (CR) tasks, such as those found in two pedagogical grammar books (Rutherford, 1988; Rutherford & Sharwood Smith, 1988), suggest that learners should be deliberately directed to attend to form. Fotos (1993, 1994) has investigated the effectiveness of consciousness-raising tasks as implemented in traditional foreign language classes. In these tasks, learners worked interactively in small groups to solve grammar problems in English, their TL. The findings of her series of studies showed that learners are more likely to notice target features in consciousness-raising tasks than when not directed in any way toward the target (i.e., in purely communicative tasks) and that the learning outcomes in consciousness-raising tasks were at least as effective in drawing learner attention to form as were those in the more traditional grammar lessons typically found in foreign language classes. Consciousness-raising tasks are not without their difficulties, however. Apart from the problem of determining whether or not noticing is actually taking place, proponents of consciousness-raising tasks must also consider the possibility that the kind of interaction that explicitly solves purely syntactic problems, such as those studied by Fotos (adverb placement, relativization, and indirect object placement) is fundamentally different from the notion of implicit cognitive processing during task- or message-based communication (Sharwood Smith, 1991, 1993). Indeed, some consciousness-raising tasks may be considered focus on forms.

The third technique, which like the dictogloss and the consciousness-raising tasks overtly directs learner attention to differences between the IL and the TL, is input processing. In input processing, learners are told *what* to pay attention to and *what* to notice and *why* they must change their processing. VanPatten, Cadierno, and Sanz (VanPatten & Cadierno, 1993a, 1993b; VanPatten & Sanz, 1995) have all argued that what they call *processing instruction* is the key to development of the learner's IL system (see Example 3, in which we have presented processing instruction in terms of task essentialness). However, it is important to note that these studies have been criticized on the basis of their assessment measures, which have been relatively nonspontaneous, and it is possible that the processing instruction is close to, if not over, the form-formS limit because of the level of explicit expression of formal features that precedes input processing. In fact, as VanPatten himself has noted, some combinations of directions to learners may actually be detrimental. VanPatten (1990) directed learners to listen simultaneously for content and note a grammatical form in the input, a condition which led to a significant drop in recall scores (see the section on Decision 6 for details).

Harley (this volume) also advocates instruction that aims to alter input processing but, in her investigation of the phonological processing of gender cues, she reduced the metalinguistic component of instruction in comparison with that of the works of VanPatten and colleagues mentioned earlier. From previous research, it had been established that, whereas younger learners seem to notice the phonological cues to grammatical gender, older learners devise a less effective system based on semantic properties. Thus the aim of the tasks was to get learners to notice the formal phonological features as they were processing the meaning. Example 9 is from an entire week of phonological focusing activities (see the Appendix of Harley, this volume, for the details of the full 5 weeks of focusing tasks). Each item in Example 9 shows how the materials were carefully developed to exemplify the relevant phonological cues to gender (M and F):

[9]   Phonological processing instruction

The students play a game of "Simon Says," with different actions for nouns with the characteristic M and F endings. "Concentration" is played again, with the class in two teams.

The students add to their M and F picture dictionaries using nouns with this week's endings. They make up rhymes about their pictures using rhyming adjectives with the same M and F endings.

As Harley reports, many of the tasks appeared to lead to item learning rather than to system learning. Although the instruction was substantially less metalinguistic than in other forms of input processing, there is some question as to the extent of task essentialness when the student is processing gender in some of the activities. For example, sometimes the labeling of M and F objects can be done correctly or incorrectly, and students cannot assess the correctness on their own. In contrast, during activities such as "Simon Says," when learners must determine correct gender assignment before continuing the game, processing gender becomes essential. It is perhaps the latter kind of task that is a more appropriate FonF technique.

In addition to developing focused tasks, the teacher may intervene, using various techniques to direct learner attention to form by employing corrective recasting or input-processing techniques. Various types of corrective recasting are clear examples of guiding or directing learners to noticing discrepancies between the IL and the TL. In our earlier consideration of responsive focus on form, we presented the four processing functions of the experimental corrective feedback employed by Carroll and Swain (1993; see Example 1 for details). In Example 2, we showed the garden path feedback technique. Both are intended to assist learner hypothesis testing. However, since the feedback in these tasks was part of decontextualized grammar instruction, the effectiveness of teacher corrective recasting when integrated in communicative tasks cannot be assumed. In other words, these kinds of corrective feedback techniques may possibly cross over the limit into focus on formS. For this reason, the integration of corrective feedback into real communication was the aim of the FonF technique employed by Doughty and Varela (this volume). All metalinguistic aspects of corrective feedback were eliminated from this technique, which aimed to attract learner attention more implicitly via intonationally segmenting out the learner error and immediately providing a recast in order to facilitate cognitive comparison. The technique was used extensively over a relatively long period of time, resulting in both short-term and long-term influences on the learners' developing ability to express events and predictions in past time. The implications of the duration of the focus on form in this study will be discussed further in the section on Decision 6.

One final example of how the teacher might increase the likelihood that learners will process linguistic form is Muranoi's interaction enhancement, a technique devised to integrate attention to form into communication-oriented instruction in a timely fashion. Interaction enhancement is based on DiPietro's strategic interaction (1987) and involves interactive problem-solving tasks in which instructors use scenarios to create contexts that guide learners to use the TL in realistic discourse. This is an instructional technique that emphasizes negotiation of meaning; minor attention is paid to grammatical accuracy. Interaction enhancement modifies strategic interaction in that the teacher leads learners' attention to a particular form while preserving the communicative characteristics of strategic interaction. Thus, *interaction enhancement* is defined as an instructional treatment in which a teacher pushes L2 learners to produce output and provides them with interactional modifications in order to lead them to notice a mismatch between their IL grammar and the TL grammar and to lead them to modify the incorrect output within the framework of strategic interaction.

Like strategic interaction, interaction enhancement has three phases: a rehearsal phase, a performance phase, and a debriefing phase. During the rehearsal phase the instructor gives the class a scenario that provides them with a problem to be solved through interaction (each scenario has many obligatory contexts for the target form). Students form pairs and prepare for the performance. During the performance phase, the scenario is performed by one student and the instructor, and this performance is observed by the entire class. The use of a student-teacher pair as a performance pair distinguishes interaction enhancement from the original strategic interaction; in the original strategic interaction, roles are performed by student-student pairs or groups. A student-teacher pair was employed in interaction enhancement so that the teacher could manipulate feedback intentionally in interaction.

Muranoi (1996) reports that, in his study, interactions were enhanced by providing requests for repetition when a student performer made overgeneralization errors with the indefinite article, which was the target form of the study. The requests for repetition had a dual function: as a flag to an incorrect form (input enhancement) and as a facilitator that guided the learner to produce modified output (output enhancement). After hearing the learner produce modified output, Muranoi repeated the learner's correctly modified form (input enhancement), or, if the learner did not modify output after receiving requests for repetition twice, he provided a corrective recast.

The performance phase in interaction enhancement is followed by the debriefing phase, in which the teacher and students (both the representative and the rest of the class) evaluate how well the interaction was carried out. In DiPietro's strategic interaction, the focus of debriefing was on meaning. That is, the degree of accuracy in conveying the meaning had the first priority. Muranoi, on the other hand, provided two types of debriefing: (1) interaction enhancement plus formS-focused debriefing involving the accuracy of the target forms, that is, explicit grammatical explanation on the use of the indefinite article; and (2) interaction enhancement plus meaning-focused debriefing involving how successfully the intended communication was carried out (the focus was on the degree of accuracy in conveying the meaning, not on the accuracy of the target forms).

The results of Muranoi's quasi-experimental study revealed that inter-action enhancement, in which L2 teachers provided targeted feedback within interactive, task-based instruction, had a positive effect on L2 learners' restructuring of the IL article system and that the impact of interaction enhancement depends on the type of debriefing that follows strategic interaction. In other words, interaction enhancement plus formS-focused debriefing had a greater effect than interaction enhance-ment plus meaning-focused debriefing. There were several instructional bonuses, as well: The effect of interaction enhancement lasted for at least 5 weeks, as measured by the delayed posttest; the positive effect of inter-action enhancement on the learning of the indefinite article was projected onto the learning of the definite article, which is less discoursally marked than the indefinite article (Chaudron & Parker, 1990); the instruction positively affected not only oral production but also production in the written mode; and finally, not only learners who participated in the inter-action enhancement but also learners who observed it improved their performance with the English article system (see also Takashima, 1994).

Summary

In discussing this range of examples of FonF techniques, it has become apparent that the consequences of crossover to focus on formS should never be taken lightly. Skehan (1996, p. 42) argues that it is important to make form-function connections clear by "devising methods of focusing on form without losing the values of communication tasks as realistic communicative motivators, and as opportunities to trigger acquisitional processes." It is also evident from the classroom studies that combina-tions of (rather than individual) FonF techniques are likely to be most useful. Some proven combinations are promoting perceptual salience plus input flooding, directing learner attention to salient or frequent linguistic features, intonational focus plus corrective recasting, and, as we have just seen, interaction enhancement. The observation that combining FonF techniques is both pedagogically and acquisitionally valid leads us directly into our discussion of the next two pedagogical decisions that must be made. In the section on Decision 5 we discuss the issue of the degree of integration of form and meaning at any one point in time. Just as we demonstrated in this section how FonF techniques are woven into classroom tasks, in the section on Decision 6 we show its integration into the entire L2 curriculum.

Decision 5: Sequential versus integrated focus on form

As we have seen, an obvious difficulty in designing FonF tasks and techniques is that, by virtue of its primary aim to draw learner attention to form, focus on form almost seems to invite explicit segmentation of language features so that learners can notice what may have been previously imperceptible. At what point does explicit segmentation cross over into linguistic isolation? This is a very fine line, indeed. Part of the solution to the problem of potential crossover is to incorporate into classroom activities tasks that are communicative, rather than language-as-object, *exercises*. The difference between *task* and *language exercises* is operationalized clearly by Loschky and Bley-Vroman (1993), who stipulate that, in *tasks,* the immediate criterion of success must be outside the grammar point itself. As has already been discussed, tasks in which the use of the form is essential are the best contexts, since the communicative pressure provides a certain opportunity for the teacher to draw learner attention to the form (see the section on Decision 2). However, since these tasks are difficult to design, and some forms are optional, task essentialness is not always feasible. This being the case, and since the most important component of focus on form is the way in which attentional resources are allocated (Long & Robinson, this volume), the remainder of the solution to potential crossover involves the requirement that *somehow and at some point* learner attention to *meaning* and *form* must be connected. It is the nature of this connection that we explore in this section.

Following Celce-Murcia (1992) and Larsen-Freeman (1995), we recognize that the term *meaning,* which is often equated only with its lexical component, in fact subsumes lexical, semantic, and pragmatic meaning. To be more accurate, we note that focus on form includes *forms, meaning,* and *function* (or *use*). To illustrate this point, Larsen-Freeman discusses the form, meaning, and function of the passive, noting in particular that both meaning and function are often overlooked in instruction. Example 10 shows the three components of focus on form.

[10]   Forms, meaning, and function

Examples (English passives)
A. The bill was paid by the company.
B. The wallet was stolen.
C. The data were collected and analyzed.
D. Spare toilet paper is stored here.
E. A mistake was made.

Forms
[NP-theme] [Auxiliary + past participle of transitive verb (by + NP-agent)]

Meaning
The events (the action expressed in the verb), the entities (the lexical
meaning of nouns), and the semantic relations (agent; theme)

Function
Use when: The theme is the topic (A, B), the agent is unknown (D), the
agent is unimportant (C), or you want to conceal the agent (E).

We suggest that the degree of effectiveness (especially over the long
term) of focus on form ultimately depends on the level of integration of
the learner's attention to all three aspects of form, meaning, and function
in the TL. Since it is often those forms that are neither perceptually salient
nor communicatively necessary that are most inaccurate in the IL of
advanced learners, the aim of FonF tasks and techniques is to engage
learner attention to facilitate more effective noticing of these form-
function-meaning relationships. To achieve this, learner attention must
be engaged at some point for a communicative purpose, either immediately or eventually. But does this mean that FonF instruction must aim
at all times to be integrated? As discussed by Lightbown (this volume),
it remains an open question as to whether the integration of form, meaning, and function must be *simultaneous* or, rather, may be *sequential,*
provided that attentional focus to each occurs within a limited time
frame.

The work of Lightbown and DeKeyser (both this volume) illustrates at
least two approaches that can be taken to increase attention to form in
the classroom. Lightbown considers what might be called the *FormS* →
FonF approach to be plausible. In this type of instruction, since in Lightbown's view any formS-focused intervention should be very *brief,* learners are first explicitly taught the forms to which the teacher will draw
their attention whenever difficulties in using them during communicative
tasks arise. Learners must also be alerted to the devices that will be used
later to attract their attention to formal errors. She discusses the unobtrusive techniques of hand signals (J. Schachter, 1981) and raised eyebrows.
Doughty and Varela (this volume) developed another unobtrusive technique for drawing learner attention to error – intonational focus in which
the learner error was repeated with rising intonation prior to the teacher
recasting the learner utterance into targetlike form without any metalinguistic comment. The more unobtrusive the signaling of the difficulty, the
more likely the learner will remain engaged with the meaning and functions aspects of the message. For this reason, it is important for the
teacher to make it clear to the learner that it is the formS and not the
message that are being briefly attended to. Lightbown suggests that prior
formS-oriented instruction plus heightened learner expectation that these
errors will be corrected are likely to combine effectively with a brief
focus on form. It is probably the case that learning cannot be guided

this unobtrusively unless there is only one learning problem in focus (Doughty & Varela, this volume; Williams and Evans, this volume).

DeKeyser (1995, this volume) also recommends a *FormS-then-FonF* instructional sequence. Based on cognitive skill acquisition theory, DeKeyser argues for the sequential roles of explicit teaching of forms (known in skill acquisition as *declarative knowledge;* see Anderson, 1993, 1995; Anderson & Fincham, 1994), controlled practice (proceduralization), and frequent opportunities to use declarative knowledge in communicative activities (automatization). The cognitive aim of this approach is to convert conscious, declarative knowledge into more automatically accessible knowledge. As DeKeyser (this volume) points out, this is not a new approach to instruction; however, he suggests, it has not been adequately implemented in the classroom. This is sometimes because not enough time has been allowed for students to fully develop declarative knowledge before they are expected to practice it or because no opportunities for practice or automatization have been made available after the declarative knowledge has been acquired. In the proceduralization phase, students must engage in target behaviors using the factual, declarative knowledge as a temporary crutch. The primary learning process that occurs during this proceduralization phase is restructuring of the factual knowledge into a more usable cognitive format.[12] It should be noted that the research basis for these claims involves the learning of miniature artificial grammars, and such findings cannot yet be generalized to the classroom setting. However, it is certainly of interest that, in these studies, the subjects are given ample time to acquire declarative knowledge, and then they are presented with *thousands* of example cases in which to proceduralize that knowledge.

As we noted in the section on Decision 3, not all aspects of language are readily amenable to focus on form. Based on the cognitive research to date, DeKeyser suggests that rules that are easy to learn (declaratively) but hard to acquire (without instruction) are prime candidates for the declarative-to-procedural-to-automatic sequencing. He also indicates that the acquisition of declarative knowledge and its proceduralization

---

12 A simple example of restructuring is found in the acquisition of computational ability. If the object is to find the total of several cases of the same number, one could take several approaches (adapted from Cheng, 1985):

First, learn the addition rule: 2 plus 2 is 4 plus 2 is 6 plus 2 is 8 plus 2 is 10.

Next, make the observation that when adding 2s, one can use the "count by even numbers" rule: 2-4-6-8-10.

Either of these approaches works very well when there are only a few numbers to be added; the second approach may be operationally faster; however, when there are twenty 2s to be counted, even the second rule is cumbersome. So, learn the multiplication rule: twenty 2s is 2 times 20 = 40.

interact with the ability level of the learners and suggests that, as learners advance, the difficulty of the declarative knowledge and the target behaviors should be increased.

In Skehan's view, proceduralization is not restricted to TL forms. It is possible, and probably likely, that nontargetlike IL knowledge is frequently proceduralized as the result of the need to communicate when linguistic proficiency is still limited. Because this knowledge is now automatic, and thus difficult to change, Skehan sees this as a "stumbling block to change in the future" (1996, p. 41). Here the role of focus on form may be to undo such procedures, replacing IL forms with more targetlike ones.

Leeman et al. (1995) make the case that, among all the possible ways to implement focus on form, it may ultimately be most worthwhile to evaluate various tasks and techniques based on whether they simultaneously integrate attention to form with attention to meaning, rather than isolating attention to form as a separate component. Because humans have a limited attentional capacity, performance on an attention-demanding task usually declines when subjects are simultaneously required to perform a second task (Tomlin & Villa, 1994; VanPatten, 1989). However, performance on the first task is not adversely affected if the two tasks are "somehow compatible" (Tomlin & Villa, 1994, p. 189). Thus tasks or enhancements designed to integrate attention to form with attention to meaning should require less diversion of learners' attentional resources. Moreover, if restructuring primarily consists of establishing new form-meaning mappings, it follows that the most efficient type of attention to form would take place *within* a meaningful context.

There are a number of studies in which researchers have experimentally attempted to increase attention to form within an overall focus on meaning. One such study was conducted by Hulstijn (1989), who compared the effects of exposing subjects to target sentences and assigning them tasks designed to require focus either on meaning or on formal properties of the input. Hulstijn then administered cued recall and repetition tasks to all subjects and found that not only did the meaning group score better than the formal group on the recall tasks but the meaning group also showed no disadvantage on at least some of the forms-oriented tasks (see also Doughty, 1991). Similarly, although Spada and Lightbown (1993, p. 218) originally set out to compare a purely communicative control group with one that was communicative but with added focus on forms, they suggest that it was the unplanned "context-embedded focus on form" that occurred unexpectedly in their control group (by the "wayward" teacher mentioned earlier) that caused comparison subjects to outperform the experimental group. In their study of the acquisition of preterit and imperfect in L2 Spanish, Leeman et al.

operationalized focus on form in the following way: The meaningful context in which all attention to form was embedded was 2 weeks of content-based instruction in Spanish history. During these 2 weeks, attention was drawn to the distinction between the preterit and the imperfect in every way possible: visual highlighting with color coding in reading material, corrective feedback from the teacher, direction of attention toward expression of time relations, and in a range of communicative activities culminating in debates and video judging of the debates. Findings showed that, in comparison with the control group, learners in the FonF group increased in their attempts at expressing past in Spanish, and there were also discernible changes in their IL production that the researchers took to be evidence of restructuring.[13]

It has also been claimed that for such instruction to be effective, the meaning associated with the forms must be grasped first. Lightbown (this volume) offers the suggestion that one of the reasons that focused instruction on questions was effective in her study (Spada & Lightbown, 1993) was that meaning was already transparent for these learners and they were therefore able to concentrate on the more formal features of the structure. VanPatten (1994a) claims that learners process more meaningful morphemes before they process less meaningful ones. It appears then, that learners must, at some level, be ready to notice and process the form. If they are already using most of their resources for other aspects of language comprehension, production, or learning, and have little attention to free up for noticing this new form, it is unlikely that focus on form will be effective. Harley (1994) makes a similar observation about learners in French immersion programs. The processing demands made on these children tend to be in terms of global comprehension of content; and this is the likely focal point of their attention, leaving few resources for focusing on forms that carry little meaning, especially those incongruent with their L1, English. Thus, salience and noticing may have as much to do with learner proficiency and task demands as with the nature of the form and its distribution in the input (Robinson, 1995b).

There are theoretical explanations and some empirical support for the limitations on how learners can allocate their attentional resources. As learners hear and comprehend language, input that is perceived is held in limited-capacity short-term memory very briefly, only to be replaced by the next wave of incoming input, unless attention is engaged so that further mental processing can occur. This further processing has been described as a stage of going from input to intake (Gass, 1988; VanPat-

---

13 It could be argued that this study also supports the formS-to-form approach, since these learners of Spanish as a foreign language were known to have about 60% accuracy in the overall use of preterit and imperfect, knowledge that they had gained via relatively traditional instruction, which could thus be considered to be a form of declarative knowledge.

ten, 1994b). Intake then undergoes additional mental processing still, and this enables the learner to encode linguistic material into long-term memory. According to these researchers, input that is not converted to intake is then lost and consequently is no longer available to any subsequent language acquisition processes. Thus the important pedagogical issue is not only whether learners pay attention to form but also how to get the attentional allocation increased, because the more one attends, the more one learns. One suggestion is that when information is presented in varying modalities, attentional capacity is increased (Allport, Antonis, & Reynolds, 1972, as reported in Schmidt, 1995).

However tempting it may be to try to increase the attentional capacity of learners, it is evident from studies that once the limit is reached, learning is no longer possible. This claim is based on experiments in cognitive psychology in which learners are presented with competing stimuli (a sequence of lights presented simultaneously with a group of tones; the learner must remember the light sequence and count the instances of a particular tone). In these dual tasks, subjects are predominantly unaware of the underlying patterns, and there is only some very limited learning (Curran & Keele, 1993).

As Schmidt (1995) points out, although learning without attention is impossible, different kinds of learning occur with differing amounts of attention. Simple item learning or the learning of very simple patterns (e.g., vocabulary words plus their collocations) seems to be possible when attention is divided, but the abstraction of more complex rules requires undivided attention. VanPatten has argued along the lines of cognitive psychologists who suggest that attention is a limited resource and that it may be impossible for learners to attend to form and meaning simultaneously. He bases this claim on his investigation of learners of Spanish who were required to count all occurrences of a lexical item (*inflación*), a free morpheme (the definite article *la*), or a bound morpheme (*-an,* which marks third person plural) while at the same time comprehending the text they were listening to (as measured by responses to questions after the passage was read). Lower-level learners could not do both kinds of processing simultaneously. Even the advanced learners had difficulty with the bound morpheme, but they were able to attend to the form and meaning of the noun and the article. VanPatten explains that the extent to which learners can process form and meaning together may be determined by the amount of knowledge that they have already acquired, a point not unlike DeKeyser's suggestion that learner level interacts with the processes involved in skill acquisition.

Summary

In this section we have discussed three possible models for the integration of form and meaning in second language instruction:

Model 1
- *Brief,* explicit instruction of formal knowledge
- FonF activities with signals and brief interventions

Model 2
- Explicit instruction of formal knowledge
- Time for the learner to grasp the declarative knowledge
- Extensive practice of the forms in controlled behaviors, using declarative knowledge as a crutch (leading to proceduralization)
- Extensive practice of the procedures in communicative activities (leading to automatization)

Model 3
- Attention to form and meaning integrated at all times, with or without explicit instruction

With regard to this important timing issue of simultaneous versus sequential integration of form, meaning, and function, we have suggested that all three models represent plausible possibilities and may be appropriate for different contexts. However, within the definition that we have set out for focus on form, that is, addressing some aspect of language in the context of *meaningful communication,* we believe that only the first and third qualify. Because of the separation of explicit provision of rules and communicative use, the second model diverges in key ways from focus on form. It is possible that this model, when properly implemented as advocated by DeKeyser, may yet prove to be effective; but this awaits classroom testing. At this juncture, however, we will concentrate on the other two models. The key difference between these two models, of course, is the extent of the integration of the forms and meaning focus. Given the task constraints that are required if simultaneous integration is to be ensured, the optimal level of focus on form may not always be practical. If sequential attention to form and meaning is all that is possible, then determining the optimal duration of the time interval between attention to form, meaning, and function becomes an urgent matter. At all times, however, the crossover limit must be borne in mind: When the focus is on linguistic form in complete isolation, and this activity is not followed by another in which the function of the formal feature becomes evident to the learner, such an activity cannot be considered to qualify as focus on form. With this limit firmly in mind, we will now turn to a consideration of the integration of focus on form into the L2 curriculum.

Decision 6: The role of focus on form in the curriculum

A number of studies we have cited purport to show the effectiveness of instruction that includes a focus on form in improving the accuracy of L2 learners. Unfortunately, however, not enough of these studies offer documentation of sustained gains. The few that are able to report lasting effects provide some insight into the long-term role of focus on form, specifically, (1) how long or intense focus on form must be in order to be effective, and (2) what sequences and combinations of tasks and techniques work best when focus on form is integrated into the curriculum.

First, it is important to acknowledge that lengthy instruction is not always necessary. It is possible, if the treatment succeeds in getting learners to notice the form, and if the form is abundant and available in the ambient input, that no further focus on form is necessary. For instance, in a recent study, Trahey (1996) followed up on an earlier study (Trahey & L. White, 1993) that documented the effectiveness of an implicit, relatively short-term, 2-week FonF treatment in improving some adverb-placement orders but not others (see the section on Decision 3 for details of the earlier study). Trahey found that the gains found in the earlier study were maintained; that is, learners who had noticed a target word order that differed from their L1 order (subject-adverb-verb-object) continued to use and accept this order a year later. Presumably, once they noticed this order, there was enough evidence in the input to strengthen this knowledge.

However, Spada and Lightbown (1993) argue that even the acquisition of forms that are abundant in the input, such as questions, may be better aided by sustained, integrated focus on form. As we noted in our discussion of classroom attempts to integrate form into meaning focus, the teacher of the class originally described as *uninstructed,* turned out to be providing continued and consistent focus on question formation. The learners in her class outperformed those in the instructed group, maintaining or improving their performance on the delayed posttest (see the section on Decision 5 for details). Harley (1989) reports a similar finding in her study of L2 French learners: The initial gains made by the classes that received specially prepared materials focusing on the *passé composé/ imparfait* distinction were matched by the uninstructed classes at the delayed posttest (see also Lightbown, 1983). However, as in the case of the teacher reported by Spada and Lightbown, Harley observed that one teacher, far more than the others, tended to focus on the *passé composé/ imparfait* distinction; her class outperformed all others.

It should be clear that determining the ideal intensity and duration of focus on form is closely tied to long-term curricular decisions. We cannot necessarily expect short-term treatment with minimal or no follow-up to have a lasting effect. Numerous studies (e.g., Harley, 1989; Spada, 1987; L. White, 1991) testify to the ineffectiveness of this type of isolated instruction. There may be initial effects, but frequently they do not endure. The studies that have thus far demonstrated long-term effects have generally had two characteristics: (1) They have integrated attention to meaning and attention to form, and (2) focus on form continues beyond a short, isolated treatment period (e.g., Day & Shapson, 1991; Doughty & Varela, this volume; Harley, 1989; Leeman et al., 1995; Lightbown, 1991; Spada & Lightbown, 1993). Examples of the success of sustained, integrated focus on form are as diverse as a middle school ESL science class (Doughty & Varela), a seventh grade immersion class (Day & Shapson), and a graduate-level class in applied linguistics (Master, 1995). Doughty and Varela found that when the primary focus was always on content, sustained and directed attention to a single form led to long-term gains on accuracy in the form in focus, the marking of past. Most important, however, was the research team's decision to integrate focus on this form, consisting of repetition and recasting, into the content class on a regular basis, throughout the course, rather than to limit it to a single activity or unit. Leeman et al. also took a curricular approach to integrating focus on form into a 2-week second language content unit. They incorporated many different FonF techniques into their treatment for the experimental class and found that those learners had higher rates of accuracy and production of the form in focus than did the learners in the class that received no FonF treatment (see the section Decision 5 for a fuller discussion).

Day and Shapson (1991) attempted to increase the use and accuracy of conditionals in L2 French immersion. Again, their approach was curricular; they planned cyclical, long-term (5 to 7 weeks) integration of focus on formS, meaning, and use of conditionals in both oral and written activities. Their approach included:

1. Cooperative planning of a future space colony. The aim of this activity was to maximize both student interaction and task-natural opportunities to use conditional.
2. Structured linguistic games or exercises that regularly preceded the first activity. The aim here was to increase the learners' metalinguistic awareness.
3. Group and self-evaluation procedures were used to promote noticing of the use of the conditional.

The experimental group performed significantly better than did the control group on immediate and delayed cloze tests and written compositions. Although the advantage of the experimental group on oral tasks was not significant, Day and Shapson argue that individual class data do show evidence of greater and more consistent development in these areas as well. Similarly, Master (1995) reports significant improvement in article choice among L2 learners of English following an instructional treatment that included detailed feedback, error awareness logs, and metalinguistic discussions that emphasized form-meaning relationships. Crucially, his FonF techniques tied article choice to the expression of meaning and continued over the period of an entire semester. Without a control group, it is, of course, impossible to determine which changes are solely a consequence of instruction. However, for many teachers, a technique that leads to any improvement in article use, an area of the grammar that is notoriously difficult, is worthy of further consideration.

It is well known to teachers and researchers alike that language acquisition takes time; restructuring is not instantaneous. Although a single encounter with a form may lead to an acquisition breakthrough, we do not know whether it is the tenth, fiftieth, or thousandth encounter that will be the crucial one or, alternatively, whether it is simply that the thousandth came at just the right time. Until we know more, we can assume that multiple encounters are required for engaging learning processes, such as noticing, hypothesis formation and testing, comparison, and restructuring. Thus, it is important that focus on form be seen within the perspective of the curriculum, rather than within the confines of a single lesson or activity.

It is also important to view the effect of FonF instruction in a broader perspective. Indeed, many studies we have reported may not have completely captured learning in progress, or therefore may not have revealed the full effect of instruction, since measures are generally in terms of target forms, that is to say, in terms of accuracy. In fact, the emergence of many intermediate IL forms, which often represent increasing IL complexity rather than increasing accuracy (Skehan, 1996), may be facilitated by focus on form. A variety of FonF studies have documented an advance in IL development – realized as increased attempts at the target – following instruction. Day and Shapson (1991) found an increased use of incipient conditionals, such as *peut être* plus adverb, future *prôche,* and *vouloir* plus infinitive. Williams and Evans (this volume) reported little effect for instruction on the passive using traditional measures, and yet there was a greater number of attempts at passives, such as the use of a *by* phrase with nontargetlike verb marking or promotion of patient to subject, again with nontargetlike verb marking, in the production of many of the instructed subjects. Similarly, Doughty and Varela (this volume) report many attempts at the past conditional in their subjects' production. They maintain that the learners first noticed the function and tried to mark it in a variety of ways, though not always in a targetlike manner. Intermediate IL forms were also noted in Leeman et al. (1995): Learners who had received FonF instruction increased their marking of tense, even though they did not always manage to mark aspect in a targetlike manner. Thus, as has also been shown in investigations of other types of instruction, focus on form does not always immediately lead to IL changes that are reflected in increased accuracy. It may also lead to restructuring that reflects increased complexity, an equally important aspect of IL development. In this respect, focus on form has the advantage of affecting both IL development and IL accuracy.

We argued earlier that task selection depends on the learners as well as the forms, and thus it is difficult to make blanket recommendations for the development of curricula that include focus on form. However, several rather general curricular formats have been proposed for the long-term teaching of formal accuracy. For our purposes, we will assume that the form in focus is available in the ambient written and/or oral input, in addition to any special instructional focus. The first task in developing a FonF component in a curriculum is to determine whether the form is emergent in the IL. By this we mean whether or not learners have begun attempting the form in output or show evidence of comprehending it in the input. If there is no evidence of even the initial stages of acquisition, the first task would be to get the learners to notice the form in question. In this case, some researchers (e.g., VanPatten, 1990) argue that FonF tasks are inappropriate, that the focus should be exclusively on meaning. However, even VanPatten and others of the same view (e.g., Terrell, 1991) support the use of advanced organizers, so-called because they provide learners with ways of organizing the subsequent meaning-focused input in structured ways. Nevertheless, within this approach, metalinguistic information is kept to a minimum. Once learners have some grasp of the meaning, more attention to form is possible. VanPatten advises beginning with activities that require learners to process only input, since input forms the building blocks of the developing IL system (see VanPatten & Cadierno, 1993a, 1993b; VanPatten & Sanz, 1995; although see also DeKeyser & Sokalski, 1996). This helps learners to notice features of the input and to establish formS-meaning relationships. Only after these forms have been incorporated into the developing system is it appropriate to include output, according to VanPatten. The primary purpose of this output would be automatization and the development of fluency.

At the other end of the scale, DeKeyser (this volume) argues for initial presentation of explicit, rule-based explanations, so that a full understanding of the form in focus can be achieved. This should be followed by formS-focused exercises but, he stresses, executed in a deliberate and thoughtful manner so that declarative knowledge can be firmly anchored. He contrasts this with traditional rapid-fire drilling. Proceduralization occurs individually, as learners reflect on their new knowledge, and most important, DeKeyser advises that activities that promote automatization should be postponed until production is nearly error-free. Essentially, then, DeKeyser's aim is to take care of the accuracy issue before non-targetlike forms can become automatic. Another technique to promote noticing in this initial stage is proposed by Bardovi-Harlig and Reynolds (1995), who used a flood of carefully chosen positive evidence combined with focused noticing activities to increase their learners' awareness of the target language use of past tense with activity and state verbs. Following Sharwood Smith (1991), they call this *elaborate,* but not *explicit,* input enhancement, since it contained numerous contextualized examples but no formal presentation of rules. Unlike the situation with the input processing approach, Bardovi-Harlig and Reynolds also included task-natural production tasks that gave learners an opportunity to use their knowledge in appropriate contexts.

Once learners have noticed the form in the input, and perhaps have begun attempting production, it is important that activities in the classroom help them to notice how their own production may differ from the target, that is, a process known as *noticing the gap.* It is possible that some of the more implicit techniques, such as input flooding and enhancement, may help them to do this, but for some learners, this may not be sufficient, especially if the IL forms represent a more general rule than the target does. Compare the results of flooding and instruction on the two forms in Williams and Evans (this volume). Acquisition of an emergent form, participial adjectives, was facilitated by the flood, but contextualized explanations were even more helpful. The opposite was true for the passive, a form that had yet to emerge in the learners' ILs. The flood apparently helped learners to notice and begin to attempt its use, but more explicit instruction was of little further use. The learners simply were not ready to sort out the complex forms-meaning-use relationship involved in the passive voice. Indeed, the passive is considerably more complex than participial adjectives. However, it is difficult to separate the effects of developmental readiness and complexity, since the level of complexity itself is sometimes the constraint that determines readiness.

This would suggest an alternative instructional strategy opposite to that proposed by DeKeyser. More direct instruction should be delayed until learners have demonstrated at least some emerging knowledge of the form (i.e., have shown learnability). Research by Swain (1995, this volume) lends support to this position. The learners in her studies were inaccurate in their use of a variety of forms, such as the *imparfait* and *passé composé,* but it is clear that they had noticed them at some level. For this population, she suggests the use of explicit rule presentation, followed by activities that require that the learners use output to reflect, in effect, on their own linguistic inadequacies, what we have called noticing the hole, and that they consult their implicit or explicit knowledge in attempting to fill in those holes. Swain is not the only proponent of tasks that include output. Foster and Skehan (1996), especially, stress the importance of planned output tasks. In tasks for which planning time is permitted, learners generally increase their accuracy and complexity (see also Crookes, 1989).

We have shown that another possible way of getting learners to notice the disparity between the target and their own production involves the provision of negative evidence, in the form of corrective feedback (Carroll & Swain, 1993; Doughty & Varela, this volume; Mackey & Philp, 1998; Oliver, 1995; Ortega & Long, 1997; Tomasello & Herron, 1988, 1989; L. White, 1991). Again, however, it is important to take a long-term approach to the use of feedback. There would seem to be little benefit in providing feedback if the learner does not have fairly firm knowledge, implicit or explicit, of the form in focus. In addition, effective feedback is sustained and focused. VanPatten (1993), in discussing input-processing activities, indeed advises that only one form be in focus in any activity, citing learners' limited attentional capacity. In providing feedback, too, there is evidence of the effectiveness of this narrow focus. Doughty and Varela (this volume) used a relatively implicit FonF technique, repetition plus recasting, to successfully improve their learners' accuracy in past time reference. These differences were largely maintained on the delayed posttest 2 months later, especially in oral production. In an experimental study, Mackey and Philp (1998) found sustained gains in question formation among a group of developmentally "ready" learners who received intensive recasting of their questions. Those who were simply allowed to interact, but did not receive the intensive recasting, showed no gains. Again, the recasting was focused, in this case, on question formation. In contrast, a similar technique did not lead to uptake in classrooms where there was recasting of diverse forms (Lyster & Ranta, 1997). Clearly, however, there is a trade-off: When one form is in focus, others cannot be. Thus it will be important to ascertain the optimum duration and intensity for focus on any given form. Individual teachers will need to determine when learners are ready to take over responsibility for accuracy on one form so that they can taper off focus on that form and move on to another.

Summary

We have discussed three distinct approaches to integrating focus on form into the curriculum, and here we present these options in summary form. The first option is the same as Model 2 discussed in the summary of the section on Decision 5, since, of course, the suggestion that focus on form need not be integrated at one point in time but, rather, can be integrated sequentially necessarily entails the need to consider FonF integration throughout the curriculum. The remaining two options offer additional curricular possibilities.

Curriculum Option 1
A. Presentation of rules → development of declarative knowledge
B. Reflection → proceduralization
C. Controlled practice → anchoring of declarative knowledge
D. Fluency practice → automatization

Curriculum Option 2
A. Input → processing meaning
B. Input processing → intake of formal features
C. Output → fluency

Curriculum Option 3
A. Preemergence: implicit techniques, for example, flood or input enhancement → noticing
B. Emergence: selection of appropriate techniques, that is, more explicit techniques, for example, focused feedback or metalinguistic reflection concurrent with production output in task-natural activities → noticing the gap or hole

These three options are by no means the only possibilities, and the decision to follow one of these options or to design any other curricular approach will depend on all the factors we have discussed throughout this chapter.

A taxonomy of FonF tasks and techniques

We conclude our discussion of the pedagogical implementation of focus on form by presenting a taxonomy of tasks and techniques; an analysis of learner, teacher, language, and mode features; and a concise summary of the underpinnings of the pedagogical decisions that we have elaborated throughout this chapter. Tables 3 to 6 comprise the taxonomy, which is based on many of the examples we have presented. Thus, it is not our intention to be exhaustive but, rather, to offer an expandable range of FonF possibilities. Our point of departure in developing the taxonomy includes only tasks and techniques that are either inherently or sequentially integrated in terms of focus on form and meaning or use. In other words, we will not deal with tasks or techniques that present only isolated metalinguistic information, since this approach would not qualify as focus on form. In Table 6, we divide the sequential types of focus on form into their component parts and analyze each separately. It is important to point out that most of the tasks and techniques listed in Tables 3 to 6 cannot guarantee that learners will focus on the intended form; they can only encourage learners to do this. And finally, it is evident that the tasks

TABLE 3. DEGREE OF OBTRUSIVENESS OF FOCUS ON FORM

	Unobtrusive ←						→ Obtrusive
Input flood	X						
Task-essential language	X						
Input enhancement[a]		X					
Negotiation		X					
Recast[b]			X				
Output enhancement			X				
Interaction enhancement				X			
Dictogloss[c]					X		
Consciousness-raising tasks[d]					X		
Input processing						X	
Garden path							X

[a]For example, typographical or intonational.
[b]As implemented by Doughty and Varela (this volume).
[c]As implemented by Swain (this volume).
[d]Here we refer specifically to tasks used by Fotos (1993, 1994).

TABLE 4. FEATURES OF FOCUS ON FORM

• Learner attention	± directed (vs. attracted)
• Learner involvement	± learner manipulation of form
• Learning condition	± deductive
• Integration	± integrated (vs. sequential)
• Inclusion of metalinguistic information	± metalinguistic
• Modes	± input
	± output
• Providers	± teacher/materials
	± other learners

and techniques can, and sometimes should, be implemented in combination with one another.

Table 3 shows how tasks and techniques can be ranged along a continuum reflecting the degree to which the focus on form interrupts the flow of communication, that is to say, on the basis of *obtrusiveness*.

In addition, as shown in Tables 4 and 5, tasks and techniques can be described and analyzed in terms of a variety of features. Note that in Table 5 some tasks and techniques have stages, each with different features.

Finally, all tasks and techniques should be designed keeping in mind the relevant components of focus on form that we have discussed in this chapter: learning context, the learners themselves, the form in focus, and,

TABLE 5. AN ANALYSIS OF FEATURES* OF FOCUS-ON-FORM TASKS AND TECHNIQUES

Task	Learner attention	Learner involvement	Learning condition	Integration	Metalinguistic	Input	Output	Provided by Teacher	Provided by Learner
Input flood	−	−	−	+	−	+	−	+	−
Task essential	−	+	−	+	−	+	+	+	−
Recast	+	±	−	+	−	+	±	+	−
Input enhancement	−	−	−	+	−	+	−	+	−
Negotiation	±	±	−	+	−	+	+	±	±
Output enhancement	+	±	−	+	−	−	+	+	−
Interaction enhancement:									
rehearsal	−	+	−	+	−	+	+	+	±
performance	+	±	−	+	−	+	+	+	−
debriefing	+	±	+	−	+	+	+	+	−
Dictogloss:									
lesson	+	±	+	−	+	+	+	+	−
modeling	+	±	+	−	+	+	+	+	−
reflection	+	+	±	+	±	+	+	−	+
CR tasks	+	+	±	−	+	+	−	+	+
Input processing:									
lesson	+	±	+	−	+	+	+	+	−
processing	+	+	+	+	−	+	−	+	−
Garden path	+	±	+	−	+	+	+	+	−

*These features are specified further in Table 4.

TABLE 6. FACTORS UNDERPINNING FONF DESIGN

- The learning context
  1. Availability of input
  2. Classroom constraints
- The learners
  1. Age
  2. Proficiency
  3. Educational background
  4. Educational goals
- The form
  1. Inherent characteristics
     a. Nature of the rule
     b. Frequency in the input
     c. Relation to L1 form
  2. Status in IL, e.g., emergent, errored, stabilized
- The learning process to be engaged
  1. Noticing
  2. Noticing gaps or holes
  3. Cognitive comparison
  4. Restructuring
  5. Hypothesis testing
  6. Automatization

---

perhaps most important of all, the learning processes to be engaged in, as recapitulated in Table 6. This list should be taken as a starting point and, by no means, represents an exhaustive list of such factors.

Conclusion

Our aim in this chapter has been to interpret the research on focus on form in classroom SLA for the language teaching professional. We hope to have convinced readers that the noninterventionist position is inefficient at best and undefinable at worst. Always leaving L2 learners to their own devices results in the sort of incomplete language learning documented extensively in the Canadian immersion studies. Fortunately, as can be seen throughout this volume and elsewhere, there is an ever-growing body of research that examines when and how the teacher can engage the cognitive processing abilities of L2 learners. We have suggested that the teacher may take either a proactive or a reactive stance in providing focus on form, depending upon the classroom context and learner variables, though the choice of one over the other has major task design and curricular ramifications that must be considered carefully. In our discussion of the nature of language features themselves and how these considerations may have an impact on all other pedagogical FonF choices, we have suggested that, occasionally, it will be best not to attend to a particular language feature, either at all or at a particular (i.e., too early) time. More often, however, the nature of the form will simply have an impact upon the decision as to whether to take an explicit or implicit approach to drawing learner attention to form. In discussing this range of possibilities, we pointed out that, contrary to earlier proposals, it is entirely possible to combine explicit and implicit FonF techniques, depending upon the particular acquisition circumstances. Such combinations should not be theoretically proscribed. Rather, their pedagogical motivations are clear, and there is growing evidence of the effectiveness of a more flexible curricular approach involving a variety of successful task-technique combinations. We did raise a warning, however, given that the possibility of crossover to focus on formS was evident in a number of the experimental and classroom studies that we examined. At the broader task and curriculum levels, we have presented a number of possible models for focusing on form, some emphasizing the psycholinguistic timing of attention to form vis à vis focus on meaning, and others emphasizing the pedagogical integration of focus on form into the overall curriculum. Finally, and most important of all, we have proposed that, whatever the pedagogical decision at hand, the primary concern of the teacher should always be the question of how to *integrate* attention to form and meaning, either simultaneously or in some interconnected sequence of tasks and techniques that are implemented throughout the curriculum.

References

Alanen, R. (1992). Input enhancement and rule presentation in second language acquisition. M.A. thesis, University of Hawai'i at Manoa.

Alanen, R. (1995). Input enhancement and rule presentation in second language acquisition. In R. Schmidt (Ed.), *Attention and awareness in foreign language learning and teaching* (pp. 259–302). Honolulu: University of Hawai'i Press.

Allen, P., Swain, M., Harley, B., & Cummins, J. (1990). Aspects of classroom treatment: Toward a more comprehensive view of second language education. In B. Harley, P. Allen, J. Cummins, & M. Swain (Eds.), *The development of second language proficiency* (pp. 57–81). New York: Cambridge University Press.

Allwright, R. (1976). Language learning through communication practice. *ELT Documents, 76*(3), 2–14.

Ammar, A. (1996). Is implicational generalisation unidirectional and applicable in foreign contexts? Evidence from relativization instruction in a foreign language. M.A. thesis, Concordia University.

Andersen, R. (1983). Transfer to somewhere. In S. Gass & L. Selinker (Eds.), *Language transfer in language learning* (pp. 177–201). Rowley, MA: Newbury House.

Andersen, R. (1984). What's gender good for, anyway? In R. Andersen (Ed.), *Second language: A cross-linguistic perspective* (pp. 77–99). Rowley, MA: Newbury House.

Andersen, R. (1993). Four operating principles and input distribution as explanation for underdeveloped and mature morphological systems. In K. Hyltenstam & A. Viberg (Eds.), *Progression and regression in language* (pp. 309–339). Cambridge: Cambridge University Press.

Anderson, J. (1982). Acquisition of cognitive skill. *Psychological Review, 89*(4), 369–406.

Anderson, J. (1983). *The architecture of cognition.* Cambridge: Cambridge University Press.

Anderson, J. (1987). Skill acquisition: Compilation of weak-method problem solutions. *Psychological Review, 94*(2), 192–210.

Anderson, J. (1990). *Cognitive psychology and its implications.* New York: Freeman.

Anderson, J. (1993). *Rules of the mind.* Hillsdale, NJ: Lawrence Erlbaum.

Anderson, J. (1995). *Learning and memory: An integrated approach.* New York: Wiley.

Anderson, J., & Fincham, J. (1994). Acquisition of procedural skills from examples. *Journal of Experimental Psychology, 20,* 1322–1340.

Atkinson, M. (1982). Explanations in the study of child language development. Cambridge: Cambridge University Press.

Baetens-Beardsmore, H. (1993). An overview of European models of bilingual education. *Language, Culture and Curriculum, 6*(3), 197–208.

Bailey, K., & Nunan, D. (1996). *Voices from the classroom.* Cambridge: Cambridge University Press.

Baker, N., & Nelson, K. (1984). Recasting and related conversational techniques for triggering syntactic advances by young children. *First Language, 13*(1), 3–22.

Bamford, J. (1989). Comments on Elisabeth Gatbonton and Norman Segalowitz's 'Creative automatization: Principles for promoting fluency within a communicative framework.' *TESOL Quarterly, 23*(2), 363–366.

Bardovi-Harlig, K. (1987). Markedness and salience in second language acquisition. *Language Learning, 27*(3), 385–407.

Bardovi-Harlig, K. (1995). The interaction of pedagogy and natural sequences in the acquisition of tense and aspect. In F. Eckman, D. Highland, P. Lee, J. Mileham, & R. Weber (Eds.), *Second language acquisition theory and pedagogy* (pp. 151–168). Mahwah, NJ: Lawrence Erlbaum.

Bardovi-Harlig, K., & Reynolds, D. (1995). The role of lexical aspect in the acquisition of tense and aspect. *TESOL Quarterly, 29*(1), 107–131.

Bates, L. (1993). *Transitions.* New York: St. Martin's.

Baudoin, M., Bober, E., Clarke, M., Dobson, B., & Silberstein, S. (1988). *Reader's Choice.* Ann Arbor: University of Michigan Press.

Beck, M., & Eubank, L. (1991). Acquisition theory and experimental design: A critique of Tomasello and Herron. *Studies in Second Language Acquisition, 13*(1), 73–76.

Berry, D. (1994). Vocabulary acquisition: Implicit and explicit learning of complex tasks. In N. Ellis (Ed.), *Implicit and explicit learning of languages* (pp. 147–164). London: Academic.

Bialystok, E. (1979). Explicit and implicit judgments of L2 grammaticality. *Language Learning, 29*(1), 81–103.

Bialystok, E. (1981). The role of linguistic knowledge in second language use. *Studies in Second Language Acquisition, 4*(1), 31–45.

Bialystok, E. (1990). The competence of processing: Classifying theories of second language acquisition. *TESOL Quarterly, 24*(4), 635–648.

Bialystok, E. (1994a). Analysis and control in the development of a second language. *Studies in Second Language Acquisition, 16*(2), 157–168.

Bialystok, E. (1994b). Representation and ways of knowing: Three issues in second language acquisition. In N. Ellis (Ed.), *Implicit and explicit learning of languages* (pp. 549–569). London: Academic Press.

Bialystok, E., & Bouchard Ryan, E. (1985). Toward a definition of metalinguistic skill. *Merrill-Palmer Quarterly, 31*(3), 229–251.

Birdsong, D. (1992). Ultimate attainment in second language acquisition. *Language, 68*(4), 706–755.

Blum, S., & Levenston, E. (1978). Universals of lexical simplification. *Language Learning, 28*(2), 399–415.

Bohannon, J., & Stanowicz, L. (1988). The issue of negative evidence: Adult responses to children's language errors. *Developmental Psychology, 34*(5), 684–689.

Bowen, J. D., Madsen, H., & Hilferty, A. (1985). *TESOL techniques and procedures.* Rowley, MA: Newbury House.

Braine, M. (1965). The insufficiency of a finite-state model for verbal reconstructive memory. *Psychonomic Science, 2,* 291–292.

Breen, M., & Candlin, C. (1980). The essentials of a communicative curriculum in language teaching. *Applied Linguistics, 1*(2), 89–112.

Brindley, G. (1991). *Learnability in the ESL classroom.* Paper presented at the RELC Seminar on Language Acquisition and the Second/Foreign Language Classrooms, Singapore.

Brooks, N. (1964). *Language and language learning: Theory and practice.* 2nd ed. New York: Harcourt Brace.

Brown, C. (1991). *My left foot.* London: Minerva.

Brown, R., & Hanlon, C. (1970). Derivational complexity and order of acquisition in child speech. In J. Hayes (Ed.), *Cognition and the development of language* (pp. 11–53). New York: Wiley.

Brumfit, C., & Johnson, K. (1979). *The communicative approach to language teaching.* Oxford: Oxford University Press.

Burt, M., Dulay, H., & Krashen, S. (1982). *Language two.* New York: Oxford University Press.

Butterworth, G. (1972). A Spanish-speaking adolescent's acquisition of English syntax. Ph.D. dissertation, University of California at Los Angeles.

Bybee, J., & Moder, C. (1983). Morphological classes as natural categories. *Language, 57*(2), 251–270.

Bybee, J., & Slobin, D. (1982). Rules and schemas in the development and use of the English past tense system. *Language, 58*(2), 265–289.

Cadierno, T. (1992). Explicit instruction in grammar: A comparison of input-based and output-based instruction in second language acquisition. Ph.D. dissertation, The University of Illinois.

Cadierno, T. (1995). Formal instruction from a processing perspective: An investigation into the Spanish past tense. *Modern Language Journal, 79*(2), 179–193.

Cancino, H., Rosansky, E., & Schumann, J. (1978). The acquisition of English negatives and interrogatives by native Spanish speakers. In E. Hatch (Ed.), *Second language acquisition: A book of readings* (pp. 207–230). Rowley, MA: Newbury House.

Carr, T. H., & Curran, T. (1994). Cognitive factors in learning about structured sequences: Applications to syntax. *Studies in Second Language Acquisition, 16*(3), 205–230.

Carroll, J. (1974). Learning theory for the classroom teacher. In G. Jarvis (Ed.), *The challenge of communication* (pp. 113–149). Skokie, IL: National Textbook Company.

Carroll, S. (1989). Second-language acquisition and the computational paradigm. *Language Learning, 39*(4), 535–594.

Carroll, S. (1993). Input and learning theory: Adults' sensitivity to different sorts of input. Paper presented at the University of Toronto Linguistics Colloquium, Toronto.

Carroll, S. (1996). The irrelevance of verbal feedback to language learning. In L.

Eubank, L. Selinker, & M. Sharwood Smith (Eds.), *The current state of interlanguage* (pp. 73–88). Amsterdam: John Benjamins.

Carroll, S., & Swain, M. (1993). Explicit and implicit negative feedback: An empirical study of the learning of linguistic generalizations. *Studies in Second Language Acquisition, 15*(3), 357–386.

Carroll, S., Swain, M., & Roberge, Y. (1992). The role of feedback in adult second language acquisition: Error correction and morphological generalization. *Applied Psycholinguistics, 13*(2), 173–189.

Ceci, S., & Howe, M. (1982). Metamemory and effects of intending, attending, and intending to attend. In G. Underwood (Ed.), *Aspects of consciousness: Vol. 3: Awareness and self awareness* (pp. 147–177). London: Academic Press.

Celce-Murcia, M. (1992). Formal grammar instruction: An educator comments . . . , *TESOL Quarterly 26*(2), 406–408.

Celce-Murcia, M., Dörnyei, Z., & Thurrell, S. (1997). Direct approaches in L2 instruction: A turning point in communicative language teaching? *TESOL Quarterly 31*(1), 141–152.

Celce-Murcia, M., & Larsen-Freeman, D. (1983). *The grammar book*. Rowley, MA: Newbury House.

Chastain, K. (1971). *The development of modern language skills: Theory to practice*. Philadelphia: The Center for Curriculum Development.

Chastain, K. (1987). Examining the role of grammar explanation, drills, and exercises in the development of communication skills. *Hispania, 70*(1), 160–166.

Chaudron, C., & Parker, K. (1990). Discourse markedness and structural markedness. *Studies in Second Language Acquisition, 12*(2), 43–64.

Cheng, P. (1985). Restructuring vs. automaticity: Alternative accounts of skill acquisition. *Psychological Review, 92*(3), 414–423.

Clahsen, H. (1987). Connecting theories of language processing and (second) language acquisition. In C. Pfaff (Ed.), *First and second language acquisition processes* (pp. 103–116). Cambridge, MA: Newbury House.

Clark, E. (1985). The acquisition of romance with special reference to French. In D. Slobin (Ed.), *The crosslinguistic study of language acquisition, Vol. 1: The data* (pp. 687–782). Hillsdale, NJ: Lawrence Erlbaum.

Clarke, M. (1994). The dysfunction of theory and practice. *TESOL Quarterly, 28*(1), 9–26.

Coady, J. (1997). L2 vocabulary acquisition: A synthesis of research. In J. Coady & T. Huckin (Eds.), *Second language vocabulary acquisition* (pp. 273–290). New York: Cambridge University Press.

Cook, V. (1991). *Second language learning and language teaching*. London: Edward Arnold.

Cook, V. (1993). *Linguistics in second language acquisition*. New York: St. Martin's.

Coppieters, R. (1987). Competence differences between native and near-native speakers. *Language, 63*(3), 544–573.

Corbett, G. (1991). *Gender*. Cambridge: Cambridge University Press.

Corder, S. P. (1967). The significance of learners' errors. *International Review of Applied Linguistics, 5*(4), 161–169.

Coughlan, P., & Duff, P. (1994). Same task, different activities: Analysis of an SLA task from an activity theory perspective. In J. Lantolf & G. Appel (Eds.), *Vygotskian approaches to second language research* (pp. 173–193). Norwood, NJ: Ablex.

Crookes, G. (1989). Planning and interlanguage variation. *Studies in Second Language Acquisition, 11*(4), 367–383.

Crookes, G. (1993). Action research for second language teachers: Going beyond teacher research. *Applied Linguistics, 14*(2), 130–144.

Crookes, G. (1997). Second language acquisition and language pedagogy: A socio-educational perspective. *Studies in Second Language Acquisition, 19*(1), 93–116.

Crookes, G., & Gass, S. (1993a). *Tasks and language learning: Integrating theory and practice.* Vol. 1. Clevedon, Avon: Multilingual Matters.

Crookes, G., & Gass, S. (1993b). *Tasks in a pedagogical context: Integrating theory and practice.* Vol. 2. Clevedon, Avon: Multilingual Matters.

Cumming, A. (1990). Metalinguistic and ideational thinking in second language composing. *Written Communication, 7*(4), 482–511.

Curran, T., & Keele, S. W. (1993). Attentional and nonattentional forms of sequence learning. *Journal of Experimental Psychology: Learning, Memory and Cognition, 19*(1), 189–202.

Curtiss, S. (1988). Abnormal language acquisition and the modularity of language. In F. Newmeyer (Ed.), *Linguistics: The Cambridge survey. Linguistic theory: Extensions and implications,* Vol. 2 (pp. 96–116). Cambridge: Cambridge University Press.

Day, E., & Shapson, S. (1991). Integrating formal and functional approaches in language teaching in French immersion: An experimental study. *Language Learning, 41*(1), 25–58.

De Graff, R. (1997). The eXperanto experiment: Effects of explicit instruction on second language acquisition. *Studies in Second Language Acquisition, 19*(2), 249–297.

DeKeyser, R. (1994). How implicit can adult second language learning be? In J. Hulstijn & R. Schmidt (Eds.), *Consciousness in second language learning* (pp. 83–96): AILA Review, Vol. 11.

DeKeyser, R. (1995). Learning second language grammar rules: An experiment with a miniature linguistic system. *Studies in Second Language Acquisition, 17*(3), 379–410.

DeKeyser, R. (1997). Beyond explicit rule learning: Automatizing second language morphosyntax. *Studies in Second Language Acquisition, 19*(2), 196–221.

DeKeyser, R., & Sokalski, K. (1996). The differential role of comprehension and production practice. *Language Learning, 46*(4), 613–642.

Delisle, H. (1985). The acquisition of gender by American students of German. *Modern Language Journal, 69*(1), 55–63.

Demetras, M., Post, K., & Snow, C. (1986). Feedback to first language learners: The role of repetitions and clarification requests. *Journal of Child Language, 13*(2), 275–292.

DiPietro, R. (1987). *Strategic interaction.* Cambridge: Cambridge University Press.

Doughty, C. (1988). The effect of instruction on the acquisition of relativization in English as a second language. Ph.D. dissertation, University of Pennsylvania.

Doughty, C. (1991). Second language instruction does make a difference: Evidence from an empirical study of ESL relativization. *Studies in Second Language Acquisition, 13*(4), 431–469.

Doughty, C. (1994a). Fine-tuning of feedback by competent speakers to language learners. In J. Alatis (Ed.), *GURT 1993: Strategic interaction and language acquisition* (pp. 96–108). Washington, DC: Georgetown University Press.

Doughty, C. (Convener) (1994b). Symposium: Focus on form – What is it? Second Language Research Forum, Montreal.

Doughty, C. (1996). SLA through conversational discourse. Paper presented at the Annual Conference of the American Association for Applied Linguistics, Chicago.

Doughty, C. (1998). Acquiring competence in a second language: Form and function. In H. Byrnes (Ed.), *Learning foreign and second languages: Perspectives in research and scholarship.* New York: Modern Language Association.

Doughty, C. (in preparation). Negotiating the L2 environment.

Doughty, C., & Williams J. (Conveners) (1995). Colloquium: Focus on form in classroom second language acquisition. Annual Meeting of the American Association for Applied Linguistics, Long Beach, CA.

Dulany, D., Carlson, R., & Dewey, G. (1984). A case of syntactical learning and judgment: How conscious and how abstract? *Journal of Experimental Psychology, 113*(4), 541–555.

Dulany, D., Carlson, R., & Dewey, G. (1985). On consciousness in syntactic learning and judgment: A reply to Reber, Allen and Regan. *Journal of Experimental Psychology, 114*(1), 25–32.

Dulay, H., & Burt, M. (1973). Should we teach children syntax? *Language Learning, 24*(2), 245–258.

Dulay, H., & Burt, M. (1974). Natural sequences in child second language acquisition. *Language Learning, 24,* 37–53.

Dulay, H., & Burt, M. (1975). Creative construction in second language learning and teaching. In H. Dulay & M. Burt (Eds.), *New directions in second language learning: Teaching and bilingual education* (pp. 21–32). Washington, DC: TESOL.

Eckman, F. (1977). Markedness and the contrastive analysis hypothesis. *Language Learning, 27,* 315–330.

Eckman, F. (1991). The structural conformity hypothesis and the acquisition of consonant clusters in the interlanguage of ESL learners. *Studies in Second Language Acquisition, 13*(1), 23–41.

Eckman, F., Bell, L., & Nelson, D. (1988). On the generalization of relative clause instruction in the acquisition of English as a second language. *Applied Linguistics, 9*(1), 1–20.

Eckman, F., & Iverson, G. (1993). Sonority and markedness among onset clusters in the interlanguage of ESL learners. *Second Language Research, 9*(3), 234–252.

Eckman, F., & Iverson, G. (1997). Structure preservation in interlanguage phonology. In S. J. Hannahs & M. Young-Scholten (Eds.). *Current issues in the acquisition of phonology,* Amsterdam: John Benjamins.

Eckman, F., Moravscik, & Wirth, J. (1989). Implicational universals and inter-rogative structure in the interlanguage of ESL learners. *Language Learning, 39*(2), 173–205.

Ellis, N. (1993). Rules and instances in foreign language learning: Interactions of implicit and explicit knowledge. *European Journal of Cognitive Psychology, 5*(3), 289–319.

Ellis, N. (1994a). Consciousness in second language learning: Psychological per-spectives on the role of conscious processes in vocabulary acquisition. In J. Hulstijn & R. Schmidt (Eds.), *Consciousness in second language learning* (pp. 37–56): AILA Review, Vol. 11.

Ellis, N. (1994b). Vocabulary acquisition: The implicit ins and outs of explicit cognitive mediation. In N. Ellis (Ed.), *Implicit and explicit learning of lan-guages* (pp. 211–282). London: Academic Press.

Ellis, N. (Ed.). (1994c). *Implicit and explicit learning of languages.* London: Academic Press.

Ellis, R. (1989). Are classroom and naturalistic language acquisition the same? A study of the classroom acquisition of German word order rules. *Studies in Second Language Acquisition, 11*(3), 305–328.

Ellis, R. (1990). *Instructed second language acquisition.* Oxford: Basil Blackwell.

Ellis, R. (1991). Grammar teaching practice or consciousness-raising? In R. Ellis (Ed.), *Second language acquisition and second language pedagogy* (pp. 232–241). Clevedon, Avon: Multilingual Matters.

Ellis, R. (1993). The structural syllabus and second language acquisition. *TESOL Quarterly, 27*(1), 91–113.

Ellis, R. (1994a). *The study of second language acquisition.* 2nd ed. Oxford: Oxford University Press.

Ellis, R. (1994b). A theory of instructed second language acquisition. In N. Ellis (Ed.), *Implicit and explicit language learning* (pp. 79–114). London: Academic.

Faerch, C., & Kasper, G. (1987). Perspectives on language transfer. *Applied Linguistics, 8*(2), 111–136.

Farrar, M. (1990). Discourse and the acquisition of grammatical morphemes. *Journal of Child Language, 17*(3), 607–624.

Farrar, M. (1992). Negative evidence and grammatical morpheme acquisition. *Developmental Psychology, 28*(1), 90–98.

Felix, S. (1981). The effect of formal instruction on second language acquisition. *Language Learning, 31*(1), 87–112.

Felix, S., & Hahn, A. (1985). Natural processes in classroom second-language learning. *Applied Linguistics, 6*(3), 223–238.

Fitts, P., & Posner, M. (1967). *Human performance.* Belmont, CA: Brooks Cole.

Flege, J. (1987). A critical period for learning to pronounce foreign languages? *Applied Linguistics, 8*(2), 162–177.

Foster, P., & Skehan, P. (1996). The influence of planning time and task type on second language performance. *Studies in Second Language Acquisition, 18*(3), 299–323.

Fotos, S. (1993). Consciousness-raising and noticing through focus on form: Grammar task performance vs. formal instruction. *Applied Linguistics, 14*(4), 385–407.

Fotos, S. (1994). Integrating grammar instruction and communicative language use through grammar consciousness-raising tasks. *TESOL Quarterly, 28*(2), 323–351.

Fotos, S., & Ellis, R. (1991). Communicating about grammar: A task-based approach. *TESOL Quarterly, 25*(4), 605–628.

Fries, C. (1945). *Teaching and learning English as a foreign language.* Ann Arbor: University of Michigan Press.

Furey, P. (1987). The relationship between advanced ESL learners' explicit rule knowledge of five English grammar patterns and performance on a grammar production task. Ph.D. dissertation, University of Pittsburgh.

Garavito-Bruhn, J. (1986). El muchacha tiene tres balón: Number and gender in the Spanish of a group of francophone learners. M.A. thesis, Concordia University.

Gass, S. (1982). From theory to practice. In M. Hines & W. Rutherford (Eds.), *On TESOL '81* (pp. 120–139). Washington, DC: TESOL.

Gass, S. (1987). The resolution of conflicts among competing systems: A bidirectional perspective. *Applied Psycholinguistics, 8*(4), 329–350.

Gass, S. (1988). Integrating research areas: A framework for second language studies. *Applied Linguistics, 9*(2), 198–217.

Gass, S., & Selinker, L. (1994). *Second language acquisition: An introductory course.* Hillsdale, NJ: Lawrence Erlbaum.

Gass, S., & Varonis, E. (1994). Input, interaction and second language production. *Studies in Second Language Acquisition, 16*(3), 283–302.

Gatbonton, E., & Segalowitz, N. (1988). Creative automatization: Principles for promoting fluency within a communicative framework. *TESOL Quarterly, 22*(3), 473–492.

Genesee, F. (1987). *Learning through two languages.* New York: Newbury House.

Green, P., & Hecht, K. (1992). Implicit and explicit grammar: An empirical study. *Applied Linguistics, 13*(4), 385–407.

Grégoire, A. (1947). *L'apprentissage du langage II: la troisième année et les années suivantes.* Paris: Les Belles Lettres.

Grimshaw, J., & Pinker, S. (1989). Positive and negative evidence in language acquisition. *Behavioral and Brain Sciences 12*(3), 341–342.

Hamilton, R. (1994). Is implicational generalization unidirectional and maximal? Evidence from relativization instruction in a second language. *Language Learning, 44*(1), 123–157.

Hammarberg, B. (1985). Learnability and learner strategies in second language syntax and phonology. In K. Hyltenstam & M. Pienemann (Eds.), *Modelling and assessing second language acquisition* (pp. 113–136). San Diego: College Hill Press.

Hardison, D. (1992). Acquisition of grammatical gender in French: L2 learner accuracy and strategies with competing cues. *Canadian Modern Language Review, 48*(2), 292–306.

Harley, B. (1979). French gender 'rules' in the speech of English-dominant, French-dominant and monolingual French-speaking children. *Working Papers on Bilingualism, 14,* 31–46.

Harley, B. (1986). *Age in second language acquisition.* Clevedon, Avon: Multilingual Matters.

Harley, B. (1989). Functional grammar in French immersion: A classroom experiment. *Applied Linguistics, 10*(3), 331–359.

Harley, B. (1992). Patterns of second language development in French immersion. *Journal of French Language Studies, 2*(2), 159–183.

Harley, B. (1993). Instructional strategies and SLA in early French immersion. *Studies in Second Language Acquisition, 15*(2), 245–260.

Harley, B. (1994). Appealing to consciousness in the L2 classroom. In J. Hulstijn & R. Schmidt (Eds.), *Consciousness in second language learning* (pp. 57–68): AILA Review, Vol. 11.

Harley, B., & Swain, M. (1984). The interlanguage of immersion students and its implications for second language teaching. In A. Davies, C. Criper, & A. Howatt (Eds.), *Interlanguage* (pp. 291–311). Edinburgh: Edinburgh University Press.

Hatch, E. (1978). Discourse analysis and second language acquisition. In E. Hatch (Ed.), *Second language acquisition: A book of readings* (pp. 401–475). Rowley, MA: Newbury House.

Hatch, E. (1983). *Psycholinguistics: A second language perspective.* Rowley, MA: Newbury House.

Hawkins, R. (1989). Do second language learners acquire restrictive relative clauses on the basis of relational or configurational information? The acquisition of French subject, direct object, and restrictive relative clauses by second language learners. *Second Language Research, 5*(2), 155–188.

Herron, C. (1991). The garden path correction strategy in the foreign language classroom. *The French Review, 64*(6), 966–977.

Herron, C., & Tomasello, M. (1992). Acquiring grammatical structures by guided instruction. *The French Review, 65*(5), 708–718.

Howatt, A. P. R. (1984). *A history of English language teaching.* Oxford: Oxford University Press.

Huebner, T. (1983). Linguistic systems and linguistic change in an interlanguage. *Studies in Second Language Acquisition, 6*(1), 33–53.

Hulstijn, J. (1989). Implicit and incidental language learning: Experiments in the processing of natural and partly artificial input. In H. Dechert & M. Raupach (Eds.), *Interlingual processing* (pp. 49–73). Tübingen: Gunter Narr.

Hulstijn, J. (1995). Not all grammar rules are equal: Giving grammar instruction its proper place in foreign language teaching. In R. Schmidt (Ed.), *Attention and awareness in foreign language learning* (pp. 359–386). Honolulu: University of Hawai'i Press.

Hulstijn, J., & De Graaff, R. (1994). Under what conditions does explicit knowledge of a second language facilitate the acquisition of implicit knowledge? In J. Hulstijn & R. Schmidt (Eds.), *Consciousness in second language learning* (pp. 97–112): AILA Review, Vol. 11.

Hulstijn, J., & Zekhnini, A. (1994). An experimental study on the learning of arbitrary and non-arbitrary gender of pseudo-Dutch nouns by non-native and native speakers of Dutch. Paper presented at the Second Language Research Forum, Montreal.

Hyltenstam, K. (1977). Implicational patterns in interlanguage variation. *Language Learning, 27*(2), 383–411.

Hyltenstam, K. (1984). The use of typological markedness conditions as predictors in second language acquisition: The case of pronominal copies in rela-

272   *References*

tive clauses. In R. Andersen (Ed.), *Second language: A cross-linguistic perspective* (pp. 39–59). Rowley, MA: Newbury House.

Hyltenstam, K. (1987). Markedness, language universals, language typology and second language acquisition. In C. Pfaff (Ed.), *First and second language acquisition processes* (pp. 55–78). Cambridge: Newbury House.

Hyltenstam, K. (1988). Lexical characteristics of near-native second-language learners of Swedish. *Journal of Multilingual and Multicultural Development, 9*(1 & 2), 67–84.

Ingram, D. (1989). *First language acquisition.* Cambridge: Cambridge University Press.

Johnson, J., & Newport, E. (1989). Critical period effects in second language learning: The influence of maturational state on the acquisition of English as a second language. *Cognitive Psychology, 21*(1), 60–99.

Johnston, M. (1985). *Syntactic and morphological progressions in learner English.* Canberra: Commonwealth Department of Immigration and Ethnic Affairs.

Jones, F. R. (1992). A language-teaching machine: Input, uptake and output in the communicative classroom. *System, 20*(2), 133–150.

Jourdenais, R., Ota, M., Stauffer, S., Boyson, B., & Doughty, C. (1995). Does textual enhancement promote noticing? A think-aloud protocol analysis. In R. Schmidt (Ed.), *Attention and awareness in foreign language learning* (pp. 183–216). Honolulu: University of Hawai'i Press.

Karmiloff-Smith, A. (1978). The interplay between syntax, semantics and phonology in the acquisition process. In R. N. Campbell & P. Smith (Eds.), *Recent advances in the psychology of language: Language development and mother-child interaction* (pp. 1–23). New York: Plenum.

Karmiloff-Smith, A. (1979). *A functional approach to child language.* Cambridge: Cambridge University Press.

Keenan, E., & Comrie, B. (1977). Noun phrase accessibility and universal grammar. *Linguistic Inquiry, 8*(1), 63–99.

Kellerman, E. (1978). Giving learners a break: Native language intuition as a source of prediction about transferability. *Working Papers on Bilingualism, 15,* 59–92.

Kellerman, E. (1985). Input and second language acquisition theory. In S. Gass & C. Madden (Eds.), *Input in second language acquisition* (pp. 345–353). Rowley, MA: Newbury House.

Kelly, L. G. (1969). *Twenty-five centuries of language teaching 500 BC–1969.* Rowley, MA: Newbury House.

Kirsner, K. (1994). Second language vocabulary learning: The role of implicit processes. In N. Ellis (Ed.), *Implicit and explicit learning of languages* (pp. 283–311). London: Academic.

Kowal, M., & Swain, M. (1994). Using collaborative language production tasks to promote students' language awareness. *Language Awareness, 3*(2), 73–93.

Kowal, M., & Swain, M. (1997). From semantic to syntactic processing: How can we promote metalinguistic awareness in the French immersion classroom? In K. Johnson & M. Swain (Eds.), *Immersion education: International perspectives* (pp. 284–309). New York: Cambridge University Press.

Krashen, S. (1977). The monitor model for adult second language performance. In M. Burt, H. Dulay, & M. Finocchiaro (Eds.), *Viewpoints on English as a second language* (pp. 152–161). New York: Regents.

Krashen, S. (1981). *Second language acquisition and second language learning.* Oxford: Pergamon.

Krashen, S. (1982). *Principles and practice in second language acquisition.* Oxford: Pergamon.

Krashen, S. (1985). *The input hypothesis: Issues and implications.* London: Longman.

Krashen, S. (1989). We acquire vocabulary and spelling by reading: Additional evidence for the input hypothesis. *Modern Language Journal, 73*(4), 440–464.

Krashen, S. (1992). Formal grammar instruction: Another educator comments . . . *TESOL Quarterly, 26*(2), 409–411.

Krashen, S. (1993). The effect of formal grammar teaching: Still peripheral. *TESOL Quarterly, 27*(4), 722–725.

Krashen, S. (1994). The input hypothesis and its rivals. In N. Ellis (Ed.), *Implicit and explicit learning of languages* (pp. 45–77). London: Academic Press.

Krashen, S., & Terrell, T. (1983). *The natural approach.* New York: Pergamon.

Kumpf, L. (1984). Temporal systems and universality in interlanguage: A case study. In F. Eckman, L. Bell, & D. Nelson (Eds.), *Universals of second language acquisition* (pp. 132–143). Rowley, MA: Newbury House.

Lado, R. (1964). *Language teaching: A scientific approach.* New York: McGraw-Hill.

LaPierre, D. (1994). Language output in a cooperative learning setting: Determining its effects on second language learning. M.A. thesis, University of Toronto.

Lapkin, S., & Swain, M. (1990). French immersion research agenda for the 90s. *Canadian Modern Language Review, 46*(4), 638–674.

Larsen-Freeman, D. (1995). On the teaching and learning of grammar: Challenging the myths. In F. Eckman, D. Highland, P. W. Lee, J. Mileham, & R. R. Weber (Eds.), *Second language acquisition theory and pedagogy* (pp. 131–150). Mahwah, NJ: Lawrence Erlbaum.

Larsen-Freeman, D., & Long, M. H. (1991). *An introduction to second language acquisition theory and research.* London: Longman.

Laufer, B. (1990). "Sequence" and "order" in the development of L2 lexis: Some evidence from lexical confusions. *Applied Linguistics, 11*(3), 281–296.

Leeman, J., Arteagoitia, I., Fridman, B., & Doughty, C. (1995). Integrating attention to form with meaning: Focus on form in content-based Spanish instruction. In R. Schmidt (Ed.), *Attention and awareness in foreign language learning* (pp. 217–258). Honolulu: University of Hawai'i Press.

Lepicq, D. (1980). Aspects théoriques et empiriques de l'acceptabilité linguistique: Le cas du français des élèves des classes d'immersion. Ph.D. dissertation, University of Toronto.

Levelt, W. (1976). Skill theory and language teaching. *Studies in Second Language Acquisition, 1*(1), 53–70.

Levin, L. (1972). *Comparative studies in foreign language teaching.* Stockholm: Almqvist and Wiksell.

Levy, Y. (1983). It's frogs all the way down. *Cognition, 15,* 75–93.

Lightbown, P. (1983). Exploring relationships between developmental and instructional sequences in L2 acquisition. In H. Seliger & M. Long (Eds.), *Classroom-oriented research in second language acquisition* (pp. 217–243). Rowley, MA: Newbury House.

Lightbown, P. (1985a). Can language acquisition be altered by instruction? In K. Hyltenstam & M. Pienemann (Eds.), *Modelling and assessing second language acquisition* (pp. 101–112). Clevedon, Avon: Multilingual Matters.

Lightbown, P. (1985b). Great expectations: Second language acquisition research and classroom teaching. *Applied Linguistics, 6*(2), 173–189.

Lightbown, P. (1991). What have we here? Some observations on the influence of instruction on L2 learning. In R. Phillipson, E. Kellerman, L. Selinker, M. Sharwood Smith, & M. Swain (Eds.), *Foreign/second language pedagogy research* (pp. 197–212). Clevedon, Avon: Multilingual Matters.

Lightbown, P. (1992). Getting quality input in the second and foreign language classroom. In C. Kramsch & S. McConnell-Ginet (Eds.), *Text and context: Cross-disciplinary and cross-cultural perspectives on language study* (pp. 187–197). Lexington, MA: Heath.

Lightbown, P. (1993). Input, instruction and feedback in second language acquisition. *Second Language Research, 7*(2), ii–iv.

Lightbown, P., & Pienemann, M. (1993). Comments on Stephen D. Krashen's "Teaching issues: Formal grammar instruction." *TESOL Quarterly, 27*(4), 717–722.

Lightbown, P., & Spada, N. (1978). Performance on an oral communication task by Francophone ESL learners. *SPEAQ Journal, 2*(4), 35–54.

Lightbown, P., & Spada, N. (1990). Focus on form and corrective feedback in communicative language teaching: Effects on second language learning. *Studies in Second Language Acquisition, 12*(4), 429–448.

Lightbown, P., and Spada, N. (1994). An innovative program for primary ESL in Quebec. *TESOL Quarterly, 28*(3), 563–579.

Lightbown, P., & Spada, N. (1997). Learning English as a second language in a special school in Quebec. *Canadian Modern Language Review, 53*(2), 315–355.

Lin, Y-H., & Hedgcock, J. (1996). Negative feedback incorporation among high-proficiency and low-proficiency Chinese-speaking learners of Spanish. *Language Learning, 46*(4), 567–611.

Logan, G. (1988). Toward an instance theory of automatization. *Psychological Review, 95*(4), 492–527.

Long, M. H. (1981). Input, interaction, and second language acquisition. In H. Winitz (Ed.), *Native language and foreign language acquisition* (pp. 259–278): Annals of the New York Academy of Sciences, Vol. 379.

Long, M. H. (1983a). Does second language instruction make a difference? A review of research. *TESOL Quarterly, 17*(3), 359–382.

Long, M. H. (1983b). Native speaker/non-native-speaker conversation and the negotiation of comprehensible input. *Applied Linguistics, 4*(2), 126–141.

Long, M. H. (1985). Input and second language acquisition theory. In S. Gass & C. Madden (Eds.), *Input in second language acquisition* (pp. 377–393). Rowley, MA: Newbury House.

Long, M. H. (1988a). Focus on form: A design feature in language teaching methodology. Paper presented at the European-North-American Symposium on Needed Research in Foreign Language Education, Bellagio, Italy: Rockefeller Center.

Long, M. H. (1988b). Instructed interlanguage development. In L. Beebe (Ed.), *Issues in second language acquisition: Multiple perspectives* (pp. 115–141). Rowley, MA: Newbury House.

Long, M. H. (1990). Maturational constraints on language development. *Studies in Second Language Acquisition, 12*(3), 251–286.

Long, M. H. (1991). Focus on form: A design feature in language teaching methodology. In K. de Bot, R. Ginsberg, & C. Kramsch (Eds.), *Foreign language research in cross-cultural perspective* (pp. 39–52). Amsterdam: John Benjamins.

Long, M. H. (1993). Second language acquisition as a function of age: Research findings and methodological issues. In K. Hyltenstam & A. Viberg (Eds.), *Progression and regression in language* (pp. 196–221). Cambridge: Cambridge University Press.

Long, M. H. (1996). The role of the linguistic environment in second language acquisition. In W. Ritchie & T. Bhatia (Eds.), *Handbook of research on second language acquisition* (pp. 413–468). New York: Academic.

Long, M. H. (1997a). Authenticity and learning potential in L2 classroom discourse. In G. M. Jacobs (Ed.), *Language classrooms of tomorrow: Issues and responses* (pp. 148–169). Singapore: SEAMEO Regional Language Centre.

Long, M. H. (1997b). Fossilization: Rigor mortis in living linguistic systems? Paper presented at EuroSLA7, Barcelona.

Long, M. H. (in press). *Task-based language teaching.* Oxford: Blackwell.

Long, M. H., & Crookes, G. (1992). Three approaches to task-based syllabus design. *TESOL Quarterly, 26*(1), 27–56.

Long, M. H., & Crookes, G. (1993a). The authors respond. *TESOL Quarterly, 27*(4), 729–733.

Long, M. H., & Crookes, G. (1993b). Units of analysis in syllabus design: The case for task. In G. Crookes & S. Gass (Eds.), *Tasks in pedagogical context: Integrating theory and practice* (pp. 9–56). Clevedon, Avon: Multilingual Matters.

Long, M. H., Inagaki, S., & Ortega, L. (1998). The role of implicit negative feedback in SLA: Models and recasts in Japanese and Spanish. *Modern Language Journal, 82*(3).

Long, M. H., & Ross, S. (1997). Modifications that preserve language and content. In M. L. Tikoo (Ed.), *Simplification: Theory and applications* (pp. 29–52). Singapore: SEAMEO Regional Language Centre.

Long, M. H., & Sato, C. J. (1984). Methodological issues in interlanguage studies. In A. Davies, C. Criper, & A. Howatt (Eds.), *Interlanguage* (pp. 253–279). Edinburgh: Edinburgh University Press.

Loschky, L. (1994). Comprehensible input and second language acquisition. *Studies in Second Language Acquisition, 16*(3), 303–323.

Loschky, L., & Bley-Vroman, R. (1993). Grammar and task-based methodology. In G. Crookes & S. Gass (Eds.), *Tasks and language learning.* Vol. 1 (pp. 123–167). Clevedon, Avon: Multilingual Matters.

Lyster, R. (1994a). The effect of functional-analytic teaching on aspects of French immersion students' sociolinguistic competence. *Applied Linguistics, 15*(3), 263–287.

Lyster, R. (1994b). Négociation de la form: stratégie analytique en classe d'immersion. *Canadian Modern Language Review, 50*(3), 447–465.

Lyster, R., & Ranta, L. (1997). Corrective feedback and learner uptake: Negotiation of form in communicative classrooms. *Studies in Second Language Acquisition, 19*(1), 37–66.

Mackey, A., & Philp, J. (1998). Recasts, interaction and interlanguage development: Are responses red herrings? *Modern Language Journal, 82*(3).

Magnan, S. (1983). Age and sensitivity to gender in French. *Studies in Second Language Acquisition, 5*(2), 194–212.

Manheimer, R. (1993). Close the task, improve the discourse. *Estudios de Linguistica Aplicada, 17,* 18–40.

Marcus, G., Pinker, S., Ullman, M., Hollander, M., Rosen, T. J., & Xu, F. (1992). Overregularization in language acquisition. *Monographs of the Society for Research in Child Development, 57*(4), 1–165.

Marinova-Todd, S. (1994). The critical period in second language acquisition: The case of gender. B.A. honors thesis, York University, Ontario.

Martens, M. (1988). Recognition and production of pronouns by francophone learners of English as a second language. M.A. thesis, Concordia University, Montreal.

Master, P. (1994). The effect of systematic instruction on learning the English article system. In T. Odlin (Ed.), *Perspectives on pedagogical grammar* (pp. 229–252). Cambridge: Cambridge University Press.

Master, P. (1995). Consciousness raising and article pedagogy. In D. Belcher & G. Braine (Eds.), *Academic writing in a second language* (pp. 183–204). Norwood, NJ: Ablex.

Mathews, R., Buss, R., Stanley, W., Blanchard-Fields, F., Cho, J. R., & Druhan, B. (1989). Role of implicit and explicit processes in learning from examples: A synergistic effect. *Journal of Experimental Psychology, 15*(6), 1083–1100.

McLaughlin, B. (1987). *Theories of second language acquisition.* London: Edward Arnold.

McLaughlin, B. (1990). Restructuring. *Applied Linguistics, 11*(2), 113–128.

Meara, P. (1984). The study of lexis in interlanguage. In A. Davies, C. Criper, & A. Howatt (Eds.), *Interlanguage* (pp. 225–235). Edinburgh: Edinburgh University Press.

Meisel, J. (1987). Reference to past events and actions in the development of natural second language acquisition. In C. Pfaff (Ed.), *First and second language acquisition processes* (pp. 206–224). Cambridge, MA: Newbury House.

Meisel, J., Clahsen, H., & Pienemann, M. (1981). On determining developmental stages in natural second language acquisition. *Studies in Second Language Acquisition, 3*(2), 109–135.

Mellow, D. (1992). Towards a theory of second language transition: Implications from constrained studies of instruction and attrition. Paper presented at the Second Language Research Forum, East Lansing, MI.

Mellow, J. D., Reeder, K., & Forster, E. (1996). Using time-series research designs to investigate the effects of instruction on SLA. *Studies in Second Language Acquisition 18*(3), 325–350.

Miller, P. (1985). Metacognition and attention. In D. Forest-Pressley, G. MacKinnon, & T. Waller (Eds.), *Metacognition, cognition and human performance, vol. 2: International practices* (pp. 181–221), Orlando: Academic Press.

Muranoi, H. (1996). Effects of interaction enhancement on restructuring of interlanguage grammar: A cognitive approach to foreign language instruction. Ph.D. dissertation, Georgetown University, Washington, DC.

Newell, A., & Simon, H. (1972). *Human problem solving*. Englewood Cliffs, NJ: Prentice Hall.

Newmark, L. (1966). How not to interfere with language learning. *International Journal of American Linguistics, 32*(1), 77–83.

Newmark, L. (1971). A minimal language teaching program. In P. Pimsleur & T. Quinn (Eds.), *The psychology of second language learning*, Vol. 32 (pp. 11–18). Cambridge: Cambridge University Press.

Newmark, L., & Reibel, D. (1968). Necessity and sufficiency in language learning. *International Review of Applied Linguistics, 6*(2), 145–164.

Newport, E. (1990). Maturational constraints on language learning. *Cognitive Science, 14*(1), 11–28.

Nicholas, H. (1986). The acquisition of language as the acquisition of variation. *Australian Working Papers on Language Development, 1,* 1–30.

Nobuyoshi, J., & Ellis, R. (1993). Focused communication tasks and second language acquisition. *ELT Journal, 47*(3), 203–210.

Nunan, D. (1992). *Research methods in language learning*. Cambridge: Cambridge University Press.

Nunan, D. (1996). Hidden voices: Insiders' perspectives on classroom interaction. In K. Bailey & D. Nunan (Eds.), *Voices from the classroom* (pp. 41–56). Cambridge: Cambridge University Press.

O'Malley, M., & Chamot, A. (1990). *Learning strategies in second language acquisition*. New York: Cambridge University Press.

Oliver, R. (1995). Negative feedback in child NS-NNS conversation. *Studies in Second Language Acquisition, 17*(4), 459–482.

Ortega, L., & Long, M. H. (1997). The effects of models and recasts on the acquisition of object topicalization and adverb placement in L2 Spanish. *Spanish Applied Linguistics, 1*(1).

Paribakht, T. S., & Wesche, M. (1997). Vocabulary enhancement activities and reading for meaning in second language vocabulary. In J. Coady & T. Huckin (Eds.), *Second language vocabulary acquisition* (pp. 174–200). New York: Cambridge University Press.

Paulston, C. (1971). The sequencing of structural pattern drills. *TESOL Quarterly, 5*(3), 197–208.

Paulston, C., & Bruder, M. (1976). *Teaching English as a second language: Techniques and procedures*. Cambridge, MA: Winthrop.

Pavesi, M. (1986). Markedness, discoursal modes, and relative clause formation in a formal and an informal context. *Studies in Second Language Acquisition, 8*(1), 38–55.

Pearson, N. (Producer), & Sheridan, J. (Director). (1989). *My Left Foot* [Film].

Pérez-Pereira, M. (1991). The acquisition of gender: What Spanish children tell us. *Journal of Child Language, 18*(3), 571–590.

Perruchet, P., & Pacteau, C. (1990). Synthetic grammar learning: Implicit rule abstraction or explicit fragmentary knowledge? *Journal of Experimental Psychology, 119*(3), 264–275.

Perruchet, P., & Pacteau, C. (1991). Implicit acquisition of abstract knowledge about artificial grammar: Some methodological and conceptual issues. *Journal of Experimental Psychology, 120*(1), 112–116.

Pica, T. (1983). Adult acquisition of English as a second language under different conditions of exposure. *Language Learning, 33*(4), 465–497.

Pica, T. (1984). Methods of morpheme quantification: Their effect on the interpretation of second language data. *Studies in Second Language Acquisition, 6*(1), 69–78.

Pica, T. (1985). The selective impact of classroom instruction on second language acquisition. *Applied Linguistics, 6*(3), 214–222.

Pica, T. (1992). The textual outcomes of native speaker-non-native speaker negotiation: What do they reveal about second language learning? In C. Kramsch & S. McConnell-Ginet (Eds.), *Text and Context* (pp. 198–237). Cambridge, MA: Heath.

Pica, T. (1994). Research on negotiation: What does it reveal about second language acquisition? *Language Learning, 44*(3).

Pica, T. (1997). Second language teaching and research relationships: A North-American view. *Language Teaching Research, 1*(1), 48–72.

Pica, T., Holliday, L., Lewis, N., & Morgenthaler, L. (1989). Comprehensible input as an outcome of linguistic demands on the learner. *Studies in Second Language Acquisition, 11*(1), 63–90.

Pica, T., Lincoln-Porter, F., Paninos, D., & Linnell, J. (1996). Language learners' interaction: How does it address the input, output, and feedback needs of language learners? *TESOL Quarterly, 30*(1), 59–84.

Pienemann, M. (1984). Psychological constraints on the teachability of languages. *Studies in Second Language Acquisition, 6*(2), 186–214.

Pienemann, M. (1985). Learnability and syllabus construction. In K. Hyltenstam & M. Pienemann (Eds.), *Modeling and assessing second language acquisition* (pp. 23–75). Clevedon, Avon: Multilingual Matters.

Pienemann, M. (1987). Determining the influence of instruction on L2 speech processing. *Australian Review of Applied Linguistics, 10*(2), 83–113.

Pienemann, M. (1989). Is language teachable? *Applied Linguistics, 10*(1), 52–79.

Pienemann, M., & Johnston, M. (1986). An acquisition-based procedure for language assessment. *Australian Review of Applied Linguistics, 9*(1), 92–112.

Pienemann, M., Johnston, M., & Brindley, G. (1988). Constructing an acquisition-based procedure for second language assessment. *Studies in Second Language Acquisition, 10*(2), 217–243.

Pinker, S. (1994). *The language instinct.* New York: Penguin.

Politzer, R., & Staubach, C. (1961). *Teaching Spanish: A linguistic orientation.* New York: Blaisdell.

Prahbu, N. S. (1987). *Second language pedagogy.* Oxford: Oxford University Press.

Quirk, R., Greenbaum, S., Leech, G., and Svartvik, J. (1972). *A grammar of contemporary English.* London: Longman.

Reber, A. (1989). Implicit learning and tacit knowledge. *Journal of Experimental Psychology, 118*(3), 219–235.

Reber, A. (1993). Implicit learning and tacit knowledge: An essay on the cognitive unconscious. Oxford: Clarendon Press.

Reibel, D. (1969). Language learning analysis. *International Review of Applied Linguistics, 7*(4), 283–294.

Richardson, M. A. (1995). The use of negative evidence in second language acquisition of grammatical morphemes. M.Ed. thesis. University of Western Australia, Graduate School of Education, Perth.

Ringbom, H. (1990). Effects of transfer in foreign language learning. In H. Dechert (Ed.), *Current trends in European second language acquisition research* (pp. 205–218). Clevedon, Avon: Multilingual Matters.

Rivers, W. (1964). *The psychologist and the foreign language teacher.* Chicago: University of Chicago Press.

Rivers, W., & Temperley, M. (1978). *A practical guide to the teaching of English as a second or foreign language.* New York: Oxford University Press.

Robinson, P. (1994). Implicit knowledge, second language learning and syllabus construction. *TESOL Quarterly, 28*(2), 160–166.

Robinson, P. (1995a). Aptitude, awareness, and the fundamental similarity of implicit and explicit second language learning. In R. Schmidt (Ed.), *Attention and awareness in foreign language learning* (pp. 303–358). Honolulu: University of Hawai'i Press.

Robinson, P. (1995b). Review article: Attention, memory and the noticing hypothesis. *Language Learning, 45*(2), 283–331.

Robinson, P. (1996a). *Consciousness, rules and instructed second language acquisition.* New York: Peter Lang.

Robinson, P. (1996b). Learning simple and complex second language rules under implicit, incidental, rule-search and instructed conditions. *Studies in Second Language Acquisition, 18*(1), 27–68.

Robinson, P. (1997a). Individual differences and the fundamental similarity of implicit and explicit adult second language learning. *Language Learning, 47,* 45–99.

Robinson, P. (1997b). Automaticity and generalizability of second language learning under implicit, incidental, enhanced, and instructed conditions. *Studies in Second Language Acquisition 19*(2), 233–247.

Rutherford, W. (1983). Language typology in language transfer. In S. Gass & L. Selinker (Eds.), *Language transfer in language learning* (pp. 358–78). Rowley, MA: Newbury House.

Rutherford, W. (1988). *Second language grammar: Teaching and learning.* London: Longman.

Rutherford, W., & Sharwood Smith, M. (1985). Consciousness-raising and universal grammar. *Applied Linguistics, 6*(3), 274–282.

Rutherford, W., & Sharwood Smith, M. (Eds.). (1988). *Grammar and second language teaching.* New York: Newbury House.

Sato, C. (1986). Conversation and interlanguage development: Rethinking the connection. In R. Day (Ed.), *Talking to learn* (pp. 23–45). Rowley, MA: Newbury House.

Sato, C. (1990). *The syntax of conversation in interlanguage development.* Tübingen: Gunter Narr.

Schacter, D. (1987). Implicit memory: History and current status. *Journal of Experimental Psychology: Learning, Memory and Cognition, 13*(3), 501–518.

Schachter, J. (1981). The hand-signal system. *TESOL Quarterly, 15*(2), 125–138.

Schachter, J., & Gass, S. (1996). *Second language classroom research.* Mahwah, NJ: Lawrence Erlbaum.

Scherer, G., & Wertheimer, M. (1964). *A psycholinguistic experiment in foreign language teaching.* New York: McGraw-Hill.

Schmidt, R. (1983). Interaction, acculturation, and the acquisition of communicative competence: A case study of an adult. In N. Wolfson & E. Judd (Eds.), *Sociolinguistics and language acquisition* (pp. 137–174). Rowley, MA: Newbury House.

Schmidt, R. (1990). The role of consciousness in second language learning. *Applied Linguistics, 11*(2), 17–46.

Schmidt, R. (1992). Psychological mechanisms underlying second language fluency. *Studies in Second Language Acquisition, 14*(4), 357–385.

Schmidt, R. (1993a). Awareness and second language acquisition. *Annual Review of Applied Linguistics, 13,* 206–226.

Schmidt, R. (1993b). Consciousness, learning and interlanguage pragmatics. In G. Kasper & S. Blum-Kulka (Eds.), *Interlanguage pragmatics* (pp. 21–42). New York: Oxford University Press.

Schmidt, R. (1994a). Deconstructing consciousness in search of useful definitions for applied linguistics. In J. Hulstijn & R. Schmidt (Eds.), *Consciousness in second language learning* (pp. 11–26): AILA Review, Vol. 11.

Schmidt, R. (1994b). Implicit learning and the cognitive unconscious: Of artificial grammars and SLA. In N. Ellis (Ed.), *Implicit and explicit learning of languages* (pp. 165–209). London: Academic Press.

Schmidt, R. (1995). Consciousness and foreign language learning: A tutorial on the role of attention and awareness in learning. In R. Schmidt (Ed.), *Attention and awareness in foreign language learning* (pp. 1–63). Honolulu: University of Hawai'i Press.

Schmidt, R., & Frota, S. (1986). Developing basic conversational ability in a second language. In R. Day (Ed.), *Talking to learn* (pp. 237–326). Rowley, MA: Newbury House.

Schneider, W., & Shiffrin, R. (1977). Controlled and automatic human information processing: Detection, search and attention. *Psychological Review, 84*(1), 1–66.

Schumann, J. (1979). The acquisition of English negation by speakers of Spanish: A review of the literature. In R. Andersen (Ed.), *The acquisition and use of Spanish and English as first and second languages* (pp. 1–32). Washington, DC: TESOL.

Schwartz, B. (1993). On explicit and negative data effecting and affecting competence and linguistic behavior. *Studies in Second Language Acquisition, 15*(2), 147–163.

Scott, V. (1989). An empirical study of explicit and implicit teaching strategies in French. *Modern Language Review, 72*(1), 14–22.

Scovel, T. (1988). *A time to speak.* Rowley, MA: Newbury House.

Segalowitz, N., & Gatbonton, E. (1994). Assessing the acquisition of second language fluency and determining input conditions for its promotion. Paper presented at the Second Language Research Forum, Montreal.

Seger, C. (1994). Implicit learning. *Psychological Bulletin, 115*(2), 163–196.

Selinker, L., & Lakshamanan, U. (1992). Language transfer and fossilization. In S. Gass & L. Selinker (Eds.), *Language transfer in language learning,* 2nd ed. (pp. 196–215). Philadelphia: John Benjamins.

Shanks, D., & St. John, M. F. (1994). Characteristics of dissociable human systems. *Behavioral and Brain Sciences, 17*(4), 367–448.

Sharwood Smith, M. (1981). Consciousness-raising and second language acquisition theory. *Applied Linguistics, 2*(2), 159–168.

Sharwood Smith, M. (1986). Comprehension vs. acquisition: Two ways of processing input. *Applied Linguistics, 7*(3), 239–256.

Sharwood Smith, M. (1991). Speaking to many minds: On the relevance of different types of language information for the L2 learner. *Second Language Research, 7*(2), 118–132.

Sharwood Smith, M. (1993). Input enhancement in instructed SLA: Theoretical bases. *Studies in Second Language Acquisition, 15*(2), 165–179.

Sharwood Smith M. (1994). *Second language learning: Theoretical foundations.* New York: Longman.

Shirai, Y. (1990). U-shaped behavior in L2 acquisition. Paper presented at the Second Language Research Forum, Eugene, OR.

Shook, D. (1994). FL/L2 reading, grammatical information and the input-to-intake phenomenon. *Applied Language Learning, 5*(2), 57–93.

Singley, M., & Anderson, J. (1989). *The transfer of cognitive skill.* Cambridge, MA: Harvard University Press.

Skehan, P. (1989). *Individual differences in second language learning.* London: Edward Arnold.

Skehan, P. (1991). Individual differences in second language learning. *Studies in Second Language Acquisition 13*(2), 275–298.

Skehan, P. (1996). A framework for the implementation of task-based instruction. *Applied Linguistics, 17*(1), 38–62.

Slimani, A. (1991). Evaluation of classroom interaction. In C. Alderson & A. Berretta (Eds.), *Evaluating second language education* (pp. 197–220). Cambridge: Cambridge University Press.

Smith, P. (1970). *A comparison of the cognitive and audiolingual approaches to foreign language instruction: The Pennsylvania Foreign Language Project.* Philadelphia: Center for Curriculum Development.

Spada, N. (1987). The relationship between instructional differences and learning outcomes: A process-product study of communicative language teaching. *Applied Linguistics, 8*(2), 137–155.

Spada, N., & Lightbown, P. (1993). Instruction and the development of questions in the L2 classroom. *Studies in Second Language Acquisition, 15*(2), 205–221.

Spilka, I. (1976). Assessment of second language performance in immersion programs. *Canadian Modern Language Review, 32*(5), 543–561.

Stein, M. (1995). What's in a fashion show? A focus-on-form task in the Spanish language classroom. Term paper, Georgetown University, Washington, DC.

Stern, H. H. (1990). Analysis and experience as variables in second language pedagogy. In B. Harley, P. Allen, J. Cummins, & M. Swain (Eds.), *The development of second language proficiency* (pp. 93–109). New York: Cambridge University Press.

Stern, H. H. (1992). *Issues and options in language teaching.* Oxford: Oxford University Press.

Stevens, F. (1984). *Strategies for second language acquisition.* Montreal: Eden.

Surridge, M., & Lessard, A. (1984). Pour une prise de conscience du genre grammatical. *Canadian Modern Language Review, 41*(1), 43–52.

Swain, M. (1984). A review of immersion education in Canada: Research and evaluation studies. In *A Collection of U.S. Educators*. California State Department of Education.

Swain, M. (1985). Communicative competence: Some roles of comprehensible input and comprehensible output in its development. In S. Gass & C. Madden (Eds.), *Input in second language acquisition* (pp. 235–253). Rowley, MA: Newbury House.

Swain, M. (1991a). French immersion and its offshoots: Getting two for one. In B. Freed (Ed.), *Foreign language acquisition: Research and the classroom* (pp. 91–103). Lexington, MA: Heath.

Swain, M. (1991b). Manipulating and complementing content teaching to maximize learning. In E. Kellerman, R. Phillipson, L. Selinker, M. Sharwood Smith, & M. Swain (Eds.), *Foreign/second language pedagogy research* (pp. 234–50). Clevedon, Avon: Multilingual Matters.

Swain, M. (1993). The output hypothesis: Just speaking and writing are not enough. *The Canadian Modern Language Review, 50*(1), 158–164.

Swain, M. (1995). Three functions of output in second language learning. In G. Cook & B. Seidlhofer (Eds.), *Principle and practice in applied linguistics* (pp. 125–144). Oxford: Oxford University Press.

Swain, M., & Carroll, S. (1987). The immersion observation study. In B. Harley, P. Allen, J. Cummins, & M. Swain (Eds.), *The development of bilingual proficiency: Final report,* Vol. 2 (pp. 190–341). Toronto: OISE.

Swain, M., & Lapkin, S. (1982). *Evaluating bilingual education: A Canadian case study.* Clevedon, Avon: Multilingual Matters.

Swain, M., & Lapkin, S. (1986). Immersion French at the secondary level: The "goods" and the "bads." *Contact, 5,* 2–9.

Swain, M., & Lapkin, S. (1995). Problems in output and the cognitive processes they generate: A step towards second language learning. *Applied Linguistics, 16*(3), 370–391.

Swain, M., & Lapkin, S. (1996). Focus on form through collaborative dialogue: Exploring task effects. Paper presented at the Annual Conference of the American Association for Applied Linguistics, Chicago.

Takashima, H. (1994). How helpful is output enhancement in promoting accuracy in communicative activities? Paper presented at the Second Language Research Forum, Montreal.

Tarallo, F., & Myhill, J. (1983). Interference and natural language in second language acquisition. *Language Learning, 33*(1), 55–76.

Tarone, E., & Liu, G.-Q. (1995). Situational context, variation, and second language acquisition theory. In G. Cook & B. Seidlhoffer (Eds.), *Principle and practice in applied linguistics* (pp. 107–124). Oxford: Oxford University Press.

Taylor-Browne, K. (1984). The acquisition of grammatical gender by children in French immersion programs. M.A. thesis, University of Calgary.

Terrell, T. (1991). The role of grammar instruction in a communicative approach. *Modern Language Journal, 75*(1), 52–63.

Tomaselli, A., & Schwartz, B. (1990). Analyzing the acquisition stages of negation in L2 German: Support for UG in adult SLA. *Second Language Research, 6*(1), 1–38.

Tomasello, M., & Herron, C. (1988). Down the garden path: Inducing and correcting overgeneralization errors in the foreign language classroom. *Applied Psycholinguistics, 9*(3), 237–246.

Tomasello, M., & Herron, C. (1989). Feedback for language transfer errors. *Studies in Second Language Acquisition, 11*(4), 384–395.

Tomlin, R., & Villa, V. (1994). Attention in cognitive science and second language acquisition. *Studies in Second Language Acquisition, 16*(2), 183.

Towell, R., & Hawkins, R. (1994). *Approaches to second language acquisition.* Clevedon, Avon: Multilingual Matters.

Trahey, M. (1992). Comprehensible input and second language acquisition. M.Ed. thesis, McGill University.

Trahey, M. (1996). Positive evidence and preemption in second language acquisition: Some long-term effects. *Second Language Research, 12*(2), 111–139.

Trahey, M., & White, L. (1993). Positive evidence in the second language classroom. *Studies in Second Language Acquisition, 15*(2), 181–204.

Tucker, G., Lambert, W., & Rigault, A. (1977). *The French speaker's skill with grammatical gender.* The Hague: Mouton.

Valdman, A. (1975). Error analysis and grading in the preparation of teaching materials. *Modern Language Journal, 59*, 422–426.

VanPatten, B. (1989). Can learners attend to form and content while processing input? *Hispania, 72*, 409–417.

VanPatten, B. (1990). Attending to form and content in the input: An experiment in consciousness. *Studies in Second Language Acquisition, 12*(3), 287–301.

VanPatten, B. (1993). Grammar teaching for the acquisition-rich classroom. *Foreign Language Annals, 26*(4), 435–450.

VanPatten, B. (1994a). Evaluating the role of consciousness in second language acquisition: Terms, linguistic features and research methodologies. In J. Hulstijn & R. Schmidt (Eds.), *Consciousness in second language learning* (pp. 27–36): AILA Review, Vol. 11.

VanPatten, B. (1994b). Cognitive aspects of input processing in second language acquisition. In P. Hashemipour, R. Maldonado, & M. van Naerssen (Eds.), *Festschrift in honor of Tracy D. Terrell* (pp. 170–183). New York: McGraw-Hill.

VanPatten, B., & Cadierno, T. (1993a). Explicit instruction and input processing. *Studies in Second Language Acquisition, 15*(2), 225–243.

VanPatten, B., & Cadierno, T. (1993b). Input processing and second language acquisition: A role for instruction. *The Modern Language Journal, 77*, 45–57.

VanPatten, B., & Oikkenon, S. (1996). Explanation versus structured input in processing instruction. *Studies in Second Language Acquisition, 18*(4), 495–510.

VanPatten, B., & Sanz, C. (1995). From input to output: Processing instruction and communicative tasks. In F. Eckman, D. Highland, P. W. Lee, J. Mileham, & R. R. Weber (Eds.), *Second language acquisition theory and pedagogy* (pp. 169–185). Mahwah, NJ: Lawrence Erlbaum.

Viberg, A. (1993). Crosslinguistic perspectives on lexical organization and lexical progression. In K. Hyltenstam & A. Viberg (Eds.), *Progression and regression in language* (pp. 340–385). Cambridge: Cambridge University Press.

Vignola, M.-J., & Wesche, M. (1991). Le savoir écrire en langue maternelle et en langue seconde chez les diplomes d'immersion française. *Études de linguistique appliquée, 82,* 94–115.

Wajnryb, R. (1990). *Grammar dictation.* Oxford: Oxford University Press.

Weinert, R. (1994). Some effects of the foreign language classroom: The development of German negation. *Applied Linguistics, 15*(1), 76–101.

Westney, P. (1994). Rules and pedagogical grammar. In T. Odlin (Ed.), *Perspectives on pedagogical grammar* (pp. 72–96). Cambridge: Cambridge University Press.

White, J. (1996). An input enhancement study with ESL children: Effects on the acquisition of possessive determiners. Ph.D. dissertation, McGill University.

White, L. (1987). Against comprehensible input. *Applied Linguistics, 8*(2), 95–110.

White, L. (1988). Universal grammar and language transfer. In J. Pankhurst, M. Sharwood Smith, & P. Van Buren (Eds.), *Learnability and second languages* (pp. 36–60). Dordrecht: Foris.

White, L. (1989). The adjacency condition on case assignment: Do L2 learners observe the subset principle? In S. Gass & J. Schachter (Eds.), *Linguistic perspectives on second language acquisition* (pp. 134–158). Cambridge: Cambridge University Press.

White, L. (1991). Adverb placement in second language acquisition: Some positive and negative evidence in the classroom. *Second Language Research, 7*(2), 133–161.

White, L., & Genesee, F. (1996). How native is near-native? The issue of ultimate attainment in adult second language acquisition. *Second Language Research, 12*(3), 223–265.

White, L., Spada, N., Lightbown, P., & Ranta, L. (1991). Input enhancement and L2 question formation. *Applied Linguistics, 12*(4), 416–432.

Wickens, C. (1989). Attention and skilled performance. In D. Holding (Ed.), *Human skills* (pp. 71–105). New York: Wiley.

Wilkins, D. (1976). *Notional syllabuses.* Oxford: Oxford University Press.

Williams, J. (1995). Focus on form in communicative language teaching: Research findings and the classroom teacher. *TESOL Journal, 4*(summer), 12–16.

Williams, J. (1997). The place of focus on form in collaborative learning settings. Paper presented at the Annual Conference of the American Association for Applied Linguistics, Orlando, FL.

Williams, J., & Doughty, C. (Conveners) (1995). Colloquium: What teachers can tell researchers. Twenty-ninth Annual TESOL Convention, Long Beach, CA.

Willis, D. (1993). Comments on Michael H. Long and Graham Crookes' "Three approaches to task-based syllabus design." *TESOL Quarterly, 27*(4), 726–729.

Winter, B., & Reber, A. (1994). Implicit learning and the acquisition of natural languages. In N. Ellis (Ed.), *Implicit and explicit learning of languages* (pp. 115–145). London: Academic Press.

Wode, H. (1981). Language acquisition universals: A unified view of language acquisition. In H. Winitz (Ed.), *Native language and foreign language acquisition* (pp. 218–234). Annals of the New York Academy of Sciences, Vol. 379.

Wolfe-Quintero, K. (1992). Learnability and the acquisition of extraction in relative clauses and Wh-questions. *Studies in Second Language Acquisition, 14*(1), 39–70.

Wong-Fillmore, L. (1976). The second time around: Cognitive and social strategies in second language acquisition. Ph.D. dissertation, Stanford University.

Wright, R. (1996). A study of the acquisition of verbs of motion by grade 4/5 early French immersion students. *Canadian Modern Language Review, 53*(1), 257–280.

Yano, Y., Long, M. H., & Ross, S. (1994). The effects of simplified and elaborated texts on foreign language reading comprehension. *Language Learning, 44*(2), 189–219.

Young, R. (1988). Variation and the interlanguage hypothesis. *Studies in Second Language Acquisition, 10*(3), 281–302.

Yuan, B. (1995). The acquisition of base-generated topics by English speaking learners of Chinese. *Language Learning, 45*(4), 567–603.

Zhou, Y.-P. (1992). The effect of explicit instruction on the acquisition of English grammatical structures by Chinese learners. In C. James & P. Garrett (Eds.), *Language awareness in the classroom* (pp. 254–277). London: Longman.

Zimmerman, C. B. (1997). Do reading and interactive vocabulary instruction make a difference? An empirical study. *TESOL Quarterly 31*(1), 121–140.

Zobl, H. (1980). The formal and developmental selectivity of L1 influence on L2 acquisition. *Language Learning, 30*(1), 43–57.

Zobl, H. (1982). A direction for contrastive analysis: The comparative study of developmental sequences. *TESOL Quarterly, 16*(2), 169–183.

Zobl, H. (1983). Markedness and the projection problem. *Language Learning, 33*(3), 293–313.

Zobl, H. (1984). The wave model of linguistic change and interlanguage systems. *Studies in Second Language Acquisition, 6*(2), 160–185.

Zobl, H. (1985). Grammars in search of input and intake. In S. Gass & C. Madden (Eds.), *Input in second language acquisition* (pp. 32–44). Rowley, MA: Newbury House.

Zobl, H. (1995). Converging evidence for the "acquisition-learning" distinction. *Applied Linguistics, 16*(1), 35–56.

Zobl, H., & Liceras, J. (1994). Functional categories and acquisition orders. *Language Learning, 44*(1), 159–180.

Author index

Subject index

clarification requests, 68, 117, 207, 238

code-focused instruction, *see* focus on formS

Cognitive Code, 51, 54–55

cognitive comparison, 118, 228, 229, 230t, 238, 241, 260

cognitive processing, 3, 67, 204

cognitive psychology, 26–30, 39, 45–47, 48–50, 56–57, 60, 231–32, 249

collaboration
classroom, 7, 75, 79–80, 239
teacher-researcher, 1, 116

communicative approach, 1, 207, *see also* communicative language teaching

communicative drills, 52–53, 60

communicative function/need, 68, 69, 137, 217, 219–221, 244

communicative language teaching, 51, 129, 135, 190, 191, 192, 205, 231, *see also* communicative approach

Communicative Orientation of Language Teaching (COLT), 36

Community Language Learning, 55

complex rules, 27–30, 43–45, 47, 155, 221–26, 232, 234t, 235t

complexity, 200, 215, 221, 254
formal, 43–44, 155, 221
functional, 44, 155, 221–22
semantic, 222–23

comprehensible input, 18, 22–23, 51, 56, 59, 62, 178, 180, 183, 190, 203

comprehension, 23, 31–32
production versus, 45, 61

comprehension tasks, 61, 209

condition, learning, *see entries under* learning

conditional past tense, 8, 38, 118–19, 120, 125–28, 252, 253

confirmation checks/requests, 68, 238

consciousness, 18, 26–30, 47–48, 57, 66, 70, 101, 157, 203, 230, 231–32, 246

consciousness-raising, 17–18, 157, 171, 239–40

consistency, 223, 224

content-based instruction, 7, 16t, 19, 20–21, 26, 65–66, 115–16, 137, 195, 248

context, classroom, for focus on form, 6, 62, 199–200

control, 48, 183, 206, 229, 230t, 238

controlled practice, 246, 250, 257

correction, self-, 192, 194–95

corrective feedback, 36–37, 38–39, 89, 123–24, 141, 142, 145, 181, 192–93, 201
nonverbal signals, 36, 38, 194, 245
recasts as, 7, 8, 23, 25–26, 38, 116–18, 123–25, 135–37, 193, 207, 241, 242, 243, 245, 252, 256
teacher reflection on, 135–37, *see also* negative feedback

course design, 3, 6, 15, *see also* curriculum; syllabus

critical periods, 202

cues/clues
formal, 156, 161, 163
morphological, 158, 161
morphophonological, 156, 164
orthographic, 9, 71
phonological, 160–61, 240–41
semantic, 160–61

curriculum, 137, 171–72
design, 6, 60, 205
models of, 256–57
sequencing in, 58–60, 244–50, 251–57

dative alternation, 207, 222, 233

declarative knowledge, 48–50, 52–53, 54, 55, 57, 58, 59, 246

deduction, 29–30, 46–47, 152–53, 204–5, 230t, 234, 258t

density, *see* frequency

detection, 30–40, 101

determiners, 156, 160, 164, *see also* articles; possessive determiners

developmental readiness, *see* readiness

developmental stages, 17, 20, 21–22, 25, 37, 73n, 97–98, 99, 100n, 104–6, 198, 213, 214
encouraging later-stage development, 180–84